Theories of
Communication

This book is part of the Peter Lang Media and Communication list.
Every volume is peer reviewed and meets
the highest quality standards for content and production.

PETER LANG
New York • Washington, D.C./Baltimore • Bern
Frankfurt • Berlin • Brussels • Vienna • Oxford

Theories of Communication

ERIC MCLUHAN and
MARSHALL MCLUHAN

PETER LANG
New York • Washington, D.C./Baltimore • Bern
Frankfurt • Berlin • Brussels • Vienna • Oxford

Library of Congress Cataloging-in-Publication Data

McLuhan, Eric.
Theories of communication / Eric McLuhan and Marshall McLuhan.
p. cm.
Includes bibliographical references.
1. Communication. I. Title.
P90.M257   302.2—dc22   2010041925
ISBN 978-1-4331-1213-3 (hardcover)
ISBN 978-1-4331-1212-6 (paperback)

Bibliographic information published by **Die Deutsche Nationalbibliothek**.
Die Deutsche Nationalbibliothek lists this publication in the "Deutsche
Nationalbibliografie"; detailed bibliographic data is available
on the Internet at http://dnb.d-nb.de/.

The paper in this book meets the guidelines for permanence and durability
of the Committee on Production Guidelines for Book Longevity
of the Council of Library Resources.

© 2011 Eric McLuhan, and The Estate of Marshall McLuhan
Peter Lang Publishing, Inc., New York
29 Broadway, 18th floor, New York, NY 10006
www.peterlang.com

Printed in the United States of America

Table of Contents

Introduction

ERIC MCLUHAN

A fundamental principle of this book is that communication entails change: the *sine qua non* of communication therefore is the matter of effect. If there is no effect, if there is no change in the audience, there is no communication. The approach is rhetoric to the core.

The centerpiece of these essays is the first chapter, which proposes a "World Communication Series" of essays on various people's Theories of Communication. In each case, it suggests, two questions need to be asked: What is the subject's intended audience? and What effect does the subject aim to produce on that audience? Such at any rate is our ideal; as with many another thing, the execution (the essays that follow) often falls short—or a bit to one side of—of the ideal. (The reader may enjoy observing just how often and how widely theory diverges from practice in these pages.) Of the essays in this collection, a few go straight to the topic; others sidle up to it; the rest are included for their contribution to the overall task of understanding culture and communication in our time. "Formal Causality in Chesterton" is one such. While it discusses Chesterton's ideas about his audience and the effect he wanted to produce, it also points out the role of the audience as the formal cause of the writer's labours. Formal causality, so widely misunderstood, is central to our topic and recurs in a number of the other chapters. We have included an appendix on formal cause.

To take another example, we can assume that Aristotle's audience consisted of his students and his colleagues. The effect he wished to achieve is clearly evident in what is taken to be his biggest contribution to logical thought: the syllogism. The syllogism breaks the mimetic thrall in which the poets held their Greek hearers, the same spell against which Plato inveighed in *Republic* and elsewhere. It posed a mortal threat to the new enterprise of reasoning, and so holds the key to Aristotle's theory of communication, as I show in Appendix One.

In 1971, Marshall McLuhan wrote to the anthropologist, Ashley Montagu, as follows:

> There are many things that I wish you were available to discuss. In recent years, I've been working on causation. More and more I feel compelled to consider causation as following from effects. That is, the effects of the telegraph created an environment of information that made the telephone a perfectly natural development. In a certain sense, therefore, the effects of the telephone provided the invention of the actual hardware instrument. This, of course, is non-lineal, non- sequential causality. In fact, it suggests that causes and effects are simultaneous, if anything.
>
> I am baffled to know why it is that in the Western world there has been no study of the effects of innovations. There is, of course, much readiness to study the inputs that are called the "content" of our technologies, but insofar as technologies create environments which alter all forms of human perception, there is a hiatus. In merely literary terms, nobody studies what sort of effect Dante or anybody else wanted to have on his time and his public. Instead, they study what they imagined the writer was saying to the public. What a man is saying is far from the effect he may wish to have, or that, in fact, he does have. Personally, I consider the effect that a writer wishes to achieve as his theory of communication. I know of no studies of anybody's theory of communication. For example, quite apart from the concern of anthropologists, and aside from the content of their work, what is the effect that they seek on their time? How do they wish to change it?[1]

"Pound, Eliot and the Rhetoric of *The Waste Land*" examines the contending approaches to communication of T.S. Eliot and Ezra Pound as registered in their work on the poem. Most remarkable is that Eliot enlisted—and submitted to—Pound's editorial surgery on his poem. Never before (or since) have two major poets collaborated on producing a single poem. The result was instantaneous and dramatic: a howl of rage and protest from every quarter. Even today, nearly a century after its appearance, *The Waste Land* puzzles and infuriates readers and critics—adequate testimony to its efficacy. Eliot played the grammarian, the man of letters; Pound, the practical rhetor, pressing always to sharpen the effect. Here, too, we encounter for the first time the uses of the five divisions of the rhetorical word in poetics—Pound's particular contribution to twentieth-century poetics.[2] "Rhetorical Spirals in *Four Quartets*," a companion piece, pursues most of the same themes in depth (though not at length) in the structures of the *Four Quartets*. It features a Dantesque layering in the four poems of the traditional four levels of interpretation—plus the four seasons, the four elements, the four causes, and so on, as penetrated by the five divisions of rhetoric—altogether an immensely rich tapestry of meaning and suggestion woven by a master poet. These two essays provide more than adequate matter to assemble a theory of communication for Eliot and for Pound.

"Poetic vs. Rhetorical Exegesis" was written as an early (1944) book review, with no thought of presenting anyone's theory of communication. It situates Practical Criticism as essentially rhetorical inasmuch as it focuses concern on audience and effect, and it discusses its limitations as contrasted with the poetic technique of F. R. Leavis. Practical Criticism can reveal nearly everything about a poem, for example, except whether or not it is a good poem. The approaches of Richards and Leavis exhibit the same complementarity as do those of Pound and Eliot; their roots are easily discerned in the traditions of rhetoric and grammar extending continuously back to Cicero and Quintilian:

> Just as Korzybski offers us a correlation of knowledge by extension of the modes of grammar (and in this respect belongs to an ancient tradition headed by Cratylus and carried on by Pliny, Philo-Judæus, Origen, St. Bonaventura, and the later alchemists) so Mr. Richards, whose *Meaning of Meaning* is a treatise of speculative grammar of curiously scholastic stamp, offers us a method for interpreting and manipulating our lives by an extension of the devices of rhetoric. In this respect Mr. Richards is a true nominalist son of Ockham, Agricola, and Ramus; and it is no accident that Harvard has welcomed this distinguished schoolman.
>
> Mr. Richards' rediscovery of the functional rhetorical relationships in speech and prose was timely, indeed, after three centuries of Cartesian contempt for metaphor and rhetoric in all its modes. However, in order to understand how Mr. Empson developed Mr. Richards' method it is worth pointing out that all four relations of "sense," "attitude," "tone," and "intention" designated by Richards are not directly applicable to the work of a poet. A speaker or a writer of prose has an intention related to an audience of some sort, but a poet's intention is entirely absorbed in the nature of the thing he is making. The thing made will stand in relation to an audience but this, while important, is only *per accidens*. Thus the "meaning" of a work of prose or rhetoric, whether pantomime, or speech, or tract is incomplete without the precise audience for which it was intended. For example, Swift's *Modest Proposal* does not have its whole meaning inherent in the internal relationships of the theme of that piece. One main "ingredient" of the composition is the relation in which its ostensible propositions stand to an audience of peculiar mental complexion. The nature of that audience must be inferred from the piece itself, and it is essential to the understanding of the work.
>
> Thus rhetoric is essentially an affair of external, as well as internal, relations, while a poem has external relations only accidentally. For example, the speech of Marvell's lover to the beloved in *The Coy Mistress* is a work of rhetoric, full of shifting attitudes to the

audience and displaying several persuasive arguments. But the audience *is in the poem.*
This is equally true for the poetic drama. A poem or play may contain any number of
rhetorical and political components needing exegesis, and yet be wholly poetic—that
is, be entirely organized with reference to a dramatic structure or movement which is
self-contained. A rhetorical work is for the sake of producing action. A poetic work is
an action produced for the sake of contemplation. This is an irreducible functional distinction between rhetoric and poetic which it is the business of the critic to manifest
point by point in judging the particular work.

The Introduction to *Paradox in Chesterton* not only places G. K. Chesterton in
relation to the traditions of rhetoric and grammar, it also situates his work and his
approach vis-à-vis his audience. Though not a formal "Theory of Communication"
essay, it nevertheless may easily be read as providing an account of Chesterton's
Theory. Much the same may be said of the essay on Innis, "The Bias of
Communication." While not a formal "Theory" essay, it does provide a more-
than-adequate account of the elements: Innis's audience and his effect on that
group. Like Marshall McLuhan, Innis wrote for two readers: one of Innis's readers is focused (narrowly) on economics and economic history; the other, a more general reader is interested in his startling and novel revelations about media and
modes of culture. Too, as with McLuhan, the academic audience—his colleagues
in Economics—despised the non-academic work and regarded it as beneath consideration, a form of intellectual and professional suicide. To this day, the same attitudes persist in departments of Economics (Innis) and English Literature
(McLuhan), though perhaps not as strenuously as heretofore. Contributing to the
richness of this essay, the reader will discover, is the fact that, in detailing Innis's
approach and technique, Marshall McLuhan exposes so much of his own: he can
be so incisive about Innis's methods because he knows them well from his own
extensive use of the same approaches. This is not to imply that he learned them from
Innis, but he found in Innis a kindred spirit.

"Media Ad-Vice" may seem at first blush an odd inclusion, yet it explores, not
for the first time, the nature and role of subliminal media effects on audiences. Its
significance in this company is not from setting forth the Theory of Communication
of one or another individual, but the Theory as it were of a profession, though the
professors be unaware they have one. Advertisers for the most part think in terms
of transporting messages and content; ironically their every motive and aim is not
to move a message but to transform non-buyers into buyers; the ad-man, like the
poet, gets most of his effects subliminally. Both ad and poem are masks. The apparent content or message serves just to keep the audience engaged long enough for
the ad to produce the intended effect. The entire process is fundamentally rhetorical; that is, it concerns the transformation of an audience.

The complementary chapters, "The Emperor's Old Clothes," and "The Emperor's New Clothes" tackle head-on the theme of the subliminal effects of media. Appearing two years after *Understanding Media: The Extensions of Man*, "The Emperor's Old Clothes" is one of several attempts to clarify the relation between any culture and the transforming power of environments imposed by new technologies. The counter-theme is the role of the artist in such situations. "We can never see the Emperor's new clothes. But we are staunch admirers of his old garb. Only small children and artists are sensuously apt to perceive the new environment. Small children and artists are anti-social beings who are as little impressed by the established mores as they are conditioned by the new. . . . If technological changes create new environments, or new processes of energy organization, what is to be the process of the new satellite environments on our perception and experience?" Here is a Theory of Communication for Art. I include it because it addresses both of our fundamental questions. Here also we find the role of environments, by definition invisible, and therefore also subliminal: present to the perceiver though not consciously present.[3] The tyranny of subliminal environments in the electric age brings up the role of the arts in acting directly on the perceptions to make visible the invisible. "Artists are the antennae of the race" in that they detect things long before the rest of us. The art administers the corrective—so it has been at least since the present renaissance began in mid-nineteenth century. Art becomes a means of survival in a time when the Emperor changes his raiment every year or so: "When the Emperor appeared in his new clothes, his courtiers did not see his nudity, they saw his old clothes. Only the small child and the artist have the immediacy of approach that permits perception of the environmental. The artist provides us with antienvironments that enable us to see the environment. Such antienvironmental means of perception must constantly be renewed in order to be efficacious. That basic aspect of the human condition by which we are rendered incapable of perceiving the environment is one to which psychologists have not even referred. In an age of accelerated change, the need to perceive the environment becomes urgent." I have included with the chapter the two Notes appended to it in *Through the Vanishing Point: Space in Poetry and Painting*.[4]

"Culture and Communication" comes from *Laws of Media: The New Science*: it critiques the reigning Theory of Communication in Western culture, and calls for a new approach to the matter that will come to grips with contemporary conditions. Our conventional (that is, commonsense) Theory of Communication—in all of its familiar variations—is rooted in the notion that communication consists in moving ideas, as if they were chunks of hardware, from place to place or from person to person. This view leaves no room to consider how media (environments) transform the users and impose on their users a new culture. It takes no account of change. *Laws of Media* called for updating our theories of communication to incorporate some provision for the transformations of person and culture that media bring about. Mid-chapter, we made this suggestion: "If literacy is to survive for another generation in the West, our writing system will soon have to be completely recast in a mould congenial to right-hemisphere sensibility and satisfactions. We might, for example, replace it with a syllabary of fifty to seventy characters." Although we tossed this note off almost casually, we were utterly serious. The present condition of postliteracy in our culture has arrived much more quickly than we had expected. The old alphabet has little to offer the reigning sensibility, offers few or no advantages to the electric world, except as a nostalgia trip. Our literature, encoded in alphabet, will submerge suddenly like an old Betamax format or obsolete computer program, taking with it the content and sensibility of literature and literary culture. The material will still be all there, whole libraries of it, but utterly inaccessible. A syllabary of course will not have the exquisite refinement of the phonetic alphabet, but it would provide a compromise or half-way meeting point for the postliterate crowd to access Western literature.

Many of my own contributions to this collection involve the five divisions of rhetoric, as will be seen in the chapters on Francis Bacon and Thomas Aquinas, and "Pound, Eliot & the Rhetoric of *The Waste Land.*" The essence of classical rhetoric is audience: everything a rhetor does begins with the audience and the effect that the speaker wants to have, as Cicero insists at every turn.[5] Marshall McLuhan's debt to the rhetorical tradition is profound, as I have tried to indicate in the essay on "Joyce and McLuhan," below, and in the concluding chapter on McLuhan's own "Theory" of communication—or lack of one. Fortunately, we now have available a cornerstone of his life's work, his doctoral dissertation, published as *The Classical Trivium: The Place of Thomas Nashe in the Learning of His Time.*[6]

Acknowledgments

Ch. 2: "Wyndham Lewis: His Theory of Art and Communication." *Shenandoah*, Vol. IV, Nos. 2–3 (Lexington, Virginia: Washington and Lee University, Summer–Autumn, 1953), pages 77–88. Reprinted in *The Interior Landscape*, pages 83–94. Notes: no footnotes in original; only one in *Interior Landscape* version (reproduced here). Nine of Lewis's paintings were printed in *Shenandoah*, none in *Interior Landscape*.

Ch. 3: "Formal Causality in Chesterton." *The Chesterton Review*, Vol. II, No. 2, Spring–Summer, 1976, pages 252–259, Saskatoon, Saskatchewan.

Ch. 4: "Francis Bacon's Theory of Communication." *Going for Baroque: Cultural Transformations 1550–1650*. Francesco Guardiani, Ed. Ottawa: Legas, 1999, pages 19–28.

Ch. 5: "Pound, Eliot and the Rhetoric of *The Waste Land*." *New Literary History*, Vol. 10, Spring 1979, pages 557–580. Copyright: McLuhan Associates Limited, 1978.

Ch. 6: "St. Thomas Aquinas's Theory of Communication." *Medievalism: The Future of the Past*. Goering, Joseph and Francesco Guardiani, Eds. Ottawa: Legas, 2000, pages 67–83.

Ch. 7: "Rhetorical Spirals in *Four Quartets*." *Figures in a Ground: Canadian Essays on Modern Literature collected in Honor of Sheila Watson*. Eds, Bessai, Diane and David Jackel (Saskatoon, Saskatchewan: Western Producer Prairie Books, 1978). Pages 76–86.

Ch. 8: "Poetic vs. Rhetorical Exegesis: The Case for Leavis Against Richards and Empson." The Spring number of *The Sewanee Review*, 1944, pages 1–11.

CHAPTER ONE

World Communication Series

ERIC AND MARSHALL MCLUHAN

One afternoon in mid-1977, a publisher-friend dropped in to the Centre for Culture and Technology to visit. Of course, the publisher in him hoped to persuade Marshall to do a book or two; by coincidence, he had brought along a few suggestions about what kind of books. As it turned out, they didn't seem half as appealing to us as they did to him, but one thing led to another and we got to talking about publishing projects and ideas for books. Marshall mentioned an idea he'd kicked around for years: little essays on various famous people's Theories of Communication. It could include anybody, from Cato the Elder to Casey Stengel, to Machiavelli or Shakespeare, Beethoven, Dali, Orwell, Einstein, Alfred Hitchcock, Martha Stewart or Madonna. Talking it over, we quickly realized that it wouldn't take much to set down someone's Theory of Communication. It could be done briefly, in only five or ten pages, so an essay of some 30 or 40 pages ought to satisfy even the most exacting pedant, making at the same time a handy small book. (We say "100 pages more or less" below: we thought "30–40" wouldn't appeal to a publisher.) The next day, we sketched the idea, as follows.

—Eric McLuhan

The themes of relevance and communication have come to occupy the centre of contemporary discussion in many fields. The issue is much related to the study of effects of existing procedures and organization. In the area of the humanities and the physical sciences alike, the focus on environmental effects has become intense.

A big American publisher is prepared to foster and to publish a series of studies in the arts and sciences which would enlist the aid of graduate students and faculty alike. The proposal is for a series of succinct monographs to cover both historical and contemporary figures. "What was Homer's theory of communication?" "What was Plato's?" "What sort of effect did they seek to create on the publics of their own times?" These questions apply not only to poets, painters, and philosophers but to geographers, and historians, to geometers, and physicists, to architects and town planners.

Creative figures at any point in history or culture seek specific effects on specific groups. It is these desired effects which constitute their "theory of communication." Few, if any, such studies exist of creative figures, past or present. Instead, attention is focussed on the components they offered for the study, on one hand, and the milieu or background of the man and his interests, on the other hand. Just what kind of change he sought to effect by the interplay of his interests and his milieu has been assumed rather than examined.

The series of studies proposed for publication would be succinct—each monograph 100 pages, more or less. Many students and faculty have already done, or [are] about to do, most of the work needed for inclusion in a book in this series. What would be needed in many cases would consist in adaptation and modification and focussing.

The series would foster patterns of relevance rather than extensive new research. However, much new research might easily result from a new sense of relevance. The basic approach to any figure in any field might be as follows:

- What were, or are, the traditional components with which he worked, or is working?

- What new arrangements did he introduce into these materials?

- What was, or is, the public or publics for which these changes and this new order were created?

- What were the new perceptions and the new awareness to be made available to these publics?

A basic principle in all media observation concerns the effect of putting one medium inside another. Siegfried Giedion pointed out the origin of visual space as occurring when the arch is put inside a rectangle, cf., the Arc de Triomphe. When any medium becomes the content of another, that which is contained becomes an art form. When the movie became the content of TV, the movie was at once elevated to the status of an art form. Prior to that, the movie had been common, or popular, entertainment. When *Sputnik* (1957) went around the planet, the planet became programmable content, and thus became an art form. Ecology was born, and Nature was obsolesced.

In the 5th century B.C. the new phoneticaly [*sic*] literate Greeks had invented Nature by classifying various phenomena and thus putting them inside the visual space of classification. It was this visually ordered "Nature" that was ended by the new environmental fact of *Sputnik*. The concept of planetary ecology came into play at once. "Spaceship Earth" was recognized as having no passengers, only crew. *Sputnik* is an information environment, i.e., a software environment which transforms the old "external" Nature. In the same way, when man is "on the phone" or "on the air," moving electrically at the speed of light, he has no physical body. He is translated into information or an image. When man lives in an electric environment, his nature is transformed and his private identity is merged with the corporate whole. He becomes "Mass man." Mass man is a phenomenon of electric speed, not of physical quantity. Mass man was first noticed as a phenomenon in the age of radio, but he had come into existence, unnoticed, with the electric telegraph.

At the speed of light, minus his physical body, man is discarnate, and discarnate man is not related to the "Natural Law." His sudden emancipation from *Natural* Law, in a sense, makes him "greater than the angels." He can be everywhere at once, whereas they are subject to limitations of space and can only be in one space at a time. This anarchic elevation of nuclear man enables individuals to be dispensed, as it were, from the moral law, a fact which was strikingly manifested in the radio age by Stalin and Hitler (and in the TV age by the universality of abortion), and helps to explain the sudden indifference of the TV generation to private morality. Politically, the same discarnate factor of electric speed seems to dissolve all constitutional and legalistic bonds, in both the private and the public sectors. Like the organization chart in its relation to job descriptions, legal bonds are pre-electric in character and seem unable to hold at the new electric speed of the information environment. (See *Take Today: The Executive as Dropout,* Marshall McLuhan and Barrington Nevitt, New York: Harcourt, Brace, Jovanovitch Inc., 1972 - and Longmans Canada Limited.)[1]

CHAPTER TWO

Wyndham Lewis
His Theory of Art
and Communication

MARSHALL MCLUHAN

For thirty years and more Wyndham Lewis has been a one-man army corps opposed to these forces which seek to use art, science, and philosophy in order to reduce our world to the nocturnal womb from which they suppose it to have been born. As he put it in *Time and Western Man*:

> For me art is the civilized substitute for magic; as philosophy is what, on a higher or more complex plane, takes the place of religion. By means of art I believe Professor Whitehead and M. Brémond wish to lead us down and back to the plane of magic, or mystical, specifically religious, experience.

The recent *Gate of Horn* by G. R. Levy presents the Greek effort to devise a civilized substitute for magic. The later dialogues of Plato "are in general of an Orphic or Pythagorean colour."

> There are the cosmic cycles, the harmony of the spheres, necessity with her whirling spindle at the centre of existence, the Judgment of the Dead, the Waters of Remembrance and Forgetfulness, and the soul's imprisonment in the Cave. In general they describe the fall from and the return to divine life.

Plato's theory of Ideas institutes a gigantic effort to establish the mystic doctrine upon an intellectual basis. The relation of created things to "the pattern laid up in heaven" is, as we saw, that *methexis*, or participation, which Aristotle equated with *mimesis*, the "imitation" by which the living world was built upon the Pythagorean numbers. Thus the relationship created by the earliest man, and the means of his growth as already described; the vehicle of the first-known religion, is now made articulate. The wheel has come full circle.

From this point of view, Greek Philosophy and science were a means of arresting the wheel of existence or of delivering us from the time mechanism of existence. In the opinion of Wyndham Lewis, that is the function of art as well. There is no need to immerse ourselves again in the destructive element of the Time flux or to return to that "Primitive Past saturated with blood and incest so generally favoured." We have, as *Finnegans Wake* also proclaims, the means to awaken permanently from the repetitive nightmare of history. This is also the basis of the Lewis attack on Spengler:

> We are perhaps in the last phases of Greek "progress"—phases that are extremely unGreek, however. Progress may even itself bring Progress to an end. Indeed, already the bottom seems to be entirely knocked out of Spengler's "historical" periodic picture by such things as wireless, air travel and so forth—actually by progress itself. How *can*, in fact, the old competitive "rising" and "declining" clashing of crowds of rising states continue at all, unless science is abolished, or else unless that state of historical rivalry is artificially maintained?

We have then, to consider that modern technology is itself mainly a product of art. It is explicitly the rival of the primitive artist. For it has been the prime characteristic of science and philosophy since Newton and Kant, that they seek to control the world rather than to understand it. We can, they say, control by magical formula what necessarily eludes our understanding or comprehension. The artist was always a magician in this sense. But the civilized artist has differed from the primitive artist in seeking to arrest the flux of existence in order that the mind may be united with that which is permanent in existence. Whereas the modern artist has used his factive or creative intelligence to manipulate matter and experience into a pattern which could arrest the mind in the presence of a particular aspect of existence, the modern scientist has sought to merge the functions of the primitive and civilized magicians. He has developed formulas for the control of the material world and then allied these to the control of the human mind. He invades the human mind and society with his patterned information. That is the key to the nature of the new "mass media."

In recent years Lewis returned to this theme in *America and Cosmic Man*, in which he took America as the laboratory in which was being produced the new ahistoric man. His attacks on the romancers of Progress and the romancers of the Past have this single aim, to deliver us from the bondage of primitive religion with its obsession with recurrence, and the way of destruction as the way of rebirth. And it has been his sense of equal menace presented to any living present by the cultist of East and West that has procured his exclusion from the public attention which they control.

Shelley, says Whitehead, "thinks of nature as changing, dissolving, transforming as it were at a fairy's touch. . . . this is one aspect of Nature, the elusive change . . . a change of inward character. That is where Shelley places his emphasis."

And that, Lewis points out, is where Whitehead, Bergson, Spengler, and their school place their emphasis. But, continues Whitehead, there is another aspect of nature, namely its opposite. And Lewis comments: "Wordsworth, we are told, because he was born upon a hill, saw the other aspect of nature. He is the poet of endurance. And Spengler tells us that all Greeks, whether born on a hill or elsewhere, always had the misfortune to see that side of the medal—the enduring and concrete as opposed to the changing."

Such is also the misfortune of Wyndham Lewis. But it is important for an understanding of his vortex view of art and civilization to notice his insistence that the world of Space as opposed to the world of memory and history is the world of a "pure Present." "The world of the 'Pure Present' of the Classical Ages is obviously the world that is born and dies every moment." By comparison with the intensity that is revealed in the contemplation of this spatial reality, the vision of the Time mind, argues Lewis, is that of the sentimental tourist:

> The pretentious omniscience of the "historical" intelligence makes of it an eternal dilettante, or tourist. It does not live in, it is *en touriste*, that is tastes its time-district, or time-climate. . . . This mental world becomes for it an interminable time-preserve, laid out for critical, disembodied journeyings.

A striking illustration of his point occurs in *The Lion and the Fox*. In Renaissance Italy:

> The prince or commander of an army or a state had often started as a free captain . . . we can agree that it must have been "singular to see these men—generally of low origin and devoid of culture—surrounded in their camps by ambassadors, poets and learned men, who read to them Livy and Cicero, and original verses in which they were compared to Scipio and Hannibal, to Caesar and Alexander." But they were all acting on a tiny scale the past that was being unearthed. . . . With the more intelligent of them like Caesar Borgia, this archaeological and analogic habit of mind assumed the proportion of a mania. His *Aut Caesar aut nihil* is the same type of literature as is concentrated in the small maniacal figure of Julian Sorel, Stendahl's little domestic Napoleon. . . . For every type of relatively small adventurer there was an antique model. . . . They

attempted to bring to life the heroes of antiquity, and recall in their own lives the events recorded in the codices, and it was this immediate application of everything to life in Italian renaissance society (like the substitution of a cinema for a history-book in a school) that made the Italian influence so vivid in the rest of Europe. Renaissance Italy was very exactly a kind of Los Angeles where historical scenes were tried out, antique buildings imitated and roughly run up, and dramatic crimes reconstructed.

In a word, Lewis' attitude to the Time-and-psychology-enchanted Bergsonian and Proustian twentieth century extends to the Renaissance. Along with T. E. Hulme he would substitute for the naturalistic values of that era those of the ahistoric cultures of Egypt and Byzantium. He is not enchanted by gimcrack approximations to past grandeur:

> When, as in the present age, life loses its exterior beauty, and all the ritual of grandeur has become extinct, the intellect and character everywhere deteriorates. "It is always the form that imposes the fact. But in its turn the form originates in some fancy or desire that seeks a ceremonious expression, just as an ardent mind seeks for itself a personal expression in some suitable medium."

It is the magical form of Shakespeare's verse which evokes the leonine splendours of his heroes:

> . . . the poetry overwhelms the prose: the chivalry substitutes itself for the self-interest, a mystical religion for a "scientific truth," the Lion for the Fox.

Lewis' theory of art and communication is a traditional one. The hero, the genius, is a god-intoxicated man. He communes with the noumenal world. And the contrast of this knowledge with the misery of his human condition constitutes his dementia or madness:

> It is as outcasts, as men already in a sense out of life, and divested of the functional machinery of their roles . . . Lear, Hamlet, Timon, Thersites, and so forth are in the position of disincarnate spirits, but still involved with and buffeted by life. Their "truth" is an angry one usually, but they have the advantage of having no "axe to grind."
>
> Thersites is always in that unfortunate position! Lear and Hamlet only become so when they grow demented . . . we assume that if undisturbed by calamity they would be respectable members of society, and not have, much less express, all these horrible thoughts. It is this assumption of conditions that do not exist at all in the plays . . . that is usually the basis of English Shakespearian criticism.

The sense in which Lewis envisages his artist as genius and as the Enemy also appears in another passage from *The Lion and the Fox*:

The child is made to feel that the individual in himself or in herself is the enemy. The death or subjection of that enemy is the task of the child. He must deaden himself before engaging as a qualified human being in the world-wide occupation of making life mechanical and uniform, and fit for even the vastest herd to live in.

Honour is not your own "good" for there is no you. Honour is a faculty of the gentleman: Its exercise consists in doing as much for somebody else (for the Not-You) as is consistent with the natural reluctance to do anything of the sort, and where the circumstances ensure complete safety: in order to get the maximum for yourself, while pretending all the while that the self does not exist, and that the Not-You (or you might say the NOT) does.

The artist, gifted with mania from above, is always confronted with the great collective mania from below:

But without the scientific organization of revolution . . . men have always had this much wider instinct for the divine—that is of course, the instinct to destroy it, to isolate it, or corrupt it to their uses. In a time when there is no accredited divinity, or "divine right," left, it is in a sense easier to observe the universal operation of this instinct. . . . So that dark competitive self, in the smallest organism, that makes it murderous, becomes organized into the type of herd-war against the head, where almost anything high, unusual and unassimilable is sighted. . . . It is the person wrenched out of the organic context by the impulses of some divine ferment, and this being suddenly appearing free, that is the signal for those dispensations and adjustments, culminating in his pathos. . . .

It must be remembered that human beings are congeries of parasites subsisting on the Individual, subsisting on a very insufficient supply of Individuals. . . . And anything representing the principle of individuality they attack. . . . On the back of every great human intelligence there are millions of contingent forms, which it propels and feeds. The relations subsisting between this lonely host and the organisms to whom he is appropriated is not very marked by a warm mutual sympathy.

In considering the meaning for art and communication of this war of the collective puppetry against the individual person there is another passage in G. R. Levy's *The Gate of Horn* which indicates the traditional bearings of the position:

Plato's theory of the Ideas constitutes a gigantic effort to establish the mystic doctrine upon an intellectual basis. . . . But it must be noted that Plato's Ideas are of two kinds, and both of the nature of the Soul. Like daemons, some of whom are conceived as descending as watchers from the higher spheres of being, and others as rising from the body or group, but infected by it, and so always drawn back into incarnation. . . .

This would seem to be the basis of Lewis' distinction between the space-mind and the Time-ridden mentality. As he writes in *Wyndham Lewis the Artist*:

If you conclude from this that I am treading the road to the platonic heaven, my particular road is deliberately chosen for the immanent satisfaction that may be found by the way. You may know Schopenhauer's eloquent and resounding words, where, in his forcible fashion, he is speaking of what art accomplishes: "It therefore pauses at this particular thing: the course of time stops: the relations vanish for it: only the essential, the idea is its object." . . . A sort of immortality descends upon these objects. It is an immortality which, in the case of painting, they have to pay for with death, or at least with its coldness and immobility.

That is, the moment of art is not a moment of time's covenant. And art emotion is specifically that experience of arrest in which we pause before a particular thing or experience. It is also, at such moments, the sense of disproportion between our mental and our physical dimensions from which Lewis derives his view both of the tragic and the comic:

It is to feel that our consciousness is bound up with this non-mechanical phenomenon of life; that, although helpless in the face of the material world, we are in some way superior to and independent of it; and that our mechanical imperfection is the symbol of that. In art we are in a sense playing at being what we designate as matter. We are entering the forms of the mighty phenomena around us, and seeing how near we can get to being a river or a star, without actually becoming that. . . . The game consists in seeing how near you can get, without the sudden extinction and neutralization that awaits you as matter, or as the machine. In our bodies we have got already so near to extinction.

This provides the perfect view of the great Lewis line in painting and his watchful game with his characters in fiction. It is a perpetual poise on a razor's edge. It explains at once his lack of enthusiasm not only for Bergson's passionate merging with the Time flux, but his scepticism about Eliot's doctrine of impersonality in art. The above views also help to explain that affinity which Lewis has with Dostoevsky despite the superficial lack of resemblance between the great Romantic and the Lewis stylization. As he himself suggests in *The Lion and the Fox*, apropos of Falstaff and Don Quixote:

Hamlet, Lear, Othello, Timon are all demented or hallucinated, as so many of the celebrated figures in nineteenth century Russian fiction were. It is the supreme liberty it is possible to take with your material. That it should be so often taken in the case of the great characters of dramatic fiction is the most evident testimony to the dependence on untruth, in every sense, in which our human nature and environment put us. In the case of Muishkin, Dostoevsky had to call in express and abnormal physiological conditions to help him incarnate his saint. And the heightening everywhere in Shakespeare is by way of madness. Since it is made to behave in the way the hero does, he has to be maddened by some means or other more often than not in order to make him at all probable.

The hero, in short, is, as such, a type of mania from above and a type of the misery as well as of the grandeur of the human condition. Along these lines it would be easy to establish the affinities not only between Lewis and Dostoevsky but between Lewis and Swift.

His theory of the comic as stated in *The Wild Body* is the exact reverse of the Bergsonian theory of laughter:

> The root of the comic is to be sought in the sensations resulting from the observations of a thing behaving like a person. But from that point of view all men are necessarily comic: for they are all things, or physical bodies, behaving as persons. It is only when you come to deny that they are "persons" or that there is any "mind" or "person" there at all, that the world of appearance is accepted as quite natural, and not at all ridiculous. Then, with the denial of "the person," life becomes immediately both "real" and very serious.

In a word, life is always serious for Bergson because our personal reality depends not on moments of detachment from the flux but on moments when we are merged in it. Lewis, on the contrary, adopts the Schopenhauer intellectualism in seeing the movements of vision as an arrest and detachment of the great mechanism of the world as will and idea: "moments of vision are blurred rapidly, and the poet sinks into the rhetoric of the will." And "no man has ever continued to live who has observed himself in that manner for longer than a flash. Such consciousness must be of the nature of a thunderbolt. Laughter is only summer-lightning. But it occasionally takes on the dangerous form of absolute revelation."

Between this view and the earlier quotation concerning art as a game played on the edge of the abyss of extinction, it is possible to get a very adequate image of Lewis's activity as a painter and novelist. He is a mystic or visionary of the comic, moving toward the pole of intelligibility instead of that of feeling. Joyce establishes a similar distinction in his notebooks as quoted by Gorman:

> When tragic art makes my body to shrink terror is not my feeling because I am urged from rest, and moreover this art does not show me what is grave, I mean what is constant and irremediable in human fortunes, nor does it unite me with the secret cause. . . . Terror and pity, finally are aspects of sorrow comprehended in sorrow—the feeling which the privation of some good excites in us.

In short, Joyce tends like Lewis to reject the way of connatural gnosis and emotion favoured by Bergson, Eliot, and theosophy, in which the emotions are used as the principal windows of the soul. And Joyce continues " . . . but a comedy (a work of comic art) which does not urge us to seek anything beyond itself excites in us the feeling of joy. . . . For beauty is a quality of something seen but terror and pity and joy are states of mind." Joyce, that is, argues that beauty is entirely of intellectual apprehension whereas the passions or states of mind are gnostic windows of the soul which cause us to be merged with that particular quality. The intellectual, comic perception is for Lewis what beauty is for Joyce. But so far as the term "beauty" goes Lewis identifies it with "ideal conditions for an organism," much as Burke does in *The Sublime and the Beautiful*. Compared with Joyce, however, there is in Lewis a Manichean abjurgation of delectation.

But Joyce, Lewis, Eliot, and Pound are perhaps nearer in agreement on the subject of the vortices of existence. If "the world of the 'pure present' of the Classical Ages is obviously the world that is born and dies every moment," it is clear that it is such a world that Lewis seeks to arrest in his paintings (and novels), especially in that "creation myth" which appears in this issue of *Shenandoah*.[1] If we can elucidate the vortex concepts in Lewis we shall be finally in a position to see his grounds for rejecting the thought and work of the Time and Flux school of this century. At first glance it might seem that Lewis was a candidate for the same school in being the observer of a "world that is born and dies every moment." But there is even at that level the habit of the observer substituted for the sympathetic merger. In place of the gnostic and nostalgic contemplation of flowers that give thoughts too deep for tears, Lewis would as soon "say it with locomotives." *In Wyndham Lewis the Artist* he writes:

> In the case of a dynamic shape like an aeroplane there is neither any reason nor any need for the collaboration of engineer and artist. All such machines, except for their colouring, or some surface design, to modify their shape, develop in accordance with a law of efficient evolution as absolute as that determining the shape of the tiger, the wasp, or the swallow. They are definitely, for the artist, in the category of animals. When we come to the static cell-structures (houses) in which we pass our lives there is far more latitude and opportunity for his inventiveness.

That is to say, Lewis is not without affinities with Samuel Butler, who viewed the evolutionary impulses as existing in an accelerated form in machinery. But Lewis is not much interested in the time vistas of evolution if only because:

> The artist goes back to the fish. The few centuries that separate him from the savage are a mere flea-bite to the distance his memory must stretch if it is to strike the fundamental slime of creation. And those are the conditions—the very first gust of creation in this scale of life in which we are set that he must reach, before he, in his turn, can create!
>
> The creation of a work of art is an act of the same description as the evolution of wings on the sides of a fish, the feathering of its fins; or the invention of a weapon within the body of a hymenopter to meet the terrible needs of its life. The ghostly and burning

growths—the walking twigs and flying stones—the two anguished notes that are the voice of a being—the vapid twitter; the bellows of age-long insurrection and discontent—the complacent screech—all these may be considered as types of art, all equally perfect, but not all equally desirable.

Corresponding to this notion of creativity is Lewis' theory of communication:

For what the artist's public has to be brought to do is to see its world, and the people in it, as a stranger would. There have been so far principally two methods of achieving this. One is to display a strange world to the spectator, and yet one that has so many analogies to his that, as he looks, startled into attention by an impressive novelty, he sees his own reality through this veil, as it were, momentarily in truer colours. The other method is the less objective one of luring the spectator to the point from which, inevitably, the world will appear as the artist sees it, and the spectator from that point of vantage paints the picture for himself, but with the artist's colours and his more expert eyes. The first of these methods can be described very roughly as the impersonal and objective method, and the second as the personal and subjective one. The latter method (contrary to what is sometimes supposed) seems to be more assured of a positive result: for a lesser effort of intelligence is required on the part of the public. . . . The artist, unless of a very lucky or privileged description, can only exist even, by pretending to be one of the audience. Nothing less democratic than that will be tolerated. . . . Bergson's view that the permanence of the work of art, or its continued interest for us, depends on its uniqueness, on the fact that such and such a thing will never happen again, would make of everything in life a work of art.

Lewis has made plain enough what he considers to be the relation between the artist and nature. He holds the traditional view of imitation as working in the way that nature works, so that art is another nature: "As much of that material poetry of Nature as the plastic vessel will stand should be taken up into the picture. Nowadays though when Nature finds itself expressed so universally in specialized mechanical counterpart, and cities have modified our emotions, the plastic vessel, paradoxically, is more fragile. The less human it becomes, the more delicate from this point of view." That suggests that as more and more of the actual material world has been brought under the manipulation of the global art of applied science, and as our emotions are attenuated by the impact of these artifacts, the balance of the individual artist becomes more precarious. It is, naturally, in relation to the artist's operating in the way that nature works that brings Lewis to a direct statement of his notion of the vortex:

Da Vinci recommends you to watch and be observant of the grains and markings of wood, the patterns found in Nature everywhere. The patterned grains of stones, marble, etc., the fibres of wood, have a rightness and inevitability that is similar to the rightness with which objects arrange themselves in life—the objects upon your work-table, for instance . . . the finest artists—and this is what Art means—are those men who are so trained and sensitized that they have a perpetually renewed power of doing what Nature does, only doing it with all the beauty of accident, without the certain futility that accident implies.

It is in this sense that art for Lewis appears as a natural vortex of patterned energy, presenting us with creative cores or vortices of causality. In the heart of these cores or vortices there is an absolute calm, but at the periphery there is violence and the unmistakable character of great energy. These "untumultuous vortices of power" are at the centre of every vital work of art as they are in any vital civilization. And it is presumably the view of Lewis that the role of the artist in society is to energize it by establishing such intellectually purified images of the entelechy of nature. The alternative mode is the swoon upon death, the connatural merging in the indiscriminate flux of life, the reflexive feeling and expressing of one's time. It is Lewis' constant theme that the art of our time has chosen the second mode and that its Mona Lisa appeal is to the death swoon.

CHAPTER THREE

Formal Causality in Chesterton

MARSHALL MCLUHAN

One reason why Chesterton exasperated many fastidious souls relates to what I am going to illustrate as his concern with formal causality. He was vividly aware of his public and of its needs both to be cheered and to be straightened out. So pervasive is this feature in Chesterton that it scarcely matters at what page one opens in order to illustrate it. For example, the first page of his book on Dickens begins as follows:

> Much of our modern difficulty, in religion and other things, arises merely from this: that we confuse the word "indefinable" with the word "vague." If someone speaks of a spiritual fact as "indefinable" we promptly picture something misty, a cloud with indeterminate edges. But this is an error even in commonplace logic. The thing that cannot be defined is the first thing; the primary fact. It is our arms and legs, our pots and pans, that are indefinable.[1]

Here Chesterton is quite aware that the problems of his time are not without a strong affinity for each other. If one looks at the opening objections in the Thomistic article, one finds a similar awareness of likeness in diversity. Aquinas always put his public on view at the opening of his disputed questions, and Chesterton usually gives strong indications of the kinds of people and the kinds of problems with which he is dealing. On the second page of the same book on Dickens, he focuses this larger awareness of audience on Dickens himself:

In everyday talk, or in any of our journals, we may find the loose but important phrase, "Why have we no great men today? Why have we no great men like Thackeray, or Carlyle, or Dickens?" Do not let us dismiss this expression, because it appears loose or arbitrary. "Great" does mean something, and the test of its actuality is to be found by noting how instinctively and incisively we do apply it to some men and not to others; above all how instinctively and incisively we do apply it to four or five men in the Victorian era, four or five men of whom Dickens was not the least. The term is found to fit a definite thing. Dickens was what it means.[2]

Joseph Conrad, addressing his public, said: "My task . . . is before all, to make you *see*."[3] He was drawing attention to a defect in his readers, a defect which he was concerned to supply and to repair. This, in turn, is to draw attention to the public as a formal cause in the sense that the public is in need of some help in some area of concern, an area in which it is ignorant, or mistaken, or confused. Ezra Pound devoted much of his work to the theme that the artist's work is to *make it new*. In this respect it is possible to point out that the formal cause, or the public itself, is in perpetual flux and always in need of clarification and re-focusing of its problems. Style itself, whether in poetry or painting or music, is a way of seeing and knowing, which is otherwise unobtainable. In his book, *The Problem of Style*, Middleton Murry pointed out "style is a way of seeing." To mention this work is to remind ourselves of the much greater work of Rémy de Gourmont, *Le Problème du Style*. The style is the response of the artist to his audience and its needs. Chesterton's style was playful in an age that was very earnest, and his perceptions and thoughts were paradoxical or multifaceted in a time that was full of intense specialism in politics and economics and religion.

Earlier I had mentioned that Aquinas put his public in full view of his readers at the beginning of each article. His public is that which shapes and patterns his discourse and takes the form of an inventory of objections which cover the whole spectrum of the confusions and inadequacies of his contemporaries. The very first objection, at the very beginning of the *Summa*, notes: "It seems that, beside the philosophical sciences, we have no need of any further knowledge. For man should not seek to know what is above reason. *'Seek not the things that are too high for thee.'* (Ecclus. III: 22)"

The answers to the objections pursue the confusions of his readers more closely still. It appears that no Thomist has considered the audience or public of a philosopher as the formal cause of his work. Yet this is truly the case in Plato and Aristotle as well as in Aquinas. If the formal cause of the Incarnation is fallen man, it is not surprising that the misguided audience of the creative person should be the formal cause of his endeavours.

Perhaps, before moving on, I should pause to indicate why Western philosophers and scholars may have shirked consideration of formal causality in the study of the arts and sciences. Since scarcely anybody has studied the audience of any writer from Plato to the present, there must surely be both a profound and a simple reason for so vast and consistent [an] omission. I suggest that this reason is to be found in the visual bias of Western man. Visual man is typically concerned with the lineal and the connected and the logical. Visual order has regard to *figure* and not to *ground*. The audience is always the hidden *ground* rather than the *figure* of any discourse. The *ground* is discontinuous, murky and dynamic, whereas the *figure* tends to be clear and distinct and static. However, without the interplay of *figure* and *ground*, no art or knowledge is possible. It might even be argued that the abrupt and bumpy and grotesquely sprockety contours of Chesterton's prose are very much a response of his sensitivity to a perverse and misbegotten public that he earnestly but good-naturedly was determined to redeem from its banalities.

Arthur Miller recently wrote a remarkable essay about his own public and its role in creating drama.[4] 1949 was the eve of network TV when a totally new public came into play. Up until then, there had been a kind of homogeneous audience from New York to San Francisco:

> In many ways it was a good audience, but the important point to remember is that it was the only one, and therefore catholic. Traditionally it could applaud the Ziegfeld Follies one night and O'Neill the next, and if it never made great hits of Odets's plays, it affected to regard him as the white-haired boy. Both O'Neill and Odets would privately decry the audience as Philistine and pampered, but it was the audience they set about to save from its triviality, for they could not really conceive there could be another.[5]

In the everyday order, formal causality reveals itself by its *effects*. There is a strange paradox in this, because since the effects come from the hidden *ground* of situations, the effects usually appear before their causes. When a Darwin or an Einstein appears, we say "the time was ripe" and that the *figure* appeared in its natural *ground*. Chesterton was almost oriental in his sensitivity to effects, his capacity for noting the consequences embedded in innovations and special attitudes or situations. In fact, Chesterton was always aware of "the law of the situation." This phrase was much used by Mary Parker Follett, the inventor of modern management studies. She was always concerned with discovering the question rather than the answer. It was she who began to ask managers: "What business do you think you are in?" They would point to the *figure* in their enterprise and she would give the *ground*, or the *effects* of the *figure*. She would point out to a windowblind manufacturer that he was really in the business of environmental light control. With this knowledge, the manufacturer is not likely to be disconcerted by an innovation like the invention of Venetian blinds.

In *Tremendous Trifles*, Chesterton observes:

> You cannot see a wind; you can only see that there is a wind. So, also, you cannot see a revolution; you can only see that there is a revolution. And there never has been in the history of the world a real revolution, brutally active and decisive, which was not preceded by unrest and new dogma in the reign of invisible things. All revolutions began by being abstract. Most revolutions began by being quite pedantically abstract.

> The wind is up above the world before a twig on the tree has moved. So there must always be a battle in the sky before there is a battle on the earth.[6]

Chesterton's awareness of the *figure*/ground consequences pervades his studies of history and human thought in general. It made it easy for him to enter the field of detective fiction, since the detective story is written backwards, starting with the effects, and discovering the cause later, and, as it were, incidentally. The history of detective fiction, at least since Edgar Poe, relates to the law of the situation very intimately.

Poe is perhaps best known for his account of the composition of "The Raven." He explained that, seeking in the first place to achieve an effect of maximal melancholy and gloom, he set about discovering the means to get this effect, noting that art must always start with the *effect*. This is another way of saying that art must start with formal cause, and with concern with the audience. Sherlock Holmes frequently explained to Watson (who was typical of the unenlightened public) that the detective must put himself in the place of the criminal. The criminal is the person who is entirely concerned with *effects*. He considers the entire situation as one to be manipulated, both *figure* and *ground*, in order to achieve a very special effect. The criminal, like the artist, takes into account both the *figure* and the *ground*, that is, the work to be done in order that the effect may be achieved. It is this interplay between *figure* and *ground*, and the confronting of the latter in the situation, which gives to the detective story so much of the poetic character. Chesterton's *Father Brown* is always sensitive to the hidden laws of the situation that are so easily obscured by the ordinary concern with *figure* and points of view: for it is of the essence of formal causality that it is not a point of view, but, rather, a statement of a situation. In "The Queer Feet," Father Brown says:

> "A crime," he said slowly, "is like any other work of art. Don't look surprised; crimes are by no means the only works of art that come from an infernal workshop. But every work of art, divine or diabolic, has one indispensable mark—I mean, that the centre of it is simple, however much the fulfilment may be complicated."[7]

He continues:

> But every clever crime is founded ultimately on some one quite simple fact—some fact that is not itself mysterious. The mystification comes in covering it up, in leading men's thoughts away from it. This large and subtle and (in the ordinary course) most profitable crime, was built on the plain fact that a gentleman's evening dress is the same as a waiter's. All the rest was acting, and thundering good acting, too.[8]

The covering-up process is done by simply introducing points of view. Points of view are inevitably alien to the law of the situation, and especially alien to formal causality. Points of view are always reserved for the police and the slow-witted. In the world of Sherlock Holmes and much detective fiction, the rational point of view, with its plodding accumulation of evidence, is reserved for Lestrade and the police in general.

Formal causality is not something that can be abstracted, since it is always a dynamic relation between the user and the ever-changing situation. Cardinal Newman recognised this *in An Essay on the Development of Christian Doctrine*:

> Moreover, an idea not only modifies but is modified, or at least influenced, by the state of things in which it is carried out, and is dependent in various ways on the circumstances which surround it. Its development proceeds quickly or slowly, as it may be; the order of succession in its various stages is variable; it shows differently in a small sphere of action and in an extended; it may be interrupted, retarded, mutilated, distorted by external violence; it may be enfeebled by the effort of ridding itself of domestic foes; it may be impeded and swayed or even absorbed by counter energetic ideas; it may be coloured by the received tone of thought into which it comes, or depraved by the intrusion of foreign principles, or at length shattered by the development of some original fault within it.[9]

It was the "rhetorical" interplay between philosophy and its public which was eliminated by Descartes in the seventeenth century with the result that formal cause was transferred from the public to the subjective life of the individual philosopher or student of philosophy. The further consequence was that the "content" of philosophy and the arts became relegated to efficient causality. Formal causality simply ceased to have any *conscious* role in the arts and sciences from then until our own day. Chesterton was part of the *avant-garde* in re-discovering formal causality in his multi-levelled grasp of his public and his themes.

CHAPTER FOUR

Francis Bacon's Theory of Communication and Media

ERIC MCLUHAN

Abstract: For centuries, Francis Bacon has been revered as a philosopher and as the founder of modern science—an honour which would have baffled him. He thought of himself as a grammarian, not a dialectician (philosopher), and as engaged in restoring the wisdom of the Ancients, not in founding scientific novelty. The "Novum" in the title of his major work, the *Novum Organum* (or *Novum Organon*) was ironic and indicated both that the work was intended to supersede the dialectical *Organon* of Aristotle and that the work was in support of traditional learning and technique in reading the Book of Nature. In Part One of the *N. O.* he sets forth his theory of the bias of communication in the celebrated doctrine of the Idols; in Part Two he presents in detail his theory of communication—a theory already present in such other works as *The New Atlantis* and *Of the Advancement of Learning*.

Francis Bacon's theory of communication and of media permeates his work. Often called the father of modern scientific method, Bacon saw his mission as that of restoring in his time the wisdom of the ancients—his program called the *Great Instauration*.

As a grammarian, Bacon could claim all of human knowledge as his province: *Of the Advancement of Learning* is an encyclopedic report on the state of the arts and sciences in his day. Bacon never for a minute ceases to view the business of the arts and sciences as being the relief of man's fallen moral state.[1] In this matter he is in perfect accord with St. Bonaventure, with his ancestor, Roger Bacon, and with a long tradition in which man's task had been defined "as the organization of our earthly exile into a sort of suburb of the heavenly kingdom. . . ."[2] Consequently, Bacon's protestations of originality are seldom to be taken seriously. His account of philosophy in Book I of the *Novum Organum*[3] is nearly identical with Cicero's. Nor is this strange, since both held the view that the arts are entirely to be judged on the basis of their usefulness to man.

The Grand Renaissance was, in the matter of the revival of grammar as the method both of science and of theology, not fully achieved until the sixteenth century. Erasmus' great work was to restore patristic theology—that is, grammatical theology. His significance in his own eyes, as well as in the eyes of his age, was that of the man who cast out the stream-lined grammars of the dialecticians of the schools and who restored the full discipline as understood by St. Jerome, the pupil of the great Donatus. "Humanism" was thus for Colet, More, Erasmus, a deliberate return to the Fathers. But that which equally marks the modern Renaissance and lends to it a character which has been much misunderstood is its "science." From the time of the neo-Platonists and Augustine to Bonaventura and to Francis Bacon, the world was viewed as a book, the lost language of which was analogous to that of human speech. Thus the art of grammar provided the sixteenth-century approach not only to the Book of Life in scriptural exegesis but to the Book of Nature, as well.

Omnis mundi creatura

Quasi liber et pictura

Nobis est, et speculum . . .

The Theory of Words and Scientific Study

In the dialogue named for Cratylus, the follower of Heraclitus, Plato has this exchange between Socrates and Cratylus:

> Socrates: But if these things are only to be known through names, how can we suppose that the givers of names had knowledge, or were legislators before there were names at all, and therefore before they could have known them?

> Cratylus: I believe, Socrates, the true account of the matter to be, that a power more than human gave things their first names, and that the names which were thus given are necessarily their true names.[4]

Obviously, with this kind of importance associated with the names of things, and of gods, heroes, and legendary beings, etymology would be a main source of scientific and moral enlightenment. And such was the case. The prolific labors of the etymologists reflected in Plato's *Cratylus*, but begun centuries before and continued until the seventeenth century, are as much the concern of the historian of philosophy and of science as of the historian of letters and culture. Indeed, it was not only in antiquity but until the Cartesian revolution that language was viewed as simultaneously linking and harmonizing all the intellectual and physical functions of man and of the physical world as well.

At any time from Plato to Francis Bacon the statement of Cratylus would have made sense and would have evoked respect even when its wider implications were rejected. With the opening of the Christian era, the doctrine of *Cratylus* gained new significance from scriptural exegesis, and especially from Genesis 2.19:

> And out of the ground the Lord God formed every beast of the field, and every fowl of the air; and brought them unto the man to see what he would call them: and whatsoever he called every living creature, that was the name thereof.

The doctrine of names is, of course, the doctrine of essence and not a naïve notion of oral terminology.

The scriptural exegetists will hold, as Francis Bacon held, that Adam possessed metaphysical knowledge in a very high degree. To him the whole of nature was a book which he could read with ease. He lost this ability to read this language as a result of his fall; and Solomon alone of the sons of men has ever recovered the power to read the book of nature. The business of art is, however, to recover the knowledge of that language which once man held by nature. The problem as to which of the arts should have priority in the work of explaining man and nature had arisen among the pre-Socratics. Grammar, or allegorical exegesis of natural phenomena, as well as of folk myths and even the works of Homer and Hesiod, enjoyed many advantages for the task. In the *Cratylus*, however, Plato asserts the superior claims of dialectics for the same work, but, as a philosopher who habitually employed the grammatical modes of poetry and myth to express his own most significant and esoteric teaching, he is far from confident that grammar can be or ought to be entirely superseded. Shortly afterwards, however, Aristotle established the nature of non-grammatical scientific method in the *Posterior Analytics*. His achievement bore no fruit until the twelfth century. Until the twelfth century, therefore, grammar reigned unrivalled as the prime mode of science, and, from the patristic period, of theology as well. But grammar was far from forgotten during the great age of dialectics. In the thirteenth century, with the triumph of Aristotle in St. Thomas Aquinas, came simultaneously the consummate achievement of the grammatical method in St. Bonaventura. The great grammarians are also alchemists. There is thus not the least incongruity in the fact that eminent humanists like Pico Della Mirandola and Cornelius Agrippa are also alchemists. The grammatical method in science, therefore, persists as long as alchemy, which is to say, well into the eighteenth century. But from the time of Descartes the main mode of science is, of course, mathematical. In our own time the methods of anthropology and psychology have re-established grammar as, at least, a valid mode of science.

Needless to say, Aristotle did not share the analogist's view of words and phenomena as interrelated by proportions and etymologies. Yet, dialectics and rhetoric in the hands of the analogists were certainly refashioned until they became not merely sciences but the queens of the sciences. This is true not merely of Ciceronian rhetoric and scholastic dialectics, but of the "system" of Francis Bacon as well.[5]

At the core of his program, Bacon puts the traditional role of the arts as providing the indispensable training for the sciences: "Our labours must therefore be directed towards inquiring into and observing resemblances and analogies, both in the whole and in its parts, for they unite nature, and lay the foundation of the sciences."[6] And at the close of the *Novum Organum* Bacon points out that it "springs from the nature of things, as well as from that of the mind," and that much care must be expended in perceptual training and practical modes of criticism and observation, either to "assist and cure the understanding and senses, or furnish our general practice."[7]

Idols and the Bias of Perception

Naturally, Bacon turned his attention to bias and corruption of the faculties and as imposed by media:

> [T]he powers of bodies are more or less impeded or advanced by the medium, according to the nature of the bodies and their effective powers, and also according to that of the medium. For one medium is adapted to light, another to sound, another to heat and cold, another to magnetic action, and so on . . .[8]

He mounted a two-pronged counterattack on the bias of communication. First, he identified the "false gods" or idols which bewitch and confuse human reason (weakened by the Fall), so that once seen they might be purged. Second, he prescribed a means of re-engaging and retuning the faculties by writing in aphoristic style.

As early as the *Advancement of Learning* the Idols appear in embryo:

> But lastly there is a much more important and profound kind of fallacies in the mind of man which I find not observed or inquired at all, and think good to place here, as that which of all others appertaineth most to rectify judgment: the force whereof is such, as it doth not dazzle or snare the understanding in some particulars, but doth more generally and inwardly infect and corrupt the state thereof. For the mind of man is far from the nature of a clear and equal glass, wherein the beams of things should reflect according to their true incidence; nay, it is rather like an enchanted glass, full of superstition and imposture, if it be not delivered and reduced. For this purpose, let us consider the false appearances that are imposed upon us by the general nature of the mind[9]

> Let us consider again the false appearances imposed upon us by every man's own individual nature and custom.[10]

> And lastly let us consider the false appearances that are imposed upon us by words, which are framed and applied according to the conceit and capacities of the vulgar sort: and although we think we govern our words, and prescribe it well, *loquendum ut vulgus, sentiendum ut sapientes*; yet certain it is that words, as a Tartar's bow, do shoot back upon the understanding of the wisest, and mightily entangle and pervert the judgment.[11]

Not surprisingly, Francis Bacon's four Idols appear in Roger Bacon. Roger's quarrel with the Schoolmen is precisely the same as that of his remote kinsman Francis; nor is there any time from Augustine to Descartes when this grammatical tradition is not very much alive. (Roger Bacon [ca. 1210–1292], educated at Oxford, spent most of his life at Paris. His *Opus Majus* is St. Augustine's *De Doctrina Christiana* put into the new formulas of the thirteenth century. What might seem to be startling anticipations of Renaissance notions turn out to be continuous traditions given the appearance of novelty or revival by the circumstances of the sudden triumph of the grammarians over scholasticism.) The eloquence of the two men is identical: Roger declares,

> There are four principal stumbling blocks (*offendicula*) to comprehending truth.... From these deadly pests come all the evils of the human race; for the noblest and most useful documents of wisdom are ignored, and the secrets of the arts and sciences ... than this, men blinded by the darkness of these four do not see their ignorance but take every care to palliate that for which they do not find the remedy ... when they are in the densest shades of error, they deem themselves in the full light of truth.[12]

Since the tradition of Descartes, Hobbes, and Newton is that not of the Fathers but of the schoolmen or *Moderni*, it is small wonder that some writers have been puzzled how to reconcile Erasmus and Bacon with the "moderns." Humanists such as Erasmus, Vives, Reuchlin, Agrippa, Mirandola, and Bacon took great pains to advertise themselves as "ancients."

Like Francis Bacon after him, Roger Bacon orders the arts with regard to their function for the relief of man's fallen estate. The principal evils of the fall are ignorance, concupiscence, and death. McKeon's statement about Roger holds for Francis and the whole grammatical tradition:

> God revealed all philosophy to man in the beginning, and the history of thought since has been the cyclical rediscovery, after periods of sin, of a wisdom the patriarchs received. Of course, the primitive revelation had to be filled by the details of science (that was why the patriarchs lived three hundred years), and Bacon therefore strikes the double posture of the prophet who heralds the return to the ancient truths and of the scientist who possesses new and strange truths with which to revivify the ancient doctrine. Wisdom is one, but items of information may be added to substantiate it without altering its outlines. Experimental knowledge is to accomplish this, and its procedure will be to work either with the Things without the mind or the Things within; God is the active intellect. The study of Bacon is chiefly the study of this theory of knowledge and of the details of reform to which knowledge of languages and of the various sciences is to be subjected.[13]

Aphoristic style

Francis Bacon envisaged two modes of delivering scientific knowledge, both functions of rhetoric: one is esoteric; the other, exoteric: "But as young men, when they knit and shape perfectly, do seldom grow to a further stature; so knowledge, while it is in aphorisms and observations it is in growth: but when it once is comprehended in exact methods, it may perchance be further polished and illustrate [*sic*: in the edition of 1605] and accommodated for use and practice; but it increaseth no more in bulk and substance."[14] Bacon makes it perfectly clear that he considered his own aphoristic style in the *Essays* as part of a scientific technique of keeping knowledge in a state of emergent evolution and thereby of constantly referring it to perception and observation.

> Another diversity of Method, whereof the consequence is great, is the delivery of knowledge in Aphorisms, or in Methods; wherein we may observe that it hath been too much taken into custom, out of a few axioms or observations on any subject, to make a solemn and formal art, filling it with some discourses, and illustrating it with examples, and digesting it into a sensible Method.

But the writing in aphorisms hath many excellent virtues, whereto the writing in Method doth not approach. For first, it trieth the writer. Whether he be superficial or solid: for Aphorisms, except they should be rediculous, cannot be made but of the pith and heart of sciences; for discourse of illustration is cut off: recitals of examples are cut off; discourse of connection and order is cut off; descriptions of practice are cut off. So there remaineth nothing to fill the Aphorisms but some good quantity of observation: and therefore no man can suffice, nor in reason will attempt to write Aphorisms, but he that is sound and grounded. But in methods,

Tantum series juncturaque pollet,

Tantum de medio sumptis accedit honoris;

—Hor. *Ep. Ad Pis.* 242

as a man shall make a great shew of an art, which, if it were disjointed, would come to little. Secondly, methods are more fit to win consent or belief, but less fit to point to action; for they carry a kind of demonstration in orb or circle, one part illuminating another, and therefore satisfy; but particulars, being dispersed, do best agree with dispersed directions. And lastly, Aphorisms, representing a knowledge broken, do invite men to inquire further; whereas Methods, carrying the show of a total, do secure men, as if they were at farthest.[15]

Knowledge in discontinuous form has specific power to involve:

. . . for the contemplation of God's creatures and works produceth (having regard to the works and creatures themselves) knowledge, but having regard to God, no perfect knowledge but wonder, which is broken knowledge.[16]

Using the traditional awareness of the impact of style on the perceptions of the audience, Bacon saw his *Novum Organum*, for example, as remedial: the choice of aphoristic style was calculated to freshen awareness and assist in purging the bias of communication. Mind as well as senses had to be cleansed to prepare them for the great task of reading and interpreting the Two Books.

Formal Cause and the Encyclopedia of Knowledge

As much as literature, Nature is an encyclopedia, so the grammarian needed full knowledge of the trivium and quadrivium as well as keen perception and critical faculties. The objective of using the arts and sciences to penetrate the Book of Nature is ever to recover knowledge of the languages in which it is inscribed, lost at the Fall.

To this task grammar brings all of its tools of interpretation and etymology and formal analysis. Bacon opens Book II of the *Novum Organum* with a report on the state of understanding in each of the four departments of causality.

> The unhappy state of man's actual knowledge is manifest. . . . It is rightly laid down that true knowledge is that which is deduced from causes. The division of four causes also is not amiss: matter, form, the efficient, and end or final cause. Of these, however, the latter is so far from being beneficial, that it even corrupts the sciences. . . . The discovery of form is considered desperate. As for the efficient cause and matter . . . they are but desultory and superficial, and of scarcely any avail to real and active knowledge.

The discovery of form united all labours on the Two Books; for, as held throughout the tradition, the forms manifest the Logos and provide the common language in which both Books are inscribed. They serve not as the *figure* but the *ground* of matter, and they underlie the analogical ratios between the Two Books. In this regard, etymology provides a major technique of scientific investigation. The whole aim of the arts and sciences therefore is to enable the discovery and understanding, and ultimately the manipulation (alchemy), of forms. This constitutes media study of a high order. The great alchemists, the Paracelsans from Raymond Lully to Cornelius Agrippa, were grammarians. Bacon is perfectly aware of how the sciences and arts are united by the study of forms and formal causes:

> On a given basis of matter to impose any nature, within the limits of possibility, is the intention of human power. In like manner, to know the causes of a given effect, in whatever subject, is the intention of human knowledge: which intentions coincide. For that which is in contemplation as a cause, is in operation as a medium. . . .

> He who knows the efficient and materiate causes, composes or divides things previously invented, or transfers and produces them; also in matter somewhat similar, he attaineth unto new inventions; the more deeply fixed limits of things he moveth not.

> He who knows the forms, discloses and educes things which have not hitherto been done, such as neither the vicissitudes of nature, nor the diligence of experience might ever have brought into action, or as might not have entered into man's thoughts.[17]

Francis Bacon's theory of communication, then, has these two main elements. For one, there is the conventional understanding of the analogical relation of the Two Books and the entire tradition of words and of forms that surrounds it. The other consists of his view of the mind as prey to Idolatry of various kinds since it was weakened by the Fall—false perception and skewed judgment—and in need of remedy. His remedy includes identifying and clearing away of Idols and employing aphorisms to reengage the faculties and restore their acuity and wonder.

Just as Bacon was later to claim in attacking the dialecticians, St. Augustine says arts and knowledge are for use, for the relief of man's estate; and, as Bacon freely admits, the greatest art is theology, since it is for the relief of man's spiritual estate.

> But the greatest error of all the rest is the mistaking or misplacing of the last or farthest end of knowledge: for men have entered into a desire of learning and knowledge, sometimes upon a natural curiosity and inquisitive appetite; sometimes to entertain their minds with variety and delight; sometimes for ornament and reputation; and sometimes to enable them to victory of wit and contradiction; and most times for lucre and profession; and seldom sincerely to give a true account of their gift of reason, to the benefit and use of men: as if there were sought in knowledge a couch whereupon to rest a searching and restless spirit; or a tarrasse, for a wandering and variable mind to walk up and down with a fair prospect; or a tower of state for a proud mind to raise itself upon; or a fort or commanding ground, for strife and contention; or a shop, for profit or sale; and not a rich storehouse, for the glory of the Creator and the relief of man's estate.[18]

CHAPTER FIVE

Pound, Eliot, and the Rhetoric of *The Waste Land*

MARSHALL MCLUHAN

I

In 1949, Hugh Kenner and I visited Ezra Pound at St. Elizabeth's Hospital. On that occasion, we discussed poetry, and I recall particularly his talking about the difference between his "Portrait d'Une Femme" and Eliot's "Portrait of a Lady." He stressed the fact that he had managed to get a good many things into his Portrait that Eliot had missed. If one turns to his "Portrait d'Une Femme": "Your mind and you are our Sargasso Sea," the poem immediately opens out as a sort of vortex of inclusive consciousness, with the lady serving as a kind of catalyst:

Oh, you are patient, I have seen you sit

Hours, where something might have floated up.

And now you pay one. Yes, you richly pay. . . .

Trophies fished up; some curious suggestion; . . .

Pregnant with mandrakes, or with something else . . . [1]

The pattern of the London vortex which she manifested to Pound reappears structurally in *The Cantos* themselves. Both Pound's "Portrait" and Eliot's constitute a kind of epyllion which, we shall see, is a pattern they used a great deal: the parallel actions function as a plot and counter-plot which enrich each other by their interplay. Poe's "Descent into the Maelstrom" has structurally much in common with the vortices of the *Cantos*. Similarly, the "Sargasso Sea" is a vortex that attracts multitudinous objects but which also tosses things up again in recognizable patterns which serve for survival. Survival for Poe's sailor had meant attaching himself to one of the recurring objects in the whirlpool. The same strategy applies to Pound's readers who need to be alert to the resonance of recurring themes. Apropos the same kind of awareness, Lewis wrote in *Blast* magazine that the vorticists defined their art as an art of the energized present, an art which has captured the point of maximum intensity. It is the presentation of "an intellectual and emotional complex in an instant of time."[2] Pound, in his note on Gaudier-Brzeska described the "radiant node or cluster . . . from which, and through which, and into which, ideas are constantly rushing."[3]

Baudelaire, admirer of Poe, in his "Envoy to the Reader" said: "Hypocrite lecteur, mon semblable, mon frère." This became a key line in *The Waste Land* itself, pointing to the vortex created by the encounter of author and reader. Muriel Bradbrook comments on the musical vortices of *The Waste Land* and *Four Quartets*: "For instance, each of the poems is concerned with one of the four elements—*Burnt Norton* with air, *East Coker* with earth, *The Dry Salvages* with water and *Little Gidding* with fire. The four elements are brought together at the beginning of the second movement of *Little Gidding*, where they are seen to be symbols of multiple meaning."[4]

Since these four-element structures (which include the four seasons) are a major Eliot vortex, it is strange that no one has remarked on the original four-part division of *The Waste Land* before Pound started to work on it.

Both the contention and collaboration between Pound and Eliot about the four levels of traditional exegesis in *The Waste Land* go deep into the theories of communication of each poet. Everyone is familiar with Eliot's declaration in *For Lancelot Andrewes*, which, he says, he made

> to refute any accusation of playing 'possum. The general point of view may be described as classicist in literature, royalist in politics, and anglo-catholic in religion. I am quite aware that the first term is completely vague, and easily lends itself to clap-trap; I am aware that the second term is at present without definition, and easily lends itself to what is almost worse than clap-trap, I mean temperate conservatism; the third term does not rest with me to define. The uncommon reader who is interested by these scattered papers may possibly be interested by the small volumes which I have in preparation: *The School of Donne*; *The Outline of Royalism*; and *The Principles of Modern Heresy*.[5]

The third of these three books appeared as *After Strange Gods* where Eliot comments on the relation between Pound's religious and poetic views:

But Confucius has become the philosopher of the rebellious Protestant. And I cannot but feel that in some respects Irving Babbitt, with the noblest intentions, has merely made matters worse instead of better.

The name of Irving Babbitt instantly suggests that of Ezra Pound (his peer in cosmopolitanism) and that of I.A. Richards: it would seem that Confucius is the spiritual adviser of the highly educated and fastidious, in contrast to the dark gods of Mexico. Mr. Pound presents the closest counterpart to Irving Babbitt. Extremely quick-witted and very learned, he is attracted to the Middle Ages, apparently, by everything except that which gives them their significance. His powerful and narrow post-Protestant prejudice peeps out from the most unexpected places: one can hardly read the erudite notes and commentary to his edition of Guido Cavalcanti without suspecting that he finds Guido much more sympathetic than Dante, and on grounds which have little to do with their respective merits as poets: namely, that Guido was very likely a heretic, if not a sceptic [*sic*]—as evidenced partly by his possibly having held some pneumatic philosophy and theory of corpuscular action which I am unable to understand. Mr. Pound, like Babbitt, is an individualist, and still more a libertarian.[6]

This passage goes far to elucidate both the collaboration and conflict between Pound and Eliot. Their contention led to the making of two (complementary) poems, which we have learned to call *The Waste Land*—one with four and one with five divisions. Eliot, as we shall see, was veered away from the original four-division *Waste Land* by Pound's editorial stress on "craft," and on the rhetorical five divisions. His "victory" over Eliot was signalized by the wry dedication "to Ezra Pound: *il miglior fabbro.*" Pound had already asserted the classical status of the five-division structure for poetry in his "Homage to Sextus Propertius" and his "Mauberly" as early as 1915 and 1917.

In his 1919 review of Pound's *Quia Pauper Amavi* (which contains three *Cantos*) entitled "The Method of Mr. Pound," Eliot echoes his earlier sentiments concerning the simultaneity of the historical vortex in "Tradition and the Individual Talent":

The historical method is, of course, the one which suits Mr. Pound's temperament; it is also a conscious and consistent application of a procedure suggested by Browning, which Mr. Pound applies more consciously and consistently than Browning did. Most poets grasp their own time, the life of the world as it stirs before their eyes, at one convulsion or not at all. But they have no method for closing in upon it. Mr. Pound proceeds by acquiring the entire past; and when the entire past is acquired, the constituents fall into place and the present is revealed. Such a method involves immense capacities of learning and of dominating one's learning, and the peculiarity of expressing oneself through historical masks. Mr. Pound has a unique gift for expression through some phase of past life. This is not archaeology or pedantry, but one method, and a very high method, of poetry. It is a method which allows of no arrest, for the poet imposes upon himself, necessarily, the condition of continually changing his mask; *hic et ubique*, then we'll shift our ground.[7]

This is a statement of a theory of communication shared by Pound and Eliot in 1919. It implies the further statement that Eliot presented in his 1921 essay on "The Metaphysical Poets":

> It is not a permanent necessity that poets should be interested in philosophy, or in any other subject. We can only say that it appears likely that poets in our civilization, as it exists at present, must be *difficult*. Our civilization comprehends great variety and complexity, and this variety and complexity, playing upon a refined sensibility, must produce various and complex results. The poet must become more and more comprehensive, more allusive, more indirect, in order to force, to dislocate if necessary, language into his meaning.[8]

II

Pound and Eliot assumed as true for their time what Dante had assumed in his time. The medieval assumption of the poet as learned, (*difficult*) is stated by E. R. Curtius: "Access to the Comedy can be gained—could and should be gained, the poet would have it—only by study. For Dante and for the Middle Ages, the basic plan for any education of the intellect is, in general, the reading of books, the "lungo studio" (Inf., 1, 83)—in contradistinction to the conversational method (διαλέγεσθας) of the Greeks."[9] Evidence of the role of erudition in medieval poetry is stressed by Robert Hollander in his study of *Allegory in Dante's Commedia*. The approach to fourfold exegesis requires encyclopedic erudition at any time, a fact that loomed large in Eliot's study of Dante before Hollander: "Essentially, however, the importance of Dante's borrowing of the technique of fourfold exegesis was lost to the critics until the twentieth century. The whole problem is densely complex when it is considered in a historical perspective."[10]

Contemporary linguistics has recovered the multi-levelled study of language in our time. However, Eliot had earlier developed his own approach to the four levels by his long and loving study of the learned grammarian Bishop Andrewes and his contemporaries. The parallel of Andrewes and Eliot is plain: "but the voice of Andrewes is the voice of a man who has a formed visible Church behind him, who speaks with the old authority and the new culture. It is the difference of negative and positive: Andrewes is the first great preacher of the English Catholic Church" (*Selected Essays*, p. 344). Eliot adds: "Andrewes may seem pedantic and verbal. . . . Andrewes takes a word and derives the world from it; squeezing and squeezing the word until it yields a full juice of meaning which we should never have supposed any word to possess" (pp. 347–48). An instance of this occurs in the passage from Bishop Andrewes that Eliot uses in *Gerontion*:

I add yet farther; what flesh? The flesh of an infant. What, *Verbum infans*, the Word an infant? The Word, and not be able to speak a word? How evil agreeth this! This He put up. How born, how entertained? In a stately palace, cradle of ivory, robes of estate? No; but a stable for His palace, a manger for His cradle, poor clouts for His array. This was His beginning. Follow Him farther, if any better afterward; what flesh afterward? *Sudans et algens,* in cold and heat, hungry and thirsty, faint and weary. Is His end any better? that maketh up all: what flesh then?[11]

Referring to his own training, Andrewes begins a discussion of typical exegetical method:

Our books tell us, the Scripture will bear four senses; all four be in this, and a kind of ascent there is in them.

1. First, after the letter and in due consequence to the word immediately next before this, the last word of the verse, which is Sinai. It is a report of Moses' ascending thither. For he, from the bottom of the Red Sea, went up to the top of Sinai, leading with him the people of Israel that long had been captive to Pharaoh; and there "received gifts," the Law, the Priesthood, but above all, the "Ark of the covenant," to be the pledge of God's presence among them. This is the literal.

2. This of Moses, by analogy, doth King David apply to himself; to his going up to mount Sion, and carrying the ark up thither. For all agree, this Psalm was set upon that occasion. The very beginning of it, "Let God arise," &c., sheweth as much;—the acclamation ever to be used, at the ark's removing, as is plain by the tenth of Numbers, verse thirty-five. Now this was done immediately upon his conquest of the Jebusites; whom a little before he had taken captives and made tributaries there. What time also, for honour of the solemnity, *dona dedit*, he dealt "bread" and "wine to all the people," gift-wise, as we find, the first of Chronicles, sixteenth chapter, and the third verse. This is the analogical; as Moses to Sinai, so David to Sion.

3. From these two we arise to the moral sense, thus. That, as whensoever God's people are carried captive and made thrall to their enemies; as then God seemeth to be put down, and lie foiled for a time, that one may well say, *Exsurgat Deus*, to Him: so when He takes their cause in hand and works their deliverance, it may well be said, *Ascendit in altum*, "He is gone up," as it were, to His high throne or judgment-seat, there to give sentence for them. Ever the Church's depressing is, as it were, God's own humiliation; and their deliverance, after a sort, His exaltation. For then He hath the upper hand. And this is the moral.

4. Now from this we ascend to the Prophetical sense, "to the testimony of Jesus, which is the spirit of all prophecy."[12]

Bishop Andrewes, Eliot's mentor, had "behind him" centuries of fourfold exegesis. Somewhat more succinct is St. Bonaventure, in the thirteenth century: "Finally, there is depth in the Scriptures, deriving from their several figurative meanings. Many Scriptural passages have, besides the direct sense, three other significations: the allegorical, the moral, and the anagogical. Allegory consists in this: that one thing signifies another thing which is in the realm of faith; moral teaching, or tropology, in this: that from something done, we learn another thing that we must do; anagogy, or lifting up, in this: that we are given to know what to desire, that is, the eternal happiness of the elect."[13] Andrewes cites Ovid frequently, as well as the other classics, ancient and medieval. In the ancient writers the four levels were also pervasive. Writing in the secular tradition, the grammarian Varro (first century B.C.) reports:

> Now I shall set forth the origins of the individual words, of which there are four levels of explanation. The lowest is that to which even the common folk has come. . . . The second is that to which old-time grammar has mounted, which shows how the poet has made each word which he has fashioned and derived. . . .

> The third level is that to which philosophy ascended, and on arrival began to reveal the nature of those words which are in common use. . . . The fourth is that where the sanctuary is, and the mysteries of the high-priest: if I shall not arrive at full knowledge there, at any rate I shall cast about for a conjecture.[14]

As the four levels of understanding and exegesis are found in both the secular and patristic traditions, they would seem to bridge the worlds of Paul and Apollo. Bishop Andrewes makes such an observation: "Why then, will some say, one of these two inconveniences will follow, that hereby we shall think the Scripture is of the devil's side, as well as of Christ's side, and so divided; as in like sort they make a division of Christ, when one holds with Paul, another with Apollos. No, it is not so, Christ allegeth not this Scripture in that sort, as one nail to drive out another; but by way of harmony and exposition, that the one may make plain the meaning of the other."[15] The four levels of meaning are simultaneous and not sequential, save for the accident imposed by narrative commentary and analysis. Because these matters of exegetical procedure were as familiar to Dante's time as to the age of Andrewes, Dante does not enlarge on this technique so basic to his work. Dante was near the middle of an unbroken tradition of exegetical practice that lasted 1600 years. He alludes to the four senses in his letter to Can Grande as casually as a musician might mention the key signature of his composition: "In evidence, then, of what should be said, let it be known that the sense of this work is not simple; nay, it may be said to be polysemous, which is to say, of a number of senses; for the first sense is that which is understood by the letter, another, that which is understood by those things signified by the letter. And the first is called literal, the second, to be sure, either allegorical, or moral, or anagogical."[16] Dante, then, uses multi-level meanings in his poem:

> Once we grasp these facts, it is manifest that the subject, around which the senses run, one after the other, is of necessity twofold. And that such is the case concerning the subject of this work ought to be clear, as is first to be understood literally, and then expounded allegorically. Thus the subject of the whole work, so far as it is to be understood in the literal sense, taken simply, is the state of the souls after death; for the process of the entire work situates itself in this and around this. If, to be sure, the work is to be understood allegorically, the subject is man, as he is liable to rewarding or punishing justice, according as he is worthy or unworthy in the exercise of the freedom of his will.[17]

Like Andrewes, Dante makes the distinction between Paul and Apollo, between theology and secular poetry, as Hollander explains: "Dante does not combine in any way at all, the allegory of the poets and the allegory of the theologians. The *Divine Comedy*, the epistle informs us, is to be understood through the techniques of allegory which are specifically and only Christian, not, as was the *Convivio*, by means of the allegory of the poets. Here there is no reference to Orpheus, only to Scripture."[18] As a close student of Dante, Eliot found these analogical approaches very familiar. In a talk on "What Dante Means to Me" Eliot acknowledged, "I still, after forty years, regard his poetry as the most persistent and deepest influence upon my own verse."[19] Eliot goes on to explain the comprehensive scope of Dante's influence on his work and how it has shaped his theory of communication: "The Divine Comedy expresses everything in the way of emotion, between depravity's despair and the beatific vision, that man is capable of experiencing. It is therefore a constant reminder to the poet, of the obligation to explore, to find words for the inarticulate, to capture those feelings which people can hardly even feel, because they have no words for them; and at the same time, a reminder that the explorer beyond the frontiers of ordinary consciousness will only be able to return and report to his fellow-citizens, if he has all the time a firm grasp upon the realities with which they are already acquainted."[20] In relation to passing "beyond the frontiers of ordinary consciousness," it might be relevant to consider St. Paul's discussion of "speaking in tongues." It is applicable to both the obscurities of modern poetry and to the levels of traditional exegesis:

1. For he that speaketh in an *unknown* tongue speaketh not unto men, but unto God; for no man understandeth *him*; howbeit in the spirit he speaketh mysteries.

2. But he that prophesieth speaketh unto men to edification, and exhortation, and comfort.

3. He that speaketh in an *unknown* tongue edifieth himself; but he that prophesieth edifieth the church.

4. I would that ye all spake with tongues, but rather that ye prophesieth; for greater *is* he that prophesieth than he that speaketh with tongues, except he interpret, that the church may receive edifying.

5. Now, brethren, if I come unto you speaking with tongues, what shall I profit you, except I shall speak to you either by revelation, or by knowledge, or by prophesying, or by doctrine?   (I Cor. 14.2–6)

Applying these observations of St. Paul to the first version of *The Waste Land* (now available in Valerie Eliot's *Facsimile and Transcript*),[21] many would say that in the first version of the poem Eliot had begun to speak in "an unknown tongue," and was speaking "not unto men but unto God." There was always some basis for this charge in Eliot's poetry. Years later, in an interview with Donald Hall in the *Paris Review*, Eliot remarked that the lack of experience and maturity often leads a poet to be obscure: "That type of obscurity comes when a poet is still at the stage of learning how to use language. You have to say the thing the difficult way. The only alternative is not saying it at all, at that stage. By the time of the *Four Quartets*, I couldn't have written in the style of *The Waste Land*. I wasn't even bothering whether I understood what I was saying."[22]

Pound, by his knowledge and "craft," transformed the poem from "an unknown tongue" to the level of prophecy and exhortation for men. Eliot, in turn, responded with the suggestion of placing *Gerontion* at the opening of *The Waste Land* as an interpretive prologue. Pound vetoed the idea; but later Eliot, possum-like, put the *Notes* at the end, for explanatory effect.

Explaining further his idea of communication in his essay on *Charles Whibley*, Eliot adapts St. Paul to his own use:

> In attaining such unity, and indeed in attaining a living style, whether in prose or in verse, the practice of conversation is invaluable. Indeed, I believe that to write well it is necessary to converse a great deal. I say 'converse' instead of 'talk'; because I believe that there are two types of good writers: those who talk a great deal to others, and those, perhaps less fortunate, who talk a great deal to themselves. It is two thousand and hundreds of years since, that the theory was propounded that thought is conversation

with oneself; all literary creation certainly springs either from the habit of talking to one-self or from the habit of talking to others. Most people are unable to do either, and that is why they lead such active lives. But anyone who would write must let himself go, in one way or the other, for there are only four ways of thinking: to talk to others, or to one other, or to talk to oneself, or to talk to God. (*Selected Essays*, pp. 500–501)

There is a deep sense in which all of the versions and parts of *The Waste Land*, including the *Notes*, and including all the commentaries ever since, are simultane-ous, and form a single poem or text.

This seeming paradox may be elucidated by Eliot's various remarks about the meaning of poems. It is also elucidated by Aquinas's classic text concerning the simultaneity of the meanings of Scripture in relation to the intention of the author and also of his commentators:

> . . . not to force such an interpretation of Scripture as to exclude any other interpreta-tions that are actually or possibly true: since it is part of the dignity of Holy Writ that under the one literal sense many others are contained. It is thus that the sacred text not only adapts itself to man's various intelligence, so that each one marvels to find his thoughts expressed in the words of Holy Writ; but also is all the more easily defend-ed against unbelievers in that when one finds his own interpretation of Scripture to be false he can fall back upon some other. Hence it is not inconceivable that Moses and the other authors of the Holy Books were given to know the various truths that men would discover in the text, and that they expressed them under one literary style, so that each truth is the sense intended by the author. And then even if commentators adapt certain truths to the sacred text that were not understood by the author, without doubt the Holy Ghost understood them, since he is the principal author of Holy Scripture. Consequently every truth that can be adapted to the sacred text without prejudice to the literal sense, is the sense of Holy Scripture.[23]

This provides a sidelight on the matter of the levels of meaning and significa-tion, and accords entirely with Eliot's idea of the "function of meaning" in poetry. In her study, *T. S. Eliot: The Making of* The Waste Land, Muriel Bradbrook remarks that "in the early 1930s, he conceded on behalf of drama, 'Its meaning to others is as much a part of it as what it means to oneself', and that 'the existence of a poem lies somewhere between the reader and the writer.'[24] Nine years later, in *The Music of Poetry*, he allowed that 'the reader's interpretation may differ from the author's and be equally valid—it may even be better. There may be much more in a poem than the author was aware of. The different interpretations may all be partial for-mulations of the one thing'" (*On Poetry and Poets*, p. 31)[25]

Another nine years, Miss Bradbrook notes, and the wheel has come full circle, with: "If the word 'inspiration' is to have any meaning, it must mean just this, that the speaker or writer is uttering something which he does not wholly understand—

or which he may even misinterpret when the inspiration has departed from him. . . . A poet may believe that he is expressing only his private experience; his lines may be for him only a means of talking about himself without giving himself away; yet for his readers what he has written may come to be the expression of both their own secret feelings and of the exultation or despair of a generation."[26]

This simultaneous and prophetic aspect of modern poetry and language has eluded even so able a student as R. P. Blackmur who remarked, in interpretation of Eliot and Yeats, that "in these various orders which Eliot has used, there is no recognizable principle of composition. Even the Sibyl and Tiresias are not enough."[27] Blackmur is more useful in relating analogy to the simultaneity of poetic structures:

> Analogy is also the deep form of reminding that there is always something *else* going on: the identity which is usually a mystery apprehended in analogy; what is lost in "mere" logic, but is carried along in the story.
>
> Analogy is like the old notion of underplot, or second plot in Elizabethan drama. Sometimes these underplots were only two logics, sometimes one and sometimes another; but sometimes they were a multiplying process. One times one equals one, but a one which is also a third thing, which is fused in the mind, in the looking of one working on the other. Emotions can be like plot and underplot. If we put two emotions of the established sorts in association (like love and hate) we get an artistic emotion differing from either but with attributes common to both. In association, emotions are fruitful, and we get a sense of living action where there had been sets of abstraction: as in the Mass.[28]

Eliot's difficulties in shaping *The Waste Land* are rehearsed in his analysis of the reason for Ben Jonson's failure in *Catiline*: "*Catiline* fails," he says, "not because it is too laboured and conscious, but because it is not conscious enough; because Jonson in this play was not alert to his own idiom, not clear in his mind as to what his temperament wanted him to do" (*Selected Essays*, p. 149). These difficulties shine through the *Facsimile and Transcript* in the way in which Pound conducted the "Caesarean Operation" of delivering *The Waste Land*.

Pound supplied just those qualities which Eliot notes as absent in the composition of *Catiline*. He whimsically wrote:

These are the poems of Eliot

By the Uranian Muse begot; . . .

If you must needs enquire

Know diligent Reader

That on each Occasion

Ezra performed the Caesarean Operation . . . [29]

III

The Waste Land that Eliot first showed to Pound was a four-part poem, both sea-sonal elegy and city pastoral. Embedded in this text was a dramatic ode to London written in the terza rima of Dante. (*Facsimile and Transcript*, p. 37). Eliot's origi-nal four-part structure of *The Waste Land* is an anticipation of the four divisions of the *Four Quartets* in respect to the four seasons, the four elements, and the four ana-logical levels of exegesis. All of these are musical and simultaneous rather than sequential. Pound modified this liturgical pattern by desacralizing it. He was alien-ated by the religious aspect of Eliot's four levels, which as a medievalist he, too, understood very well. He had an alternative classical pattern in mind, which we will come to presently.

Looking more closely at Eliot's original four-part poem, we first encounter the heading from *Our Mutual Friend* of the great Londoner, Charles Dickens. The title of the novel has the sinister overtone of the devil himself, everybody's friend. Eliot's title phrase, "He Do the Police in Different Voices" refers to the lad Sloppy, who reads to Betty Higden. She says: "I do love a newspaper. You mightn't think it, but Sloppy is a beautiful reader of the newspaper. He do the Police in different voic-es."[30] The non-literate Betty has a special appreciation of the subtleties of oral per-formance. At the same time, Eliot's highly literate awareness of multi-levelled nuances of meaning in "voices" ("Three Voices of Poetry") evokes the idea of the levels (different voices) of interpretation. Taken in order, the four parts of the first *Waste Land* move through the four seasons in sequence.

First, "The Burial of the Dead" (Spring): "April is the cruelest month" (*Facsimile and Transcript*, p. 7, l. 55). Then, "In the Cage," with summer showers; followed by "The Fire Sermon" (Autumn):

> The river's tent is broken and the last fingers of leaf
>
> Clutch and sink into the wet bank.

(P. 25, ll. 1–2)

Finally, "Death by Water" (Winter) occurs in northern latitudes where the ship ends up in the Arctic ice pack:

> And dead ahead we saw, where sky and sea should meet,
>
> A line, a white line, a long white line.
>
> . . . towards which we drove
>
> My God man there's bears on it.

(P. 61, ll. 75–78)

The four elements and the four levels also resonate in this structure. "The Burial of the Dead" is in the "earth" of the city, beginning with the pub-crawl through the cultural labyrinth of the town. This is followed by

> . . . breeding
> Lilacs out of the dead land.

(P. 7, ll. 55–56)

Next, "In the Cage" (air) includes the strange synthetic perfumes and the play of the wind under the door (p. 11, l. 42), with accent on the social "airs" of the two women. The third element is "The Fire Sermon" itself, and the fourth is drowning ("Death by Water").

Parallel to the elements and the seasons are the four levels, beginning with the burial of the spiritually dead, as the literal basis of the poem, which is exhibited in a variety of vignettes of perversity:

> I read, much of the night, and go south in the winter.

(P. 7, l. 72)

"In the Cage" affords the allegory of the two complementary women, the one representing Asian opulence, the other embedded in lower-class Western squalor. "The Fire Sermon" is an eloquent presentation of the moral level of the lusts of the flesh, from Fresca's affairs to the typist's teatime fling. "Death by Water" attains the anagogic level, where the ascent is to the pure and ethereal regions of Arctic snow and ice, and death.

To these same four levels or aspects of the Books of Man and Nature, Ernst Robert Curtius devotes an entire section of *European Literature and the Latin Middle Ages*. From the ancient world through Shakespeare there is a continuous study of the two Books. For example there is "the philosophical speculation of a Plotinus": "Writing affords him comparisons intended to serve cognition, not literary effect. Thus, the stars for him are "like letters forever being written in the sky, or like letters written once and for all and forever moving" (II, 3, 7; Müller, 1, 93, 8). The motion of the stars serves to maintain the universe but it also has another use: "If they are regarded as letters (γράμματα) he who knows that alphabet (γραμματική) reads the future according to the figures they form." Concerning the seer, Plotinus says that his art is 'to read the written characters of Nature, which reveal order and law.'"[31]

For centuries men turned their eyes to the page of Nature as well as to the *sacra pagina*, using the grammars of the trivium and the quadrivium respectively to read them. St. Bonaventure was working in the midst of this flourishing tradition which had in his time persisted for over 1000 years, a tradition of which all educated men, including Dante and Chaucer, were fully aware. Etienne Gilson summarizes Bonaventure's approach:

Since the universe was offered to his eyes as a book to read and he saw in nature a sensible revelation analogous to that of the Scriptures, the traditional methods of interpretation which had always been applied to the sacred books could equally be applied to
the book of creation. Just as there is an immediate and literal sense of the sacred text,
but also an allegorical sense by which we discover the truths of faith that the letter signifies, a tropological sense by which we discover a moral precept behind a passage in
the form of an historical narrative, and an anagogical sense by which our souls are raised
to the love and desire of God, so we must not attend to the literal and immediate sense
of the book of creation but look for its inner meaning in the theological, moral and mystical lessons that it contains. The passage from one of these two spheres to the other is
the more easily effected in that they are in reality inseparable.[32]

In the same way, each theme of *The Waste Land* resonates allegorically with all
of the others, and includes them, just as Tiresias is the corporate embodiment of
all the characters. The novel, *In the Cage*, by Henry James, is most helpful for
understanding the role and function of Tiresias. The novel opens: "It had occurred
to her early that in her position—that of a young person spending, in framed and
wired confinement, the life of a guinea-pig or a magpie—she should know a great
many persons without their recognizing the acquaintance. That made it an emotion the more lively—though singularly rare and always, even then, with opportunity still very much smothered—to see any one come in whom she knew outside,
as she called it, any one who could add anything to the meanness of her function."[33]

The girl in the telegraph cage is described as having "a whimsical mind and
wonderful nerves; she was subject, in short, to sudden flickers of antipathy and sympathy." James tells us, "What she could handle freely, she said to herself, was com-
binations of men and women," and Eliot originally had the lines,

> And we shall play a game of chess: The ivory men make company between us.

> (*Facsimile and Transcript*, p. 13, ll. 62–63)

James's heroine is a kind of Madame Sosostris, who, he tells us, observed
"Ladies wiring to different persons under different names. She had seen all sorts of
different things"—like Tiresias—"and pieced together all sorts of mysteries."[34]
"How did she guess all sorts of impossible things, such as, almost on the very spot,
the presence of drama at a critical stage and the nature of the tie with the gentleman at the Hotel Brighton? More than ever before it floated to her through the bars
of the cage that this at last was the high reality, the bristling truth that she had hitherto only patched up and eked out—one of the creatures, in fine, in whom all the
conditions for happiness actually met, and who, in the air they made, bloomed with
an unwitting insolence."[35] Like Tiresias, she reads the book of the world.

Having said in his (later) "Notes": "What Tiresias *sees*, in fact, is the substance
of the poem," Eliot adds, "The whole passage from Ovid is of great anthropolog-

ical interest." He then gives the episode from Ovid in full, in which Ovid's four levels are clearly manifested. At the *literal* level is the encounter with the snakes— Tiresias "knows" their knowing. Representing the *figurative* level, he is punished by being made an allegory—a "knower" of both man and woman. As the *moral* mode, he is blinded for not "knowing better" than to take a playful dispute seriously. Finally (*anagogically*), in return for his loss of sight, Jove gave him the power to "know" the future. This quotation is one of the several ways which Eliot uses to train the perceptions of the reader in multi-level awareness. Mythic "narrative" is not sequential but simultaneous, requiring prolonged meditation.

IV

When Pound confronted Eliot's *Waste Land* manuscript, he moved quickly to alter the four-part structure, which his secular bias told him was loaded with spirituality and mysticism. His aversion to the mode of meditational four-level exegesis prompted him to urge a five-division pattern of classical oratory. The poem, which Eliot had begun as a four-part meditation, emerged as a five-division oration. Pound's bias was towards the manifesto and public declaration, as appears in "Hugh Selwyn Mauberly":

> The age demanded an image
>
> Of its accelerated grimace. . . .
>
>   (*Personae*, p. 188)

This "classic" poem has the claim to be truly classic in respect to its structural use of the five divisions of classical rhetoric. Seven years before the appearance of *The Waste Land*, Pound had developed the style of classical eloquence in contemporary poetry. He divided "Mauberly" into five numbered sections which are simultaneous, rather than sequential, resonant rather than logical, as are the five divisions of classical oratory as understood by Cicero and Quintilian. The importance of this simultaneity concerns the classical claim to embody the Logos in the resonant interplay of these divisions.

Pound's five divisions are: invention, or the finding of the theme or matter: "For three years, out of key with his time" (*Personae*, p. 187); the arrangement (disposition) of that matter: "The age demanded an image" (p. 188); elocution or ornament in accord with the occasion: "What god, man, or hero/ Shall I place a tin wreath upon" (p. 189); memory: "frankness as never before . . . trench confessions" (p. 190); and delivery: "There died a myriad, . . . / For a botched civilization, . . . / Quick eyes gone under earth's lid" (p. 191). Not only did Pound develop this structure of eloquence for his own poetry, but he communicated it to W.B. Yeats, who was persuaded to use it in some of his major poems.

In May, 1914, (*Poetry* IV), Pound reviewed Yeats's *Responsibilities* under the heading, "The Later Yeats," in which occur several poems structured by the five rhetorical divisions including "Beggar to Beggar Cried," "A Song from 'The Player Queen,'" and "The Magi." The latter uses the five divisions within the single stanza, as also occurs in some of the later poems, such as "The Circus Animals' Desertion." Here there are five stanzas, with also the five divisions *within* each stanza. It is easiest to see Pound's insistence on using the five divisions in such "later" five-stanza poems as "Under the Round Tower," "The Wild Swans at Coole," and "Byzantium."

Just as [the] "later Yeats"[36] of course owes a great deal to Pound, so does the "later Eliot." Once he had published *The Waste Land*, finally firmed up by the structural use of classical rhetoric, Eliot made this form his own immediately in "The Hollow Men" (1925). As M.C. Bradbrook points out, in the early 'twenties, "Eliot is concerned to defend rhetoric, and the 'artificial style' in drama."[37] In his essay on Ben Johnson (1919), Eliot defines the advantages of formal rhetoric: "And you may say: rhetoric; but if we are to call it 'rhetoric' we must subject that term to a closer dissection than any to which it is accustomed. What Jonson has done here is not merely a fine speech. It is the careful, precise filling in of a strong and simple outline, and at no point does it overflow the outline . . . they do not exhibit prolixity or redundancy or the other vices in the rhetoric books; there is a definite artistic emotion which demands expression at that length (*Selected Essays*, p. 150).

As preparation for viewing the structural changes that Pound effected in *The Waste Land* we can look back from the form given to *Four Quartets* where Eliot made a wedding of the diverse patterns of the four levels of exegesis, on the one hand, and of the five divisions of classical rhetoric, on the other. As already remarked, both patterns are synchronic and simultaneous, rather than diachronic or sequential. The simultaneity of the four levels, as used by the grammarian, constitutes the resonance of the Logos, just as the five divisions, when used by the orator, constitute the presence of the word. This is what the linguists now call *la langue*, and Eliot calls "the auditory imagination." The "auditory imagination" includes both the four levels and the five divisions: "What I call the 'auditory imagination' is the feeling for syllable and rhythm, penetrating far below the conscious levels of thought and feeling, invigorating every word; sinking to the most primitive and forgotten, returning to the origin and bringing something back, seeking the beginning and the end. It works through meanings, certainly, or not without meanings in the ordinary sense, and fuses the old and obliterated and the trite, the current, and the new and surprising, the most ancient and the most civilized mentality."[38]

That inclusive consciousness, which the ancients called eloquence, emanated from encyclopedic knowledge, and is central to the work of both Pound and Eliot. Pound evokes it by vortices, and Eliot, by the "auditory imagination." As cited before, in Eliot's (1919) review, "Mr. Pound proceeds by acquiring the entire past . . . at which point the constituents fall into place and the present is revealed." This is the Pound "vortex," and also the key to Mr. Eliot's idea of Tradition: "a feeling that the whole of the literature of Europe from Homer and within it the whole of the literature of his own country has a simultaneous existence, thus: composes and simultaneous order. This historical sense, which is a sense of the timeless as well as of the temporal and of the timeless and of the temporal together, is what makes a writer traditional" (*Selected Essays*, p. 14).

In Book I of *The Institutes of Oratory*, Quintilian sets forth the program for schooling in eloquence, which includes the study of languages and the cultivation of both Grammar and Rhetoric:

> This profession may be most briefly considered under two heads, the art of speaking correctly and the interpretation of the poets; but there is more beneath the surface than meets the eye. For the art of writing is combined with that of speaking, and correct reading precedes interpretation, while in each of these cases criticism has its work to perform. . . . Nor is it sufficient to have read the poets only; every kind of writer must be carefully studied, not merely for the subject matter, but for the vocabulary; for words often acquire authority from their use by a particular author. Nor can such training be regarded as complete if it stop short of music, for the teacher of literature has to speak of metre and rhythm: nor again if he be ignorant of astronomy, can he understand the poets; for they, to mention no further points, frequently give their indications of time by reference to the rising and setting of the stars. Ignorance of philosophy is an equal drawback.[39]

In Book III, following Cicero (who, in turn, continued the program of Isocrates), he presents the divisions of rhetoric and their basic characters:

> The art of oratory, as taught by most authorities, and those the best, consists of five parts:—*Invention, arrangement, expression, memory*, and *delivery* or *action* (the two latter terms being used synonymously). But all speech expressive of purpose involves also a subject and words. If such expression is brief and contained within the limits of one sentence, it may demand nothing more, but longer speeches require much more. For not only what we say and how we say it is of importance, but also the circumstances under which we say it. It is here that the need of arrangement comes in. But it will be impossible to say everything demanded by the subject, putting each thing in its proper place, without the aid of memory. It is for this reason that memory forms the fourth department. But a delivery, which is rendered unbecoming either by voice or gesture, spoils everything and almost entirely destroys the effect of what is said. Delivery therefore must be assigned the fifth place.[40]

It was in accordance with the structure indicated by these traditional five divisions, still current in classical training in Pound's day, that Pound shaped *The Waste Land*.

For compression and to enhance discontinuity and intensity (the "Caesarean operation") Pound and Eliot began by cutting out the narrative sections. These were: the first fifty-five lines of the "Burial of the Dead" (*Facsimile and Transcript*, p. 3), the seventy-two lines (Fresca's morning toilette) of "The Fire Sermon" (pp. 23, 27), and eighty-three of the ninety-three lines of "Death by Water" (pp. 55–61), leaving only the Phlebas passage which had itself been retrieved from the earlier poem "Dans le Restaurant." This last cut destroyed Eliot's original four-part structure: with the cancelled lines went the fourth season and the fourth level; the fourth element (water) alone remained. Pound also persuaded Eliot to add a fifth section, using for the purpose some untitled additional lines Eliot had written, but not marked for inclusion (pp. 71–81). This became the part now called "What the Thunder Said."

The switch from the private narrative to the public declamation appears immediately in the contrast between the openings of Eliot's and Pound's "Burial of the Dead": "First we had a couple of feelers down at Tom's place" is personal, narrative recollection, and contrasts with the rhetorical thrust of "April is the cruellest month, breeding . . ."

Another way of detecting the change of form and tone is to note the shift from the Conrad to the Petronius epigraph, from "The horror! The horror!" to Latin and the Greek cry of the Sibyl, "I want to die." The context for "The horror! The horror!" provided by Eliot, is that of a tragic narrative of replay and recall of an entire life: "Did he live his life again in every detail of desire, temptation, and surrender during that supreme moment of complete knowledge? He cried in a whisper at some image, at some vision,—he cried out twice, a cry that was no more than a breath—'The horror! The horror!'" (*Facsimile and Transcript*, p. 3).

These echo the themes of memory, drowning, death and an inclusive moment of knowledge and (spiritual) recognition, all of which are consonant with the original four-level meditational scheme. In this regard, Eliot wrote to Pound, commenting on the Conrad epigraph, "Do you mean not use the Conrad quote or simply not put Conrad's name to it? It is much the most appropriate I can find, and somewhat elucidative" (*Letters*, p. 171).

The difference between the context of the Conrad epigraph and that of Petronius is between the "Uranian" muse of theology and the satiric muse, between tragedy and comedy. The death in Conrad echoes Phlebas's sudden clairvoyance, whereas Petronius's Sibyl blends with Madame Sosostris and satire. At the wealthy Trimalchio's Menippean banquet, all is frivolous:

Needless to say, we pointedly applauded all of Trimalchio's sallies.

"But tell me, my dear Agamemnon," continued our host, "do you remember the twelve labors of Hercules or the story about Ulysses and how the Cyclops broke his thumb trying to get the log out of his eye? When I was a kid, I used to read all those stories in Homer. And, you know, I once saw the Sybil of Cumae in person. She was hanging in a bottle, and when the boys asked her, 'Sybil, what do you want? she said, 'I want to die.'"[41]

Whereas the context for Conrad's "The Horror! The Horror!" is gloomy and sinister, the context of the Cumaean Sybil is boisterous and festive:

We think we're awful smart, we think we're awful wise, but when we're least expecting, comes the big surprise. Lady Luck's in heaven and we're her little toys, so break out the wine and fill your glasses, boys![42]

The tone of bizarre and dishevelled frivolity is mimed in Eliot's Madame Sosostris, who "had a bad cold" (World War I slang for venereal disease) "nevertheless/Is known to be the wisest woman in Europe,/With a wicked pack of cards."[43] These Tarot cards are the contemporary form of Sibyl's leaves.

As contrasted to the devotional pattern of the exegetical levels, satire is usually focused on an audience which is itself in part the target of the satire. Again, we have the change from passive meditation in a melancholy mood, to active penetration of the foibles of the time: in other words, a shift from the mode of Mr. Eliot to the mode of Ezra Pound. In this matter, one need go no further than Pound's annotations on the original *Waste Land* manuscript to discover the contrast between the somewhat mournful Eliot and the energetic Pound. Pound's sprightliness naturally favoured vigorous assertion and playful teasing of the audience. In other words, Pound liked to "put on" his public. Pound always favoured the rhetorical thrust of art. Apropos the great opening passage of *A Game of Chess*: "The Chair she sat in, like a burnished throne," with its overtones of Cleopatra, Pound punctures Eliot's solemnity with "Too tum-pum at a stretch" (*Facsimile and Transcript*, p. 11). And, further down, "Too penty" (p. 11), referring to the full-blown pentameter. And, later, "verse not interesting enough as verse to warrant so much of it" (p. 45), showing a typical rhetorical concern for the attention of the audience.

In the final version of the poem "imposed" by Pound, the five numbered sections strongly manifest the characteristic modes of the five divisions of rhetoric. Taking them in order, "The Burial of the Dead" (*Inventio*) designates the themes and the matter of the entire poem "mixing memory and desire," the rootless "living dead," and the "unreal city." "A Game of Chess" (*Dispositio*)—the new title points entirely to the world of "games people play," and concerns the humours, whims and indispositions of the two women, upstairs and downstairs: bad nerves, on the one hand, and an abortion on the other. *Elocutio* is the eloquence of "The Fire Sermon" and presents the mask of Tiresias, who embodies all the figures of the poem. As Eliot describes him in the "Notes," he is "the most important personage in the poem, uniting all the rest. . . . all the women are one woman, and the two sexes meet in Tiresias. What Tiresias *sees*, in fact, is the substance of the poem."

Like a good classical oration, "The Fire Sermon" includes memorable exempla. The fourth section, "Death by Water," is entirely concerned with Memory. It opens: "Phlebas the Phoenician. . . . /Forgot. . . ." Then he recalls "the stages of his age and youth" in a synchronic moment, as remarked earlier. The section's rhetorical function is succinctly stated by R.P. Blackmur: "it is a lyric interlude put in to remind you what the rest of the poem is about."[44] Of the fifth section, "What the Thunder Said," the "delivery" or "action" of the poem, Eliot wrote to Bertrand Russell (1923): it "is not only the best part, but the only part that justifies the whole, at all." This remark to Bertrand Russell indicates Eliot's awareness of rhetorical pattern in the poem and his acceptance of Pound's artistic judgment and his midwifery.

V

Eliot was far from passive in his initial response to Pound's editing. Eliot's attachment to the four-part structure involved his devotion to *Grammatica* and its *figure/ground* structure included in the text itself. By contrast, Pound's insistence on the primacy of the public outside the poem as the real *ground*, led him to prefer the use of rhetoric.

Eliot had tried several ploys to veer the poem back into the orbit of *Grammatica*. First he had suggested to Pound that they print his editorial comments as a marginal (grammatical) gloss to the poem. Pound refused: "My squibs are now a bloody impertinence. I send 'em as requested; but don't use 'em with *Waste Land*. You can tack 'em onto a collected edtn, or use 'em somewhere where they would be decently hidden and swamped by the bulk of accompanying matter. They'd merely be an extra and wrong note with the 19 page version" (*Letters*, p. 169).

Alternatively, Eliot suggested adding "Gerontion": "Do you advise printing 'Gerontion' as a prelude in book or pamphlet form?" (p. 171). To which Pound replied, "I do *not* advise printing 'Gerontion' as preface. One don't miss it *at* all as the thing now stands. To be more lucid still, let me say that I advise you NOT to print 'Gerontion' as prelude" (p. 171). Had Eliot managed to get "Gerontion" into the poem as prelude, he would have obviated Pound's rhetorical structure.

Eliot next asked whether he had "Perhaps better omit Phlebas also???" (p. 171) Had Phlebas—that is, "Death by Water"—been omitted, the poem would have reverted to the four-part structure. This would have had the effect of restoring almost all of Eliot's original scheme: "What the Thunder Said" would serve to present the element of water (as it rains) and also the final or spiritual "levels." It omits only the season (winter). Pound's response was decisive: "I DO advise keeping Phlebas. In fact, I more'n advise. Phlebas is an integral part of the poem; the card pack introduces him, the drowned phoen. sailor. And he is needed ABSOLOOT-LY where he is. Must stay in" (p. 171).

Eliot made further gestures for evading the five-part rhetorical structure. In *T.S. Eliot and Ezra Pound*, Donald Gallup reported that Eliot continued, after Pound's editing, to think of the work as a series, and even suggested "to Scofield Thayer that the poem could go into as many as four issues of the *Dial*. Even as late as 21 September 1922, Eliot was planning to print *The Waste Land* in two instalments in his own *Criterion*—Parts I–II in October 1922 and Parts III–V in January 1923. It was only Pound's 'howling to high heaven that this was an outrage' that kept the poem from being split in this fashion in its original periodical appearances."[45]

Had Eliot published *The Waste Land* in four issues of the *Dial*, he would have restored his favourite pattern of four. On the other hand, had he broken the poem in half, in his own *Criterion*, he would again have by-passed Pound's rhetorical structure, and would have had instead a two-part pastoral epyllion. Much the same epyllion effect would have resulted from using "Gerontion" as preface.

The discontinuous epyllion, or mythic, structure as Marjorie Crump explains,[46] requires a plot and digression, or a double plot, which constitutes a metamorphic structure of *figure* in interplay with *ground*—necessary to the aetiological epic, a study of origins and causes. Eliot explicitly discusses the epyllion structure in his celebrated review of "*Ulysses*, Order and Myth":

> In using the myth, in manipulating a continuous parallel between contemporaneity and antiquity, Mr. Joyce is pursuing a method which others must pursue after him. They will not be imitators, any more than the scientist who uses the discoveries of an Einstein in pursuing his own, independent, further investigations. It is simply a way of controlling, of ordering, of giving a shape and a significance to the immense panorama of futility and anarchy which is contemporary history. It is a method already adumbrated by Mr. Yeats, and of the need for which I believe Mr. Yeats to have been the first contemporary to be conscious.[47]

Yeats's "adumbration" appears in his short (1903) note on "Emotion of Multitude,"[48] which he begins by explaining why he dislikes "the clear and logical construction which seems necessary if one is to succeed on the modern stage. . . . The Shakespearian drama gets the emotion of multitude out of the sub-plot which copies the main plot, much as a shadow upon the wall copies one's body in the firelight." After illustrating from *Lear* and *Hamlet*, he adds, "It is so in all the plays . . . the sub-plot is the main plot working itself out in more ordinary men and women, and so doubly calling up before us the image of multitude." In 1934, writing on John Marston, Eliot distinguishes the epyllion perceptual experience from the merely allegorical and conceptual:

> It is possible that what distinguishes poetic drama from prosaic drama is a kind of doubleness in the action, as if it took place on two planes at once. In this it is different from allegory, in which the abstraction is something conceived, not something differently felt, and from symbolism (as in the plays of Maeterlinck) in which the tangible world is deliberately diminished—both symbolism and allegory being operations of the conscious planning mind. In poetic drama a certain apparent irrelevance may be the symptom of this doubleness; or the drama has an under-pattern, less manifest than the theatrical one. (*Selected Essays,* p. 229).

The "Notes" Eliot put in apposition to *The Waste Land* are not only a grammatical gloss and an analogy to the poem, but they constitute a second plot, "a shadow of the main plot" which, as Yeats points out, evokes an emotion of multitude, or the sense of universality. Of course, this epyllion, this parallel structure, is not only mythic but pervasive in the work of Pound, Eliot, Yeats and Joyce. In one perspective, the "Notes" evoke the whimsical and multitudinous image of a "simultaneous order" of innumerable grammarians and commentators, past and present.

Eliot at last published the poem in the form preferred by Pound (in the *Criterion*, and in the *Dial*, October and November, 1922, respectively). Ezra later remarked that the poem's obscurities were reducible to four Sanskrit words, three of which are "so implied in the surrounding text that one can pass them by . . . without losing the general tone or the main emotion of the passage. They are so obviously the words of some ritual or other."[49] This was a characteristic rhetorical gesture of contempt for the meticulous solicitude of grammarian Eliot.

Old Possum, having been overruled many times, got in the last word . . . with the "Notes." These, added some months after the first publication, finally turned the poem away from rhetoric and back into the world of *Grammatica* and multi-level exegesis and learned commentary. Pound's reaction to the "Notes" is a testimony to the fact that there had been two poems in the process of making from the start, one by Eliot, the *Grammaticus*, and one by Pound, *Rhetor*. Pound resolutely brushed aside the "Notes" as irrelevant:

> For the rest, I saw the poem in typescript, and I did not see the notes till 6 or 8 months afterward; and they have not increased my enjoyment of the poem one atom. The poem seems to me an emotional unit. . . .
>
> I have not read Miss Weston's *Ritual to Romance*, and do not at present intend to. As to the citations, I do not think it matters a damn which is from Day, which from Milton, Middleton, Webster, or Augustine. I mean so far as the functioning of the poem is con-

cerned. One's incult pleasure in reading *The Waste Land* would be the same if Webster had written "Women Before Woman" and Marvell the *Metamorphoses*.[50]

As Kenner remarks, Pound's "parting shot deserves preservation": "This demand for clarity in every particular of a work, whether essential or not, reminds me of the Pre-Raphaelite painter who was doing a twilight scene but rowed across the river in day time to see the shape of the leaves on the further bank, which he then drew in with full detail."[51]

Four Quartets requires a separate essay,[52] but the student of classical rhetoric need look no further than the fifth (delivery) section of each *Quartet* to find a full treatment of language and poetics. The four-part structure of the poem, "the complete consort dancing together," was Eliot's triumphant marriage of Paul and Apollo, of theology and art, that capped the years of Pound's masterly tuition.

CHAPTER SIX

St. Thomas Aquinas's Theory of Communication

ERIC MCLUHAN

The problem of discussing St. Thomas's theory of communication is made difficult not because it is subtle and obscure but because it appears everywhere in his
work. It arises in his constant references to principles of formal causality and
ground. It arises in his preference for the position of Realism against that of
Nominalism.[1] It surfaces—to take a few random examples—

- in his doctrine of essences: "in everything the essence is identical with the
ground of its being"[2]

- in *De Potentia Dei*, where he points out that formal cause is the *ground* of
being: " . . . being is the term and proper effect of creation . . . [and] . . .
all being derives from a form"[3]

- in his doctrine of all being as derived by analogical ratio with its formal cause
in God[4]

- in his doctrine of the process of knowing as operating by analogy; that is,
by mimesis and formal cause ("the cognitive agent is and becomes the thing
known"): "Once in act through this species as through its own form, the
intellect knows the thing itself"[5]; and "For the likeness of the known in the
knower is the form by which the operation takes place"[6]

- in his doctrine of faith as knowledge enabled by grace[7]

In fact, Thomas's entire discussion of the action of supernatural graces as formal causes in human understanding and human affairs, at the end of the *Summa contra Gentiles*, Book III, part 2, forms a comprehensive "theory of communication" unto itself.

To discuss someone's theory of communication it is necessary to locate two things: one is that writer's audience; the other, the effect that the writer proposes to produce in that audience and the manner of doing it. In the *Summa for the Gentiles*, St. Thomas discusses these things briefly in Chapter 2 of the first book. (This passage has often attracted attention because of Thomas's uncharacteristic use of the first person "I.") It is plain that work is composed for the use of teachers: in it he sets out material for teachers to use in discussion with "gentiles" and in refuting errors. But his audience is never more in evidence, or more explicitly than when he uses the famous "Thomistic article."

Before discussing Thomas's theory of communication it would be useful to revisit how he brought some of the resources of traditional rhetoric to bear on the matter of the *logos*, and also how he used rhetoric in attacking his audience. St Augustine, himself a professional rhetor, wrote about some of the problems that rhetoric poses for Christianity. (For example, if someone is persuaded to become a Christian by force of rhetoric rather than by inner conviction, is the conversion valid or invalid?) These and other problems Thomas sidestepped by his innovation, the article. Thomas used rhetoric as much more than a persuasive logos when he applied it analytically to the problem of proving to a skeptical inquirer that God exists.

St. Thomas's amazing doctrine of the "five ways" of proving God's existence shows that Practical Criticism is at least as old as the Middle Ages. As an exegetical performance, it derives from the conventional understanding of the natural world as a speech uttered by God at the Creation: when God said "let there be—" He was not posing a suggestion but simultaneously naming and creating each thing. The universe then is a sort of text, the Book of Nature written (as it were) in parallel to the text of Holy Scripture. Since Nature and Scripture were written in parallel, the mode of science and the mode of literary analysis were the same. The same or parallel methods of explicating texts should be used. To cite just one illustration of this conventional understanding of the Book of Nature, Alan of Lille wrote the little mnemonic,

Omnis mundi creatura

Quasi liber et pictura

Nobis est et speculum . . . [8]

St. Thomas's "five ways" of proving the existence of God begin with the Book of Nature, that is, with reference to experience of the natural world, of things, and of the senses.

The traditional Doctrine of the *Logos* held, among other things, that God created the natural order by uttering it, that the Divine *fiat* itself was the act of creation; name and thing were identical and univocal. To utter the name, "tulip," or "whale," was also to utter tulip or whale, to bring it into being. From this awareness flowed a powerful rationale for the traditional science of names and etymologies as directly related to understanding material essences and as embodying esoteric knowledge.

St. Thomas's technique in this article (*Summa Theologiae*, Part I, Question 2, Article 3) is to work backwards from the evidence provided by the fact of the utterance to the existence of the utterer. Of the arts of the *logos* as then practised (the trivium), only one provided the necessary tools for examining the relation of an utterance to its utterer. Dialectic, as the science of abstract thought and of testing for truth, is unsuitable. Grammar had several facets, including encyclopedic humanism, natural science, and the science of etymology and multi-leveled signification. While basic to interpreting *meaning* in both "texts" (Scripture and Nature), grammar yet did not provide any means to deduce from the character of either "book" the nature or existence of its Author. Rhetoric, on the other hand, specifically concerns itself with both utterances and utterers, and it was to this science of the *logos* that St. Thomas turned to find his "five ways." *To be* is an act; indeed, it is the ultimate act, and we know from the *Logos* of Creation that it is a rhetorical act.

St. Augustine had based his ideal Christian, the *doctus Christianus,* on Cicero's ideal rhetorician (*doctus orator*), a man of encyclopedic wisdom and eloquence. Cicero had derived his ideal by grammatical means, from the Roman translation of the Greek word, *logos*: *ratio et oratio*, reason and speech. On this ideal combination of wisdom and eloquence was founded the West's tradition of Christian humanism and learning; and the twinned arts of rhetoric and grammar had, continuously from Cicero to St. Augustine and onward through to the Renaissance, been treated as entirely complementary. The tradition of encyclopedic education for the ideal man—prince, poet, or Christian—continues unbroken from Isocrates to Erasmus. Cicero's ideal statesman/orator served as the model for the medieval theologian and prince alike largely owing to St. Augustine.

> How this came about is discussed by H.-I. Marrou *in St Augustin et la fin de la culture antique*, a study of the traditional education of the ancient world as it was adapted to the business of educating the great Christian exegetist and the great preacher. Thus the main stream of classical culture flows in the channel of scriptural exegesis as practised by the encyclopaedic humanist, a stream which was much reduced in volume by the

scholastic theologians between the twelfth and fifteenth centuries but which reached new levels with the Erasmian effort to restore the "old theology."[9]

It is natural then that St. Thomas, as a *doctus-orator-theologus*, would perform a rhetorical analysis (of creation by means of a *logos*) which assumed as its *ground* a grammatical trope (of nature as "quasi liber et pictura . . . et speculum").

For over five hundred years before Cicero, rhetoricians had been investigating the character of rhetorical utterances, and the rhetorical *logos*, for clues to its structural composition and the source of its power to transform. By Cicero's and Quintilian's time it had been decided that this rhetorical *logos* had five, and only five, components or "divisions." The first of these was *inventio*, which consisted of techniques of inventing or discovering material. The second division, *dispositio*, involved the manner of laying out an oration, the sequential disposition or arrangement of its material. *Elocutio*, the third division and the heart of the enterprise, governed all aspects of a rhetor's activities. It determined what would be selected from *inventio* and how that matter would be disposed. As regards the choice of ornament and style, it guided the use of figures—schemes and tropes—to fine-tune the material. It decided all aspects of delivery—inflection, gestures, etc. *E-loqui*, meaning speaking out or eloquent utterance, was the discipline of putting-on and putting together harmoniously the audience and its sensibilities, the occasion, and the desired effect: the sensibilities form a direct route to the mode of being of the audience and also to changing it.[10] Under the fourth division, *memoria*, were gathered various memory techniques; and the fifth division, *pronuntiatio* or *actio*, was the reservoir of vocal delivery and techniques of stagecraft, the "delivery system" by means of which the entire *logos* had its impact. Cicero maintained that these five processes informed every aspect of every speech, from the whole down to the least detail. St. Thomas, taking him literally, worked backwards and used each division of the rhetorical *logos* as a route to demonstrate the existence of the speaker.

St. Thomas's "first way" is the "argument from motion":

> It is certain, and evident to our senses, that in the world some things are in motion. Now whatever is in motion is put in motion by another, for nothing can be in motion except it is in potentiality to that towards which it is in motion; whereas a thing moves inasmuch as it is in act. For motion is nothing else than the reduction of something from potentiality to actuality. But nothing can be reduced from potentiality to actuality, except by something in a state of actuality. Thus that which is actually hot, as fire, makes wood, which is potentially hot, to be actually hot, and thereby moves and changes it. Now it is not possible that the same thing should be at once in actuality and potentiality in the same respect, but only in different respects. For what is actually hot cannot simultaneously be potentially hot; but it is simultaneously potentially cold. It is therefore impossible that in the same respect and in the same way a thing should be both mover and

moved, i.e. that it should move itself. Therefore, whatever is in motion must be put in motion by another. If that by which it is put in motion be itself put in motion, then this also must needs be put in motion by another, and that by another again. But this cannot go on to infinity, because then there would be no first mover, and, consequently, no other mover; seeing that subsequent movers move only inasmuch as they are put in motion by the first mover; as the staff moves only because it is put in motion by the hand. Therefore it is necessary to arrive at a first mover, put in motion by no other; and this everyone understands to be God.

By "motion," he explains, he means "the reduction of something from potentiality to actuality." The argument turns on the necessity of there being a "first mover" who is "put in motion by no other," and who is responsible for bringing things into a created state: an inventor. The "first way" derives from the process of invention—*inventio*.

St. Thomas's "second way is from the nature of the efficient cause":

In the world of sense we find there is an order of efficient causes. There is no case known (neither is it, indeed, possible) in which a thing is found to be the efficient cause of itself; for so it would be prior to itself, which is impossible. Now in efficient causes it is not possible to go on to infinity, because in all efficient causes following in order, the first is the cause of the intermediate cause, and the intermediate is the cause of the ultimate cause, whether the intermediate cause be several, or only one. Now to take away the cause is to take away the effect. Therefore, if there be no first cause among efficient causes, there will be no ultimate, nor any intermediate cause. But if in efficient causes it is possible to go on to infinity, there will be no first efficient cause, neither will there be an ultimate effect, nor any intermediate efficient causes; all of which is plainly false. Therefore it is necessary to admit a first efficient cause, to which everyone gives the name of God.

Of the four causes—formal, efficient, material, final—only the efficient cause operates sequentially. The other three are simultaneous, fully present from the first moment. Now, dialectic, the governing art of the time and the scholastic's main mode of exposition, reserves for itself only two of the five rhetorical divisions: *inventio* and *dispositio*, matter and arrangement. In dialectic and rhetoric, the convention of *dispositio* was that of logical, linear sequence in argument and of efficient cause in reason and science. Via efficient cause, the "second way" links directly to *dispositio*.

St. Thomas's "third way is taken from possibility and necessity," and is concerned with observation of modes of being:

We find in nature things that are possible to be and not to be, since they are found to be generated, and to corrupt, and consequently, they are possible to be and not to be. But it is impossible for these always to exist, for that which is possible not to be at some time is not. Therefore, if everything is possible not to be, then at one time there could have been nothing in existence. Now if this were true, even now there would be nothing in existence, because that which does not exist only begins to exist by something already existing. Therefore, if at one time nothing was in existence, it would have been impossible for anything to have begun to exist; and thus even now nothing would be in existence—which is absurd. Therefore, not all beings are merely possible, but there must exist something the existence of which is necessary. But every necessary thing either has its necessity caused by another, or not. Now it is impossible to go on to infinity in necessary things which have their necessity caused by another, as has been already proved in regard to efficient causes.[11]

These various modes and degrees of being and of not-being are taken as manifesting, as "showing forth," a fundamental and original of being:

> [as the paragraph concludes] . . . we cannot but postulate the existence of some being having of itself its own necessity, and not receiving it from another, but rather causing in others their necessity. This all men speak of as God.

The third division of the rhetorical logos, *elocutio*, embraces the same two concerns—"showing-forth" or "speaking-out" (*e-loqui*), and the "modes" or figures of that speaking-out in the sense of con-figurations of speech[12] and postures of the mind as realized in the modes or configurations of beings in creation. Each rhetorical figure is a vivisection of the mind and sensibilities in action. The "third way," then, derives from *elocutio*.

St. Thomas's "fourth way" is a much simpler matter. As Thomas remarks, "the fourth way is taken from the gradation to be found in things." The concern is not, as might appear superficially, with some sort of simple hierarchical arrangement:

> Among beings there are some more and some less good, true, noble and the like. But "more" and "less" are predicated of different things, according as they resemble in their different ways something which is the maximum, as a thing is said to be hotter according as it more nearly resembles that which is hottest; so that there is something which is truest, something best, something noblest and, consequently, something which is uttermost being; for those things that are greatest in truth are greatest in being, as it is written in Metaph. ii. Now the maximum in any genus is the cause of all in that genus; as fire, which is the maximum heat, is the cause of all hot things. Therefore there must also be something which is to all beings the cause of their being, goodness, and every other perfection; and this we call God.

Some have adduced as a source here St. Anselm's "ontological argument"[13]; I propose instead (or in addition) that St. Thomas here argues that the observables in the created order, to the degree that they have being, are redolent of the fount and maximum of all being and all good and all perfection. This principle of redolence, of recall, derives from the fourth division of rhetoric, *memoria*.

St. Thomas's "fifth way" is "taken from the governance of the world":

> We see that things which lack intelligence, such as natural bodies, act for an end, and this is evident from their acting always, or nearly always, in the same way, so as to obtain the best result. Hence it is plain that not fortuitously, but designedly, do they achieve their end. Now whatever lacks intelligence cannot move towards an end, unless it be directed by some being endowed with knowledge and intelligence; as the arrow is shot to its mark by the archer. Therefore some intelligent being exists by whom all natural things are directed to their end; and this being we call God.

This concern, with "conduct" and "governance" and being "shot to the mark"[14] has its locus in the fifth and final division of rhetoric, *pronuntiatio* or delivery. Just as the five divisions of rhetoric form a simultaneous whole, so do the five proofs cited above. None of the arguments was entirely new, but Thomists agree that St. Thomas developed and arranged them in this article to form a "coherent whole."[15]

St. Thomas, in using rhetoric thus, has simply applied the traditional divisions of the integral *logos* analytically instead of prescriptively—in the way a rhetor would normally employ them—to the grammatical Doctrine of the Logos. He retraced the labyrinth of the speech from the fact of its existence to that of the speaker, a procedure that in our time inheres in that literary discipline called Practical Criticism. Another novelty of the "five ways" is that they are empirical, based on reading and "criticism of text" of the Book of Nature: all begin with direct experience: "In the world of sense   "; "It is certain and evident to our senses that in the world . . ."; "We find in nature . . ."

I have dwelt in some detail on this one case-study as it were of St. Thomas's use of the divisions of the rhetorical *logos*, but it is not the only such use. He employed them occasionally, as far as I can ascertain, when discussing one or another aspect of the *logos* or *fiat* of creation. (Another use, for example, occurs in *De Potentia Dei*, Book I, Question 3, Article 4.) I should also point out that St. Thomas was not the first to make analytical use of the five divisions of classical rhetoric in this manner. Writers deployed them from time to time in both sacred and secular literature, and they have been continuously in use in literature and the arts from ancient times to our own. Two precedents are the *Pentateuch* of the Old Testament, the five books of which are patterned after the five divisions of rhetoric so that they form a simultaneous whole; and Cicero's five books on oratory, the three of *De Oratore* along with the *Brutus* and *Orator*, which Cicero noted formed a single work. Subsequent to St. Thomas, the Tridentine Mass was deliberately shaped using the five divisions of rhetoric: the first two divisions structure the first part of the Mass, "The Mass of the Catechumens"; in the remaining "Mass of the Faithful," the Offertory, Canon, and Communion perform the functions of elocutio, memoria, and delivery. The Mass, of course, is a single complex prayer. In our time, the five divisions have been used extensively by poets such as W. B. Yeats, T. S. Eliot, and Ezra Pound.

St. Thomas used the five divisions analytically, rather like a microscope, to turn the gaze inward upon a matter and anatomize it. He used them in a parallel manner when he turned the gaze outwards, towards his audience. In both cases, however, the form of the operation is that of the word (*logos*) understood through rhetoric.

Professor Etienne Gilson often remarked that the Thomistic article presents "one of the big mysteries" of medieval philosophy: where did Thomas get that article? By any measure, the article seems rather an odd and convoluted form to use in structuring an argument—when compared, say, to the syllogism or other (and more efficient) scholastic forms of article or dialectical procedure. And why did he use it some times and not others? One can discern in it a *kind* of *exitus* et reditus pattern, or a *sort* of thesis-antithesis-synthesis system, but both are gravely distorted from their ideal forms. When looked at from outside philosophy and theology, from the standpoint of literature, the article makes another kind of sense:

> Anyone familiar with the persistent use which Joyce makes of the labyrinth figure as the archetype of human cognition will have noticed the same figure as it appears in the dramatic action of a Thomistic "article." There is first the descent into the particular matter of the "objections." These are juxtaposed abruptly, constituting a discontinuous or cubist perspective. By abrupt juxtaposition of diverse views of the same problem, that which is in question is seen from several sides. A total intellectual history is provided in a single view. And in the very instant of being presented with a false lead or path the mind is alerted to seek another course through the maze. Baffled by variety of choice it is suddenly arrested by the "sed contra" and given its true bearings in the conclusion. Then follows the retracing of the labyrinth in the "respondeo dicendum." Emerging into intellectual clarity at the end of this process it looks back on the blind alleys proffered by each of the original objections. Whereas the total shape of each article, with its trinal divisions into objections, respondeo, and answers to objections, is an "S" labyrinth, this figure is really traced and retraced by the mind many times in the course of a single article. Perhaps this fact helps to explain the power of Thomas to communicate a great deal even before he is much understood. It certainly suggests why he can provide rich esthetic satisfactions by the very dance of his mind—a dance in which we participate as we follow him.
>
> His "articles" can be regarded as vivisections of the mind in act. The skill and wit with which he selects his objections constitute a cubist landscape of great intellectual extent seen from an airplane. The ideas or objects in this landscape are by their very contiguity set in a state of dramatic tension; and this dramatic tension is provided with a dramatic peripeteia in the respondeo, and with a resolution in the answers to the objections.[16]

The drama of dialectical oppositions plays on the surface of the article in the contradictions between topic and objections, objections and *Sed contra* and replies to objections. But beneath this surface tension there lies a different structure, and another drama, a further unity. The five elements of St. Thomas's article comprise a simultaneous order since they too use the rhetorical pattern.

In keeping with rhetorical form, each article begins with a quest—an *inventio*. With this opening "Utrum" ("Whether . . ."), the topic is located, placed on centre stage: and discovered *via* doubt, not propositional certainty:

- Whether God can do what nature cannot . . .

- Whether God's power is infinite . . .

- Whether there be but one God . . .

The second element, the list of objections, provides the *ground* for the enterprise, the direction for the quest *(questio)* and the formal cause for the article. Here St. Thomas parades the ignorance—the *in*disposition *(dispositio)*—that will be used to probe and to winkle out the truth. St. Thomas's audience is put front and centre every time in the objections: it is the target of the article/*logos* and its ignorance supplies the form. Limning the ignorance in the objections is a technique for manipulating the probe of *inventio* across the bounding line between ignorance and truth, anticipating the *Respondeo* and, as a sort of exploratory gloss, the subsequent replies to the objections.

The third component of the Thomistic article always begins with the words, *Sed contra* . . . , and offers a statement of the true path. The words may come from Thomas's own reason or from an indisputable authority. (Occasionally, the *Sed contra* takes the form of another extreme view—the authority's—which is not always in harmony with Thomas's own views.) This is the *elocutio* moment, that of showing-forth or bestowing of right reason. It is normally brief, having the character of epiphany. This and the fourth element comprise a turn or reversal that flips the reader back across the bounding line that circumscribes the ignorance limned in the earlier parts of the article. The *Respondeo*, which complements the *Sed contra*, brings to bear on the quest the full measure of wisdom and eloquence, tradition and reason. It supplies the *memoria* function in the rhetorical *logos*. In the last section, the objections are "delivered" systematically, one by one, in the light of the foregoing.

The foregoing explains not only the source and the structure of the celebrated article, but also why it had that particular pattern and had to have all five elements. But why bother to pattern the article after a rhetorical *logos* at all?

The reasons are spelled out in St. Augustine's *De Doctrina Christiana*. Augustine frequently reiterates the traditional Ciceronian formula for the ideal orator as a man of encyclopedic wisdom and eloquence as that of his ideal Christian teacher. The formula derives from the Roman translation of the Greek term, *logos*: having no single-word translation, they used the hendiadys, *ratio atque oratio*—wisdom and eloquence. In turn, this pairing symbolized the pairing of grammar (encyclopedism) and rhetoric (eloquence), a traditional alliance which Martianus Capella immortalized in his monumentally popular *De nuptiis mercurii et philologiae*.[17]

"We have all known," writes Prof. Muller-Thym, "St. Augustine's dependence on Cicero in many details."

> By a stroke of sheer genius Henri-Irénée Marrou read in St. Augustine this remarkable sentence:
>
> O, would that on both these matters (i.e., *de vi et potentia animae*) we could question some most learned, and not only that, but most eloquent, and wholly most wise and perfect man.
>
> For who can this *doctissimus* and *eloquentissimus* be if not the *doctus orator*, the *vir doctus et eloquens* of Cicero? And thence, after a most remarkable reading of all the text of St. Augustine, we are forced with Marrou to the conclusion that all his life St. Augustine was a grammarian and an eloquent man in the best Ciceronian and Quintilianian sense of the word. It was the whole gamut of grammarial technique he applied to the exegesis of Scripture. It was a reworked *puerilis institutio* and *politior humanitas* whose treatises he began to write, but which were not completed. Cicero wanted to become an historian; St. Augustine did become one, in the best Latin and Roman tradition in the *De Civitate Dei*. And to make clear to Christians the state of and the preparation for Christian eloquence, as Cicero had written *De Oratore*, St. Augustine wrote that charter of Christian education, the *De Doctrina Christiana*. Here, in a word, was a man in whom eloquence was coming back to life in the purity of the Ciceronian ideal. But instead of addressing men to guide them toward the common good of the city, as Brutus, Cassius, and Cicero had done, Augustine and the Christian orators had to resort to eloquence to guide the Christians to God, the common good of the City of God.[18]

St. Augustine is wary of the power of rhetoric, which so easily can shift its effect from neutral teaching to active (even if inadvertent) persuasion, with unfortunate results. The difficulty is simply stated: any conversion that owes its impetus to a rhetor's pressure is to that degree not a valid conversion. The impetus must come from inside the convert, not from outside. Christian oratory, then, continually walks a tightrope. These matters concern the very essence of any theory of communication.

According to the textbooks, rhetoric persuades by one of the three established routes: *ethos* (appeal through character), *pathos* (appeal through sentiment), or *logos* (appeal through reason). These routes are as commonplace as the layout of an oration from exordium to peroration. But behind this civilized cliché lies the raw power of primal utterance. Thomas's *article* sidesteps the conventional routes to persuasion; instead, it deploys the rhetorical *logos* in attack mode, not so much to change the reader's mind or thinking as to set the reader himself to rights. It brings the ancient integral *logos* to bear on the reader's faculties, not one at a time as with the usual modes of rational appeal, but from all sides at once. Thomas's article is neither neutral nor passive nor objective, but an active agent on the attack. It functions medicinally. The form of the article—its formal cause—is the ancient rhetorical *logos*, the *logos prophorikos* of the Stoics. In their medicinal aspect, then, the five divisions of Thomas's article function as follows.

- The "*Utrum*" (*inventio*) identifies the area of weakness or illness addressed by the physician.

- The objections (*dispositio*) detail the wounds, the forms the disease takes.

- *Sed contra* (*elocutio*) by way of contrast puts the healthy condition on display.

- *Respondeo* (which could be written using the familiar R-sub-x) gives the medicinal prescription.

- The replies to the objections (delivery) show the medicine being applied to the wounds, the healing process.

St. Thomas's radical article tackled head-on the problem St. Augustine identified. St. Thomas did not invent the technique of using rhetoric therapeutically: medicinal literature and poetry has a long and varied tradition. A principal function of literary satire is therapeutic—and it could well be said that there is a large satiric (in the serious sense) dimension to the Thomistic article. Another well-known "medicinal" work that uses the same five-part structure is Boethius's *Consolation of Philosophy*.

That Thomas deployed the article in some of his works and not in others suggests that an exact decorum governs how and when it may be used. It appears in works throughout his career, e.g., from the *De veritate* (1256–1259) and *Quodlibetal questions* (1256–1259) to the *Summa Theologiae* (1266–1273), so it is not just something he stumbled across mid-career. (More likely the basic knowledge formed part of his training by Albertus Magnus.) It was not used, on the other hand, in discursive writings, such as the *Summa contra Gentiles*, and would have been inappropriate there: that *summa* is intended to supply teachers with material to heal not *their* ills (so there is no need to apply the medicine to *them*) but the mental "ills" or misconceptions of their audiences. Obviously, this very large and complex matter merits a separate study.

If St. Thomas's theory of communication is difficult to locate, it is because it is everywhere evident and in plain sight; and he is everywhere consistent. He adheres closely to the principles of formal causality and bases his communication strategy on them. He employs traditional rhetoric, not for argument in the expected manner, but both analytically, where the *logos* of being or of creation is concerned, and prescriptively, in shaping the celebrated article. In both cases, the form (formal cause) is the *logos prophorikos*, the rhetorical *logos*. The Thomistic article, then, is an active agent to be applied therapeutically not for the purpose of persuading the audience in the usual manner but to attack or cure an illness of the understanding or the imagination—to restore the patient's mental and spiritual balance and empower him or her to recover right reason.

References

Aquinas, St. Thomas. *Summa Theologiae*. New York: Benziger Brothers, Inc. (Dominican translation, in 3 vols.), 1947.

———, *On Being and Essence / De Ente et Essentia*. Trans., George G. Leckie. New York: Appleton-Century-Crofts, Inc., 1937; Rpt., 1965.

———. *Summa Contra Gentiles* (*On The Truth of the Catholic Faith*). *Book One: God, Newly Translated, with an Introduction and Notes by Anton C. Pegis* (New York: Doubleday / Image Books, 1955). *Book Two: Creation, Newly Translated, with an Introduction and Notes by James F. Anderson* (Image Books, 1956*). Book Three; Providence, Part I,* and *Book Three: Providence, Part II,* [both] *Newly Translated, with an Introduction and Notes by Vernon J. Bourke* (Image Books, 1956).

Augustine, St. *De Doctrina Christiana*, any edition.

Boethius, *Tractates, Consolatione Philosophiae*, Trans. H. F. Stewart, E. K. Rand, S. J. Tester. Cambridge, Mass.: Harvard University Press; London: William Heinemann, Ltd: Loeb Classical Library. Or any edition.

Capella, Martianus. *De Nuptiis Philologiae et Mercurii* (The Marriage of Mercury and Philology). Ed. Adolfus Dick, 1925. Rpt. Stuttgart: B. G. Teubner, 1969. Trans. William Harris Stahl, Richard Johnson, E. L. Burge, *Martianus Capella and the Seven Liberal Arts*. 2 vols. New York: Columbia University Press, 1970.

Chenu, M. D. "The Plan of St. Thomas' *Summa Theologiae*" in *Cross Currents*, Vol. II, No. 2. New York: Cross Currents Corporation, Winter, 1952.

Chesterton, G.K. *Saint Thomas Aquinas—"The Dumb Ox."* New York: Doubleday / Image Books, 1956.

Cicero. *De Oratore*. 2 vols. Trans. E. W. Sutton and H. Rackham. Loeb, 1942, 1967–8.

———. *Brutus* and *Orator*. Trans. G. L. Hendrickson and H. M. Hubbell. Loeb, 1939, 1971.

Copleston, F. C. *Aquinas*. Great Britain: Penguin Books, New York: Viking / Penguin, 1955.

Curtius, E. S. *European Literature and the Latin Middle Ages*. Trans. Willard R. Trask. New York and Evanston: Harper & Row, Harper Torchbooks / The Bollingen Library, 1953.

Gilson, Étienne. *Being and Some Philosophers* (Second Edition) Toronto: Pontifical Institute of Medieval Studies, 1949, 1951.

Gilson, Étienne. *The Spirit of Mediaeval Philosophy.* Trans., A. H. C. Downes. New York, 1936.

Marrou, Henri-Irenée, *Saint Augustin et la Fin de la Culture Antique.* Paris, 1938.

McLuhan, H. M. "Henry IV, a Mirror for Magistrates." Toronto: *University of Toronto Quarterly*, Vol. XVII, No. 2, January, 1948.

————. "Joyce, Aquinas and the Poetic Process." *Renascence*, Vol. IV, No. 1, Autumn, 1951, pages 3–11.

Muller-Thym, Bernard J. "St. Thomas and the Recapturing of Natural Wisdom," in *The Modern Schoolman*, May, 1941.

Quintilian. *Institutio Oratoria.* Trans. H. E. Butler. 4 vols. Loeb Classical Library, 1920–1922.

Weisheipl, James A. *Friar Thomas D'Aquino.* Garden City, New York: Doubleday & Company, Inc., 1974.

CHAPTER SEVEN

Rhetorical Spirals in Four Quartets

MARSHALL MCLUHAN

Mr. Eliot's designation of himself as "classical in literature and royalist in politics" has long been pushed aside. However, there is a great deal of sense in his "classical" claim if we turn to the traditions of Greek and Roman oratory. Eric McLuhan's essay on "The Rhetorical Structure of *Finnegans Wake*"[1] draws attention to the pervasive use of the five classical divisions of rhetoric as well as the four traditional levels of exegesis cultivated by classical *Grammatica* and *Philologia*. Both the five divisions (not to be confused with the six parts of an oration) and the four levels also pervade the work of T. S. Eliot, as I hope to show in an examination of *Four Quartets*. Each of the *Four Quartets* has five movements corresponding to the five aspects of the *Logos*, and each is also assigned to one of the traditional levels of interpretation. Dante's use of the four levels is well-known, but he also takes for granted the five divisions of rhetoric as the basis for organizing each of the *Cantos*; since, unlike the mere parts of a speech, the five divisions are, in fact, nothing else than the five mental faculties of man, perceived comprehensively. The *Logos*, especially as understood by the pre-Socratics, includes them all, but rhetoric and later philosophy alike tended to fragment and specialize the *Logos* which was translated as *ratio et oratio* by the Romans. Both the ideal poet and orator shared the encyclopedic training indispensable to true eloquence.

Turning first to the five divisions as they appear in the work of Cicero:

> And, since all the activity and ability of an orator falls into five divisions, I learned that
> he must first hit upon what to say; then manage and marshal his discoveries, not
> merely in orderly fashion, but with a discriminating eye for the exact weight as it were
> of each argument; next go on to array them in the adornments of style; after that keep
> them guarded in his memory; and in the end deliver them with effect and charm. . . .
>
> (*De Oratore*, I, xxxi, 142; Loeb Classical Library, p. 99)

To the five divisions he adds the six parts, which helps to distinguish the structural character of the divisions (synchronically and structurally seen) from the merely *diachronique* character of the sequential parts of an oration. That is to say, the divisions are structural and simultaneous, whereas the parts are sequential and distinct. It is probably this simultaneous character of the divisions (which involve all the mental faculties at once) that has confused many students before and since Cicero, including the misunderstanding of Horace's "five acts" in the drama of speech.

Cicero returns to the theme of the "fivefold divisions of rhetoric" again in the second book of *De Oratore* where he reproves some orators as working with theories that are "utterly ludicrous":

> After that they set forth a sort of fivefold division of rhetoric, to choose what to say, to
> marshal the chosen material, next to express it elegantly, then to commit it to memory, and in the end actually to deliver it.
>
> (II, xix, 79–84; Loeb, p. 257)

This kind of streamlining in the interests of dialectical simplicity and logical force also dominated the scholastic period and reached a special intensity in the work of Peter Ramus in the sixteenth century. The Ramistic "Method" was to reduce the five divisions to two and was caught up by Descartes and transmitted to the eighteenth century in a direct line through the *Port Royal Grammaire* (1660). Noam Chomsky, in *Language and Mind*, takes the story from there to modern structural and descriptive linguistics and to "the great Swiss linguist Ferdinand de Saussure, who at the turn of the century laid the groundwork for modern structural linguistics. . . ."[2] Chomsky further pursues the genealogy of linguistics: "Levi-Strauss models his investigations quite consciously on structural linguistics, particularly on the work of Troubetzkoy and Jakobsen."[3]

Quintilian in his *Institutes* gives full credit to Cicero for his insistence on the role of the five divisions in contributing to plenary eloquence. He moves from the role of rhetoric in creating cities and laws:

The art of oratory, as taught by most authorities, and those the best, consists of five parts:—*invention*, *arrangement*, *expression*, *memory*, and *delivery* or *action* (the two latter terms being used synonymously). But all speech expressive of purpose involves also a *subject* and *words*. If such expression is brief and contained within the limits of one sentence, it may demand nothing more, but longer speeches demand much more. For not only what we say and how we say it is of importance, but also the circumstances under which we say it. It is here that the need of arrangement comes in. But it will be impossible to say everything demanded by the subject, putting each thing in its proper place, without the aid of memory. It is for this reason that memory forms the fourth department. But a delivery, which is rendered unbecoming either by voice or gesture, spoils everything and almost entirely destroys the effect of what is said. Delivery therefore must be assigned the fifth place.   (III.iii, 2–3; Loeb, pp. 383, 385)

In many places both Cicero and Quintilian make occasion to expound the qualities involved in each of the five divisions of rhetoric, or the five faculties of man. Thus, invention or discovery was synonymous with genius and inspiration, yet was closely allied to erudition and encyclopedic learning. In *De Oratore II* Cicero notes:

And so, since in oratory three things are necessary to discovery of arguments, first acuteness, secondly theory, or art, as we may call it if we like, and thirdly painstaking, I must needs grant pride of place to talent, though talent itself is roused from lethargy by painstaking, painstaking, I repeat, which is always valuable, and most of all in fighting a case. (P. 305)

In *Ad Herennium* Cicero explains *inventio* further:

Invention is used for the six parts of a discourse: the Introduction, Statement of Facts, Division, Proof, Refutation, and Conclusion. The Introduction is the beginning of the discourse, and by it the hearer's mind is prepared for attention. The Narration or Statement of Facts sets forth the events that have occurred or might have occurred. By means of the Division we make clear what matters are agreed upon and what are contested, and announce what points we intend to take up. Proof is the presentation of our arguments, together with their corroboration. Refutation is the destruction of our adversary's arguments. The Conclusion is the end of the discourse, formed in accordance with the principles of the art.   (I, iii, 4; Loeb, pp. 9, 11)

It is important to notice that the divisions of rhetoric, or the faculties of the mind, are quite distinct from these parts of a discourse which are merely lineal and sequential; whereas the divisions or faculties of the mind are simultaneous and structural. As Quintilian noted above: "all speech expressive of purpose involves also a subject and words. If such expression is brief and contained within the limits of one sentence, it may demand nothing more, but longer speeches require much more." Hence he was saying that all educated people in Greece and Rome took for granted that the *Logos* included the five human faculties and that these were deployed alike in large treatises, in the individual parts of a speech, and in single sentences. It is not surprising, therefore, that T. S. Eliot also understood this in arranging the five movements of each of the *Quartets*.

Before turning to the five themes, it would be well to consider the four-part structure of the *Quartets* as this pattern relates to a classical doctrine of philology that precedes Christianity, namely the four levels of exegesis of the Book of Nature, including man and society. Varro in *De Lingua Latina* explains the four levels as follows:

> Now I shall set forth the origins of the individual words, of which there are four levels of explanation. The lowest is that to which even the common folk has come. . . . The second is that to which old-time grammar has mounted, which shows how the poet has made each word which he has fashioned and derived. . . .
>
> The third level is that to which philosophy ascended and on arrival began to reveal the nature of those words which are in common use. . . . The fourth is that where the sanctuary is, and the mysteries of the high-priest: if I shall not arrive at full understanding there, at any rate I shall cast about for a conjecture. . . .   (V, 7–8; Loeb, p. 9)

Ernst Curtius in *European Literature and the Latin Middle Ages* has a rich section on "The Book as Symbol" in which he notes: "The Humanism of the twelfth century, like every true humanism, delights simultaneously in the world and in the book." He cites the vision of a man transformed into a book:

> On his brow shines astrology, grammar governs his teeth, rhetoric brightens on his tongue, from his lips spouts logic, etc.; the mechanical arts are drawn on his back, on his right hand is written: "*Dux ego previus, et to me sequere.*"[4]

The "trope" of the book served to organize the verbal universe including both the "text" of Nature and that of Scripture. Etienne Gilson explains the relevance of "the trope of the book" for medieval theologians and scientists alike:

> Since the universe revealed itself to his eyes as a book to read and he saw in nature a sensible revelation analogous to that of the Scriptures, the traditional methods of interpretation which had always been applied to the sacred books could equally be applied to the book of creation. Just as there is an immediate and literal sense of the sacred text, but also an allegorical sense by which we discover the truths of faith that the letter signifies, a tropological sense by which we discover a moral precept behind a passage in the form of an historical narrative, and an anagogical sense by which our souls are raised to the love and desire of God, so we must not attend to the literal and immediate sense of the book of creation but look for its inner meaning in the theological, moral, and mystical lessons that it contains. The passage from one of these two spheres to the other is the more easily effected in that they are in reality inseparable.[5]

Eric McLuhan, in his essay on "The Rhetorical Structure of *Finnegans Wake*," explains how Joyce has used the five divisions of rhetoric and the four levels of exegesis in arranging the patterns of the *Wake*, alluding to the same structures as they occur in *Ulysses*:

> Signatures of all things I am here to read, seaspawn and seawrack, the nearing tide, that rusty boot. Snotgreen, bluesilver, rust: colored signs. Limits of the diaphane. But he adds: in bodies.[6]

I am going to look at first at the four-level structure of the *Four Quartets*, merely as it relates to the conventional levels of traditional exegesis of the Books of Nature and of Scripture. Since Eliot's text is easily accessible (but also expensive to quote) I shall be mainly descriptive. Each of the *Four* ties in the seasons and the elements and specific geographical locations:

"Burnt Norton"—autumn and air,

"East Coker"—summer and earth,

"The Dry Salvages"—late spring and water,

"Little Gidding"—winter and fire.

In the epigraph the words of Herakleitos relate to all four: "The law of reason is common. The majority of people live as if they had an understanding of their own." And second: "The way up and the way down are one and the same."

In terms of the levels of exegesis, "Burnt Norton" is the literal level (the literal contains all the other levels[7]). The theme is time—past, present, and future. It is a world of deceptions and hopes and memories: "Disturbing the dust on a bowl of rose-leaves" (1.17). The title refers to a "burnt-out case," a fallen world. Redemption is achieved by the simultaneity that is "consciousness" which liberates us from time (1.88). Liberation is by pattern recognition.

"East Coker" is the second level, which is to say figurative or allegorical and genealogical, since it includes an allusion to Eliot's ancestor, Andrew E. Eliot, who set out from East Coker for Beverly, Massachusetts, in 1670. Further figurative extensions of the family theme include the Eliot family motto: *Tace et Fac* ("We must be still and still moving").

"The Dry Salvages" represents the tropological or moral level of exegesis. Full of the world of practical observation concerning the human situation, it is concerned with action and the quest for survival and meaning. The ambivalence of the final line—"The life of significant toil"—binds the seeking and toiling of the behavioral *Quartet*.

"Little Gidding" is the fourth or anagogical and mystical level of spiritual concentration. It is a kind of confessional meditation that interlaces the great mystical themes of both East and West.

Turning now to the five movements of each *Quartet*, it is possible to be brief, since Eliot spirals and weaves with unbroken consistency through the four levels and the five divisions of the rhetorical structures. That is not to say that there is a merely mechanical repetition of the five modes of the *Logos* as they are traditionally embedded in the idea of the five divisions. Since these five movements resonate with the inclusive Word or *Logos*, and relate to diverse mental faculties, there is no limit to the variety of adaptation to the poetic situation.

In "Burnt Norton" the opening movement, concerning time and its intersection with place in human consciousness, opens the door into many forgotten gardens.

The second movement which implies the modes of order and arrangement invokes a variety of orders—mythical, anthropological, biological, and astrological. The contemplation of the multiple orders of "the turning world" occurs at "the still point" (l. 64) which is the resonant interval *where the action is*—the world of touch.

The third movement, which is the division of *elocutio*, puts on the mask of "a place of disaffection." The third movement of each of the *Quartets* presents a mask—the "put on," the *persona* of a place and a condition. Here it is "the gloomy hills of London" (l. 114) and "in this twittering world" (l. 117).

The fourth movement is *memoria*, and the theme is nostalgia—"Will the sunflower turn to us . . ." (l. 133)

The fifth movement of *pronunciatio* or delivery and performance is, here and in each of the *Quartets*, devoted to the theme of language, which "will not stay in place" (l. 156). Language is man's way of catching "in the form of limitation" (l. 171) the interplay between "Un-being and being" (l. 172).

The first movement or *inventio* of "East Coker" (consider Bach's two- and three-part inventions as strictly relevant to this rhetorical term) plays with primal processes of birth and death—"Houses live and die" (l. 9). Matrimony—the beginnings and ends (l. 51).

The second movement (*dispositio* or arrangement) presents a world of disorder at many levels—November is late (l. 52) and spring is disturbed (l. 53)—the hollyhocks "aim too high" (l. 56), which leads him to notice that he is tending to "a worn-out poetical fashion" (l. 70), and that his "knowledge imposes a pattern, and falsifies" (l. 85). The disorder becomes Dantesque "in a dark wood, in a bramble" (l. 91), human disorder born of the "fear of fear and frenzy" (l. 96), but there is the sudden "wisdom of humility" (l. 99).

The third movement, *elocutio*, puts on the mask or *persona* of the blind Samson, and *The Heart of Darkness*, and the darkened theatre (ll. 14–15). It is an empty artificial world in which the "motive of action" (l. 110) has been lost. The artifice of bureaucracy and organization suddenly yields to a darkened theatre (ll. 14–15) and "an underground train" (l. 120) and "mental emptiness" of the pilgrims (l. 123). There is a spiraling out of the depth which begins with "I said to my soul, be still" (l. 126), and ends "where you are not" (l. 150).

Section IV (*memoria*) opens with the surgeon (a figure which Paul Valéry uses for the artist—*Variété* V, p. 55) which for Eliot is a figure of Christ and a rehearsal of the Passion. This section is eminently reverie and memoria.

Section V (*delivery*), with its "wholly new start" (l. 179) and its spiraling "Into another intensity" (l. 209), is readily identifiable, in rhetorical terms.

"The Dry Salvages" opens with the spiral of "the river" (l. 1) which moves at many levels and in many situations: "The river is within us" (l. 15). The river weaves through all levels of creation, both natural and human, and is a kind of evolutionary thrust appearing equally in "the whale's backbone" (l. 19) and "the shattered lobsterpot" (l. 23). The river is *figure* against the *ground* of the sea: "the sea is all about us" (l. 15), and there is the interplay between *figure* and *ground* which "Clangs / The bell" (ll. 49–50).

Section II (judgment, arrangement and *dispositio*) takes the theme of I and pursues its pattern through the different levels of existence, natural and human, from "The prayer of the bone on the beach" (l. 55) to "the fishermen sailing / Into the wind's tail" (ll. 69–70). The spiral moves through the stages of human life from "a very good dinner" (l. 94) to "the moments of agony" (l. 106) and "the bite in the apple" (l. 119).

Earlier I cited Cicero to show that invention is equally used for the six parts of a discourse. To those unfamiliar with the rhetorical terms, it may appear quite arbitrary which division or faculty of rhetoric is in play at any one time. It is necessary, therefore, to remember that all five of the divisions or faculties are present in any sentence, but the art of rhetoric consists in taking advantage of the properties or functions of each of these to enhance larger discourse, so that to have a surefooted knowledge of the structural characteristics of each of the five divisions permits the poet to move with confidence among his themes. Eliot is, of course, using all of the divisions of rhetoric simultaneously but is also giving fuller structural play to the individual divisions in each of his five movements.

Section III (*elocutio*) puts on the mask of Krishna ornamenting it with rich metaphors: "a faded song, a Royal Rose"—the "yellow leaves of a book." The transmigration theme blends with the transportation theme of a railway train (l. 139) and "the drumming liner" (l. 144)—"The murmuring shell of time" (l. 150).

Section IV (*memoria*) is enriched by Dantesque references and the theme of recall in prayer "for those who were in ships" (l. 183). I have noted that spiritual recollection and reverie is the character of IV and it is so in each of the *Quartets*.

Section V (*delivery*) opens with the themes of escape, and release from the human condition by occult means—"converse with spirits" (l. 188); "sortilege, or tea leaves" (l. 194); "barbituric acids" (l. 196); by Freudian interpretation of dreams (l.

198); and the sensations of the "press" (l. 199). And then "The point of intersection of the timeless/With time" (ll. 205–206)—the Cross—is indicated as the real "escape." Delivery is finally indicated as "we have gone on trying" (l. 233).

It is characteristic of the *Quartets* that each interlaces with the other, particularly the fifth section, as here. The themes of the Cross and Incarnation spiral directly into "Little Gidding," which is devoted to the fourth level of exegesis, the anagogical or mystical. The opening *inventio* stresses the paradox of "midwinter—Spring," the union of frost and fire (l. 4). Paradox is an essential mode of the mystical and of the Incarnation of spirit in matter, a theme which pervades "Little Gidding." The first section is lyrical, with the encounter between "Now and in England" (l. 40).

Section II (arrangement, pattern) establishes fragile and delicate form in a single calligraphic gesture: "Ash on an old man's sleeve" (l. 56) and "Dust in the air suspended" (l. 58). The interplay here between body and soul includes the developing pattern of the *Four Quartets* in their sequence—the death of air ("Burnt Norton," l. 63), the death of earth ("East Coker," l. 71), the death of water and fire ("The Dry Salvages," and "Little Gidding," (l. 79). The death of water and fire is a special paradox because of the role they play in the delivery section. The interval of interplay between body and soul provides a special liberation in the encounter with "a familiar compound ghost" (l. 97), where it is not only the interplay between the shades of "Pound" and Eliot: "In the uncertain hour before the morning" (l. 80); and it takes place "Between three districts" (l. 87) which is entirely appropriate to the idea of the intervals between the trivium of Grammar, Logic and Rhetoric. No more splendid a means of considering the role of art in the world could be imagined than the structure and arrangement of the second movement of "Little Gidding."

The poem is moving at the fourth or mystical level of exegesis, and the theme of art, itself a supreme mode of order, becomes the means of presenting the *dispositio* of this movement. For Dante the rhetorical arts are indispensable. The image of "the familiar compound ghost" (l. 97) merges between the two faces: "What! Are *you* here?" (l. 100). (As in a two-part invention by Bach, the music is not to be found in one or other of the two voices but in interplay. It is the contrapuntal mode of *dispositio* or arrangement which Eliot uses here.) The entire section, down to line 148, is a discourse on the order of art and poetry in the *ground* of a living culture. It includes both the poet and his public function, both tradition and the individual talent.

Section III (*elocutio*) explicitly concerns the "putting on" of the self and things and persons (l. 154), and the creative interval of indifference "growing between them" (l. 155), the *persona* and its *ground*. The enrichment of the *elocutio* is aided by the memory of the past (ll. 161–162) and the "love of a country" (l. 162). History enriches the corporate mask or *persona* of the poet. He rallies to include in his *persona* the figure of the Norwich mystic: "Sin is Behovely" (l. 169) and "the king at nightfall" (l. 178) and Milton (l. 182). The elocutionary enrichment invokes the drama of other cultures, Russian and Greek (especially Aeschylus in lines 155–205).

Section IV (*memoria*), like the other *memoria* movement, is a meditation on the spiritual life, both private and corporate. This one (ll. 210 ff.) rehearses the love-hate themes, and examines *philos-aphilus*, of Aeschylus and Greek tragedy. The movement begins downward with "The dove descending" (l. 203) and moves upward from line 210 to the end, reminding us of the Heraclitean epigraph: "The way up and the way down are the same." "The intolerable shirt of flame" is the Nessus shirt which can only be consumed, or become fire. Hercules, tormented by the Nessus shirt, threw himself on the funeral pyre and was transformed into a "star" ("fire or fire," l. 216). This delivery from fire by fire interlaces with V (*delivery*) which is a *ricorso* or replay of all the themes of the poem. "And every phrase/And sentence that is right" (ll. 219–220) spirals into the modes of the traditional rhetorical art, meditating and illustrating the themes of decorum: "The common word exact without vulgarity" (l. 224) explaining that "every sentence" (l. 227) involves the whole man and the whole art, as in the *Logos* of the Herakleitos epigraph at the opening of the poem. The theme is of liberation through involvement in the "timeless moments" (l. 238), between the way up and the way down. "Between two waves of the sea" (l. 254) is the resonant interval, the stilling of the unheard music that assures that "all shall be well" (l. 258).

CHAPTER EIGHT

Poetic *vs.* Rhetorical Exegesis

The Case for Leavis Against Richards and Empson

MARSHALL MCLUHAN

It was said ten years ago that American critics once alerted to the new movements in English criticism would probably bog down in the rhetorical exegesis of Richards and Empson rather than adapt it, as F. R. Leavis did, as a means in a critical journey to the full act of plenary critical judgment. At first it may seem simply absurd to say that neither Richards nor Empson is a fully equipped critic. That, however, is not to say for one moment that the critic can dispense with their techniques. The fallacy consists in supposing that the excellent devices for observing and describing "what is going on in a poem" which they have contributed to the art of criticism is a technique of evaluation.

The fact is that neither Richards and Empson nor their disciples have met with success in the evaluation of poems. It is only fair to add that neither Richards nor Empson has ever aimed at evaluation. Those, however, who have employed their method as the method of critical judgment itself have had occasion to be embarrassed. Mr. Kenneth Burke, for example, admits the validity of R. P. Blackmur's observation: "I think on the whole his [Burke's] method could be applied with equal fruitfulness to Shakespeare, Dashiell Hammett, or Marie Corelli." Not only could it be so applied but it is so applied throughout Mr. Burke's very stimulating essays. One can say with equal validity of Mr. Empson that his method is quite as fruitfully applicable to a nursery rhyme or a headline. That is not to damn his method at all. It is merely to say that it doesn't involve literary evaluation.

Within the limits of their method neither Richards nor Empson can say why the nursery rhyme is superior in value as a human product. Involved in the fascinating game of explicating the rhetorical or psychological relations of symbolic statements (and let us recall that Aristotle found it necessary to treat psychology and rhetoric together, just as he presupposes that the poet will first of all have become a rhetorician), Mr. Burke is unable to assign any ground for detecting the pseudo quality of such a writer as E. E. Cummings. Likewise Mr. Empson can delight us with the rhetorical-psychological implications of *Alice in Wonderland* as readily as of Marvell's *Garden*.

Just as Korzybski offers us a correlation of knowledge by extension of the modes of grammar (and in this respect belongs to an ancient tradition headed by Cratylus and carried on by Pliny, Philo-Judæus, Origen, St. Bonaventura, and the later alchemists) so Mr. Richards, whose *Meaning of Meaning* is a treatise of speculative grammar of curiously scholastic stamp, offers us a method for interpreting and manipulating our lives by an extension of the devices of rhetoric. In this respect Mr. Richards is a true nominalist son of Ockham, Agricola, and Ramus; and it is no accident that Harvard has welcomed this distinguished schoolman.

Mr. Richards' rediscovery of the functional rhetorical relationships in speech and prose was timely, indeed, after three centuries of Cartesian contempt for metaphor and rhetoric in all its modes. However, in order to understand how Mr. Empson developed Mr. Richards' method it is worth pointing out that all four relations of "sense," "attitude," "tone," and "intention" designated by Richards are not directly applicable to the work of a poet. A speaker or a writer of prose has an intention related to an audience of some sort, but a poet's intention is entirely absorbed in the nature of the thing he is making. The thing made will stand in relation to an audience but this, while important, is only *per accidens*. Thus the "meaning" of a work of prose or rhetoric, whether pantomime, or speech, or tract is incomplete without the precise audience for which it was intended. For example, Swift's *Modest Proposal* does not have its whole meaning inherent in the internal relationships of the theme of that piece. One main "ingredient" of the composition is the relation in which its ostensible propositions stand to an audience of peculiar mental complexion. The nature of that audience must be inferred from the piece itself, and it is essential to the understanding of the work.

Thus rhetoric is essentially an affair of external, as well as internal, relations, while a poem has external relations only accidentally. For example, the speech of Marvell's lover to the beloved in *The Coy Mistress* is a work of rhetoric, full of shifting attitudes to the audience and displaying several persuasive arguments. But the audience *is in the poem*. This is equally true for the poetic drama. A poem or play may contain any number of rhetorical and political components needing exegesis, and yet be wholly poetic—that is, be entirely organized with reference to a dramatic structure or movement which is self-contained. A rhetorical work is for the sake of producing action. A poetic work is an action produced for the sake of contemplation. This is an irreducible functional distinction between rhetoric and poetic which it is the business of the critic to manifest point by point in judging the particular work.

This brings us to the crucial point. Faced with a work full of rhetorical, and, therefore, political and psychological complexity, the rhetorician-psychologist can perform prodigies of ingenious and helpful exegesis but cannot possibly, within the limits of his method, determine whether the work is a poem or not. He cannot even decide how much exegesis of technique of imagery is relevant to a particular passage of the work, as the reader of Empson is frequently aware. Mr. Richards and Mr. Empson are thus rhetoricians. Mr. Richards is a rhetorician with one foot in the camp of the speculative or dialectical grammarians and one foot in the camp of the psychologists. Mr. Empson ignores the grammarians and provides a forensic-psychological approach to letters which is naturally congenial to the Southern intellectual. As rhetorician, Mr. Empson has brilliantly availed himself of the new insights of Freud and Jung into traditional speaker-audience relations. The *Seven Types of Ambiguity* is an ingenious and valid application of Freud's analysis of wit and of dreams to some of the material of poetry. Insofar as political and social myth-making is inevitably part of the material of poetry, as it is of language, it too can be subjected to psychoanalytic scrutiny with fascinating results. But the utmost extension and refinement of the methods for observing speaker-audience relations brings one no nearer the problem of deciding whether a particular work is a poem, and if so, whether it is a significant or an insignificant one.

The whole problem for the critic to determine in poetic judgment has been precisely indicated by Mr. Eliot in *Tradition and the Individual Talent*: "For it is not the 'greatness'; the intensity of the emotions, the components, but the intensity of the artistic process, the pressure, so to speak, under which the fusion takes place, that counts." Richards and Empson offer no clues whatever for approaching evaluation of this sort. Mr. Empson, for example, can offer no clues which would help to determine whether the components of *Alice in Wonderland* are merely an aggregate, whether they are excogitated, or whether they are genuinely fused in a unifying vision which makes of them a dramatic integrity. Similarly, Mr. Kenneth Burke, examining Odets' *Golden Boy*, notes the contrasting cluster-symbols of "violin-prizefight," but he offers no basis for evaluating the pressures and significances which Odets gets or fails to get from the interaction of these components. He offers some shrewd psychological insights into the imagery of *The Ancient Mariner* without indicating whether the work is internally organized, whether it really hangs together at all.

However, in *The Philosophy of Literary Form*, Mr. Burke, whom I am here considering as an able rhetorical exegetist in the Empson line, appears for a moment to emerge as a critic of poetry: "We should watch for the dramatic alignment: what is *vs.* what. As per Odets': violin *vs.* prizefight. Or in Hitler's *Mein Kampf*: where we found the discordant principle of parliament . . . placed in dramatic or dialectic opposition to the one voice of Hitler." Here Burke begins with a basic principle of poetic judgment only to switch, significantly, to a rhetorical example. He recovers himself momentarily later on: "We should watch for 'critical points' within the work, as well as at beginnings and endings. . . . There is such a moment in *Murder in the Cathedral*, where the medium shifts from verse to prose. . . ." Again he selects a rhetorical feature for isolated comment without heeding the dramatic unity, if any.

In a word, the primarily rhetorical exegesis of Richards, Empson, and their very able exponents in America has obscured the essentially poetic exegesis of F. R. Leavis. Leavis doesn't "belong" among the rhetoricians and they have tended to ignore him. However, he has not ignored them and he can turn out a psychological elucidation of a cluster-symbol as deftly as anyone—as, for example, when he tackles Mr. Empson's "mountains as a totem or father-substitute" in his Wordsworth essay (*Revaluation*, p. 159). The ready hospitality which Leavis accords Richards and Empson as offering preliminary training in poetic exegesis is everywhere evident, and it is explicit in *How to Teach Reading*: "Further education in analysis may be derived from Mr. Wm. Empson's *Seven Types of Ambiguity*; those who are capable from learning from it are capable of reading it critically, and those who are not capable of learning from it were not intended by Nature for an advanced 'education in letters.' Besides these books there is, at this point, little to recommend." (p. 26).

However much Leavis may welcome Richards and Empson as coadjutors in the matter of training students how to read, he himself derives his method from T. S. Eliot: "Literary study, of course, cannot stop at the analysis of verse—and prose texture. How to go beyond and, without forgetting that everything done by the artist and experienced by the reader is done and experienced here, here, and here at an advancing point in a sequence of words, to deal with all that a critic has to deal with, the student will be able to learn from Mr. T. S. Eliot's *The Sacred Wood* or not at all. It is only because of their content that the essays in this book are (for those who master them) an education in themselves; they are models of critical method. Let the student consider for instance how Mr. Eliot in the essay on Massinger, starting with comparisons between passages of Massinger's and Shakespeare's verse, arrives at judgments of the relative value of two ages. He will then, at any rate, understand the injunction to attach, as far as possible, all that he wants to say about a given work to observations concerning technique, and will be safe from the kinds of interest in 'technique' that produced Mr. Pound's 'Melopoeia,' 'Phanopoeia,' and 'Logopoeia,' and the vowel-and-consonant analysis of the school manuals." (p. 27).

It is noteworthy that, as Mr. Leavis points out, Mr. Eliot achieves a qualitative political judgment as a by-product of evaluing particular poems. There is no paradox here. Since poems are actions the quality or precise degree of intensity among diverse components or vehicles of the action is the index to the moral quality of the age that "produced" the poems. Valuations of this sort must be undertaken by the critic and must be honestly based on detailed and verifiable particulars of a particular passage of poetry. It is not, on the other hand, possible to arrive at a critical evaluation of a poem or an age from the point of view of rhetorical exegesis, as one can see in the work of Richards and Empson. Basically a rhetorical exegesis is concerned with indicating the "strategy" employed by a writer in bringing to bear the available means of persuasion. One can go on indefinitely describing the situation from which the strategy emerges, elaborating whole psychological and political treatises without ever reaching the point of critical evaluation.[1]

It is impossible to survey here the critical achievement of F. R. Leavis, but it is clear on every page that his method is that of an artistic evaluation which is inseparable from the exercise of a delicately poised moral tact. He is not a critic of isolated comments as the mere titles of his works show. For example, *New Bearings in English Poetry* is concerned with assessing the precise changes in the poetic climate which have occurred in consequence of the impact of Yeats, Eliot, Hopkins, and Pound on our language. On the other hand, *Revaluation* "was planned," he tells us, "when I was writing my *New Bearings in English Poetry*, . . . indeed, the planning of one book was involved in the planning of the other."

The function of both these books is, with reference to particular poets and poems, to show what has happened to that existing order of traditional English poetry, of which Mr. Eliot speaks, once genuinely new work has arrived. For order to persist, says Mr. Eliot, "after the supervention of novelty, the whole existing order must be, if ever so slightly, altered; and so the relations, proportions, values of each work of art toward the whole are readjusted; and this is conformity between the old and the new." The basic implication in this statement is that the entire literature of Europe is to be viewed as a single emergent work of art, having a dramatic principle of its own. Genuinely new work is thus like a new development in a play. It tells us something about the preceding events of the play which we could not have seen before, and it alters the relations and tensions between the events which have already occurred. At the same time the new event must be seen as inherent in the earlier dramatic movement. How profoundly Mr. Eliot has since interpreted this dramatic view of history the reader of *Four Quartets* need not be told,

The entire effort of Mr. Leavis has been to realize by detailed judgments of selected poems this insight in such a way as to make it available for general recognition and experience among intelligent readers. It represents not only a major crit-

ical effort but the extension and refinement of sensibility as the very mode of critical activity and of discriminatory reading and response.

There are further implications of importance for poetry in this position. All
poetry, past and present, as forming a simultaneous order, becomes equally available for contemplation, and for the extension and ordering of sensibility. The perception of the traditional in modern poetry is thus an inevitable feature of enjoying
the contemporaneity of past poetry. It is clear, however, that that which is contem-
poraneous in Shakespeare and that which is traditional in Hopkins is not the
rhetoric, the psychology, or the politics. At least, this fact could be shown if need
be. And so the rhetorical exegetist of poetry has no available technique for directing attention to one of the most essential facts which the critic of poetry must be
able to focus at all times. Naturally, this elusive trait resides in the inevitable dramatic character of poems; and Mr. Leavis has concentrated attention on this feature in tracing "the line of wit."

There is thus a direction, an economy, and a concentrated relevance in the critical judgments of Leavis which are obviously lacking in Richards and Empson. Their
virtuosity of erudition notwithstanding, Leavis, in his method of criticism, is dealing simultaneously with a greater variety of factors than Empson or Richards. He
is in fact the more difficult writer. This can be illustrated quite easily from any of
his essays. It is most convenient, however, to cite an exegesis of a passage from
Macbeth (I, vi) since it is one of the few in his work which stand in isolation. Mr.
Leavis submits it as an example of method in *How to Teach Reading* (pp. 29–31):

> . . . one's caveat against the habit of regarding Shakespeare as a great "creator of char-
> acters" is not a mere pedantic whim. One turns up, say, Act I, Scene vi, of *Macbeth*—
> the scene under the battlements at Dunsinane:

Duncan.	This castle hath a pleasant seat; the air Nimbly and sweetly recommends itself Unto our gentle sense
Banquo.	This guest of summer, This temple-haunting martlet, does approve, By his lov'd mansionry, that the heaven's breath Smells wooingly here; no jutty, frieze, Buttress, nor coign of vantage, but this bird Hath made his pendent bed, and procreant cradle: Where they most breed and haunt, I have observ'd, The air is delicate

> Here is a good instance of Shakespeare's marvellous power of using words to compel
> on the reader or listener a precise complex response, to evoke the combination of emo-
> tions and associations appropriate to the context ("appropriate" clearly calls for analy-

sis). We note the insistence, throughout the passage, of the element represented by "pleasant," "sweetly," "gentle"; it is so insistent that it appears in a place so apparently inappropriate (on editorial inspection) as to elicit from the Arden editor the comment: "probably a proleptic construction." But the air *Nimbly* and sweetly recommends itself, and the set of associations represented by "nimbly" is equally important in the whole: we are in hill air, which is not only sweet, but fresh and vital—a sharp contrast to the smothering sense, already evoked, of the "blanket of the dark." But that is not all; every word in the passage contributes. Why, for instance, "temple-haunting"? It coöperates with "guest" and "heaven" to evoke the associations belonging to the "sanctity of hospitality," for "heaven," reinforced by "temple," is not merely the sky where the fresh winds blow. Nevertheless the suggestion of altitude is potent: no jutty, frieze, Buttress, nor coign of vantage, . . .

—"above the smoke and stir of this dim spot." But why "martlet"? The bird, with its swift vitality and exquisite frail delicacy, represents a combination analogous to "nimbly and sweetly." But more; its "pendent bed," secure above the dizzy drop, is its "procreant cradle"; and "procreant" is enforced by "breeds": all these suggestions, uniting again with those of "temple" and "heaven," evoke the contrast to "foul murder"—life springing swift, keen and vulnerable from the hallowed source.

There is no need to enlarge upon the dramatic potency of the effect thus roughly analysed. And yet it is to a great extent independent of the speakers (though, of course, Banquo and Duncan bring in an intensifying irony). At any rate it will be granted that an attention directed upon "character" and "psychology" is not favourably disposed for doing justice to the kind of thing Shakespeare does here with words.

Notice here how the rhetorical components of "character" and "speech" deriving from Banquo and Duncan are vigorously subordinated. At every point the imagery of these lines is considered as dramatically emergent from an earlier passage, contributing something startlingly new which is yet natural and prophetic of further development. The reader as spectator or contemplator is compelled to "a precise complex response." However, this compulsion is dictated not by any rhetorical persuasiveness or strategy but simply by the exigencies of a dynamic dramatic moment. There are a dozen points in this analysis where a rhetorical exegesis would have led us down exciting semantic and synecdochal vistas at the cost of missing the way in which the fusion of the elements occurred and is significant for the play as a whole.

It would be wholly unfair to leave the impression that Mr. Leavis merely derives from Mr. Eliot's extraordinarily fruitful criticism. The intense relevance of view and novelty of insistence in Mr. Eliot's early criticism was a by-product of his own problems as a craftsman. His poetic problems solved, his line of development assured, a distressing slackness overtook Mr. Eliot's prose. He ceased to function as a critic, or rather his critical comments became less and less related to his basic interests as a writer. Since his poetry has in no way suffered from this fact, it can be dismissed as a matter of little consequence. In the meantime, however, Mr. Leavis, with a rare sense of tact and without any chance of popular recognition, was engaged in executing the program which Mr. Eliot had indicated but relinquished. Just how well he succeeded the reader who has worked for six years with *Revaluation* is best able to say.

In a word, then, the method of Leavis has superior relevance to that of Richards and Empson because he has more clearly envisaged not only the way in which a poem functions, but the function of poetry as well. A poem in itself functions dramatically, not strategically or persuasively. It is for contemplation, and functions for the spectator or reader as a means of extending and refining moral perception or dramatic awareness. Where Mr. Leavis sees the function of poetry as the education or nourishment of the affections, Richards and Empson tend to regard it pragmatically and rhetorically as a means of impinging on a particular situation. Since the material or vehicle of all art is necessarily social symbol and experience, Richards and Empson have done a great service by insisting on the discriminating perception of the complex implications of this matter. They have made art respectable and redoubtable once more for all intelligent men. So much so that it is tempting to take up residence in their halfway house and to overlook the arduous stage of the journey which remains to be accomplished before winning an overall view, which is plenary critical judgment.

CHAPTER NINE

Joyce and McLuhan

ERIC MCLUHAN

Marshall McLuhan was not at all reticent about the debt he owed to James Joyce, and frequently uttered and published such statements as this: "Nobody could pretend serious interest in my work who is not completely familiar with all of the works of James Joyce and the French symbolists." He intended such statements to be taken quite literally. and truly, a full appreciation of McLuhan's work is impossible without the sort of perceptual training that such familiarity instils. Needless to say, that is not an attractive proposition, particularly to those from fields other than literature who resent any imputation that the training afforded by their own studies is in any measure inadequate. Consequently, such statements have come to be regarded as nothing more than provocative hyperbole. McLuhan, however, like Joyce, demanded the highest scholarship and erudition of those who would take him seriously or who would attempt to share his vision. He remarked once to me, as I know he did to many others, that his work on media and culture was, in the main, "applied Joyce." In that case, it might be fair to say that no-one can claim a serious appreciation of Joyce's work without a complete familiarity with the full spectrum of McLuhan's work. Joyce himself claimed to be "the greatest engineer who ever lived." Unquestionably, he is the towering figure in twentieth century language and letters; McLuhan occupies much the same position vis-à-vis the study of communication in this century, having done for that field what Joyce did for expression in prose. Yet he is the only scholar to maintain that he has taken up where

Joyce left off and pressed on to explore new areas of experience and understanding. Neither McLuhan nor Joyce worked in isolation from the main stream of our intellectual tradition; rather, each was quite aware of that tradition in all of its complexity and quite conscious of his role in it.

It has been fashionable in recent years to downplay or denigrate, privately and publicly, Marshall McLuhan's knowledge and use of Joyce's work and insights, a trend that does no-one credit. After *Work in Progress* and *Finnegans Wake,* Joyce himself was widely regarded as a lunatic. But twenty or thirty years after Joyce's death, just when he was beginning to be regarded as academically safe, a good many of the literati would wince and gnash their teeth whenever McLuhan cited Joyce or used his work to illuminate (or obscure) a point about contemporary culture. It was as if they felt some crass and unworthy popularizer were poaching on their private preserve. Even today, one finds condescending slights. I hope that my own study of Joyce and Menippism will, in some measure, illuminate a few of the many insights that McLuhan derived from Joyce and the *Wake,* and afford some glimmering of why he insisted that his work on culture and technology owed Joyce a great debt.[1]

On the day that it appeared in American bookstores, Marshall McLuhan and Bernard J. Muller-Thym bought copies of *Finnegans Wake* and excitedly repaired to a local bar in St. Louis to examine them. Both men, of course, knew what to expect, having followed with consuming interest the samples published in *Transition* magazine under the title, *Work in Progress.* True to the—even by then—accepted practice, they began reading it aloud to each other. Imagine them on that warm, sunny afternoon, declaiming slightly, as the atmosphere in a friendly neighbourhood bar might encourage you to do. They hadn't been at it long when another patron, who had been drinking there somewhat longer than they, wandered over and interrupted them and asked to see the page. They willingly showed it to him. He took a long, long, silent look. Then he handed the book back solemnly, slurred "I've had enough" and left the place. Some say he never returned.

Marshall McLuhan was a modern grammarian; that is, he was concerned with reading and interpreting not only literary texts but also what traditional grammarians call the "book of nature," the world around him. He consequently maintained a keen interest in writers and poets of all periods and their methods of observation of men and affairs, as his writings demonstrate. In this regard, although he did his doctoral work on Nashe and the Elizabethans (he wrote it, as he remarks from the outset, "from the point of view of grammar"), he frequently consulted *Finnegans Wake* in particular and Joyce in general, not just for ideas, but also for sharpening and training. Such is one of the great traditional uses for the arts. He was the first (and for many years the only one) to offer courses in "the moderns"—Joyce, Eliot, Pound, Lewis, Yeats—at the University of Toronto, having recently completed his studies at Cambridge where Eliot and Richards and Empson were all the rage. He had drunk the heady excitement of being near those intellects and their discoveries, and was not backward in conveying it to his students.

Today, nearly sixty years after Joyce's death, is there any reason to suppose his work has contemporary relevance? As its impact on readers and literature is undiminished, it is clearly as vital and relevant to understanding and perceptual training as when it appeared. Joyce wasn't "ahead of his time" so much as ahead of his contemporaries. Richard Lanham had this to say in *The Electronic Word* about the effect of the personal computer on the teaching of literature. He might easily have been discussing *Finnegans Wake.*

> Conventional literary study is pretty much stood on its ear by a changeable, interactive, and nonlinear text that has no final beginnings, middles, and endings, no unchanging dominant tonalities, and no non-negotiable rules about verbal excess and expressive self-consciousness. . . . If the reader can adjust the writing by becoming the writer, and to any extent desired, a great deal of the current controversy about the role of the reader can be conveniently shelved. There is as much connection between reader and writer, or as little, as you want to dial in. Is ever critic a creator and vice-versa? Is textual order a product of our rage for it, more than of the text itself? We can shelve that debate too: contrive whatever mixture you want. Is there a neutral language of conceptual expression or is all expression radically metaphorical? If we cannot settle this controversy finally, we can at least point now to a very broad spectrum of expressivity that includes not only words but also images and sounds, a spectrum controlled by a general theory of expressivity (which is what a theory of prose must become). This spectrum runs from least to most metaphorical, and you can locate yourself wherever you want. An identical spectrum exists for the reader as well as the text. Mix and match as you like, anywhere along either one.[2]

Let me offer three snapshots, taken about a dozen years apart, to display the character and the progression of Marshall McLuhan's interest in Joyce and his work. The first shows his awareness of how Joyce's awareness relates to our entire intellectual tradition. He portrays Joyce as the *Doctus grammaticus.* It comes from an article written barely a decade after *Finnegans Wake* appeared:

> In the *Wake,* Shem the penman is, like Moses, an "outlex." The seer cannot be a rhetor. He does not speak for effect, but that we may know. He is also an outlet, a shaman, a scapegoat. And the artist, in order that he may perform his katharsis-purgative function, must mime all things. (The katharsis-purgative role of the Herculean culture-hero dominates the night world of the *Wake* where the hero sets Alpheus, the river of speech and collective consciousness, to the task of cleansing the Augean stables of thought and feeling.) As mime, the artist cannot be the prudent and decorous Ulysses, but appears as a sham. As sham and mime, he undertakes not the ethical quest but the quest of the great fool. He must become all things in order to reveal all. And to be all he must empty himself. Strictly within the bounds of classical decorum, Joyce saw that,

unlike the orator the artist cannot properly speak with his own voice. The ultimate artist can have no style of his own, but must have an "outlex" through which the multiple aspects of reality can utter themselves. That the artist should intrude his personal idiom between thing and reader is literally impertinence. Decorum permits the artist as a young man (the *Portrait*) to speak with his master's voice—the voice of Pater, his father in art. (Joyce like Chesterton delighted in the multivalent wit of nature and reality so that, no matter how far-fetched his analogues and paradoxes, they are never concocted or forced. They not only bear but require intense scrutiny.)

Whereas the ethical world of *Ulysses* is presented in terms of well-defined human types the more metaphysical world of the *Wake* speaks and moves before us with the gestures of being itself. It is a night world and, literally, as Joyce reiterates, is "abcedminded." Letters ("every letter is a godsend"), the frozen, formalized features of remote ages of collective experience, move before us in solemn morrice. They are the representatives of age-old adequation of mind and things, enacting the drama of the endless adjustment of the interior acts and dispositions of the mind to the outer world. The drama of cognition itself. For it is in the drama of cognition, the stages of apprehension, that Joyce found the archetype of poetic imitation. He seems to have been the first to see that the dance of being, the nature imitated by the arts, has its primary analogue in the activity of the exterior and interior senses. Joyce was aware that this doctrine (that sensation is imitation because the exterior forms are already in a new matter) is implicit in Aquinas. He made it explicit in *Stephen Hero* and the *Portrait*, and founded his entire poetic activity on these analogical proportions of the senses.

Delivery

The doctrine of decorum, the foundation of classical rhetoric, is a profoundly analogical doctrine, so that to discuss it as it operates in Joyce is to be at the center of his communications network. In *Ulysses*, each character is discriminated by his speech and gestures, and the whole work stands midway between narrative and drama. But the *Wake* is primarily dramatic and the techniques proper to this form are taken from the [fifth division] of rhetoric, "*pronuntiatio*" or action and delivery. This division of rhetoric was a crux of communication theory in former times, being the crossroads of rhetoric, psychology, and other disciplines. St. Thomas discusses the issue, for example (*S. T.* I, 57, 4, ad 3), apropos of the modes of communication between men and angels:

> Since, therefore, the angels knew corporeal things and their dispositions, they can thereby know what is passing in the appetite or in the imaginative apprehension of brute animals, and even of man, in so far as man's sensitive appetite sometimes acts under the influence of some bodily impression . . .

The analogical relation between exterior posture and gesture and the interior movements and dispositions of the mind is the irreducible basis of drama. In the *Wake* this appears everywhere. So that any attempt to reduce its action, at any point, to terms of univocal statement, results in radical distortion. Joyce's insistence on the "abcedminded" nature of his drama can be illustrated from his attitude to the alphabet throughout. He was familiar with the entire range of modern archaeological and anthropological study of pre-alphabetic syllabaries and hieroglyphics, including the traditional kabbalistic lore. To this knowledge he added the Thomistic insights into the relations of these things with mental operations. So that the polarity between H.C.E. and A.L.P. involves, for one thing, the relation between the agent and the possible intellect. H.C.E. is mountain, male and active. A.L.P. is river, female and passive. But ALP equals mountain and historically "H" is interfused with "A," and "A" is both ox-face and plough first of arts and letters; so that, dramatically, the roles of H.C.E. and ALP are often interchangeable. Punning on "Dublin," he constantly invites us to regard his drama as the story of "doublends joined." Irremediably analogical, Joyce's work moves as naturally on the metaphysical as on the naturalistic plane.[3]

The next snapshot shows McLuhan probing Joyce's attention to media of communication. It appears in *The Gutenberg Galaxy,* under the heading, *Only a fraction of the history of literacy has been typographic* (pp. 74–5):

From the fifth century B.C. to the fifteenth century A.D. the book was a scribal product. Only one-third of the history of the book in the Western world has been typographic. It is not incongruous, therefore, to say as G. A. Brett does in *Psychology Ancient and Modern* (pp. 36–7):

> The idea that knowledge is essentially book learning seems to be a very modern view, probably derived from the mediaeval distinctions between clerk and layman, with additional emphasis provided by the literary character of the rather fantastic humanism of the sixteenth century. The original and natural idea of knowledge is that of "cunning" or the possession of wits. Odysseus is the original type of thinker, a man of many ideas who could overcome the Cyclops and achieve a significant triumph of mind over matter. Knowledge is thus a capacity for overcoming the difficulties of life and achieving success in the world.

Brett here specifies the natural dichotomy which the book brings into any society, in addition to the split within the individual of that society. The work of James Joyce exhibits a complex clairvoyance in these matters. His Leopold Bloom of *Ulysses,* a man of many ideas and many devices, is a free-lance ad salesman. Joyce saw the parallels, on one hand, between the modern frontier of the verbal and pictorial and, on the other, between the Homeric world poised between the old sacral culture and the new profane or literate sensibility. Bloom, the newly detribalized Jew, is present in modern Dublin, a slightly detribalized Irish world. Such a frontier is the modern world of advertisement, congenial, therefore, to the transitional culture of Bloom.

In the seventeenth or Ithaca episode of *Ulysses* we read: "What were habitually his final meditations? Of some one sole unique advertisement to cause passers to stop in wonder, a poster novelty, with all extraneous accretions excluded, reduced to its simplest and most efficient terms not exceeding the span of casual vision and congruous with the velocity of modern life."

In *The Books at the Wake*, James S. Atherton points out (pp. 67–8):

> Amongst other things, *Finnegans Wake* is a history of writing. We begin with writing on "A bone, a pebble, a ramskin . . . leave them to terracook in the muttheringpot; and Gutenmorg with his cromagnom charter, tintingfats and great prime must once for omniboss stepp rubrickredd out of the wordpress" (20.5). The "muttheringpot" is an allusion to Alchemy, but there is some other significance connected with writing, for the next time the word appears, it is again in a context concerning improvements in systems of communication. The passage is: "All the airish signics of her dipandump helpabit from an Father Hogam till the Mutther Masons. . ." (223.3). "Dipandump helpabit" combine the deaf and dumb alphabet's signs in the air—or airish signs—with the ups and downs of the ordinary ABC and the more pronounced ups and downs of Irish Ogham writing. The Mason, following this, must be the man of that name who invented steel pen nibs. But all I can suggest for "mutther" is the muttering of Freemasons which does not fit the context, although they, of course, also make signs in the air.

"Gutenmorg with his cromagnom charter" expounds by mythic gloss the fact that writing meant the emergence of the caveman or sacral man from the audile world of simultaneous resonance into the profane world of daylight. The reference to the masons is to the world of the bricklayers as a type of speech itself. On the second page of the *Wake*, Joyce is making a mosaic, an Achilles shield, as it were, of all the themes and modes of human speech and communication: "Bygmeister Finnegan, of the Stuttering Hand, freemen's maurer, lived in the broadest way immarginable in his rushlit toofarback for messuages before joshuan judges had given us numbers. . . ." Joyce is, in the *Wake*, making his own Altamira cave drawings of the entire history of the human mind, in terms of its basic gestures and postures during all phases of culture and technology. As his title indicates, he saw that the wake of human progress can disappear again into the night of sacral or auditory man. The Finn cycle of tribal institutions can return in the electric age, but if again, then let's make it a wake or awake or both. Joyce could see no advantage in our remaining locked up in each cultural cycle as in a trance or dream. He discovered the means of living simultaneously in all cultural modes while quite conscious. The means he cites for such self-awareness and correction of cultural bias is his "collideorscope." This term indicates the interplay in colloidal mixture of all the components of human technology as they extend our senses and shift their ratios in the social kaleidoscope of cultural clash: "deor," savage, the oral and sacral; "scope," the visual or profane and civilized.

The third snapshot is from the book, *War and Peace in the Global Village: An inventory of some of the current spastic situations that could be eliminated by more feed-forward*, which was written about seven years after *The Gutenberg Galaxy*. *War and Peace* opens with this hymn to Joyce:

> The frequent marginal quotes from *Finnegans Wake* serve a variety of functions. James Joyce's book is about the electrical retribalization of the West and the West's effect on the East:

> The West shall shake the East awake. . . . while ye have the night for morn . . .

> Joyce's title refers directly to the Orientalization of the West by electric technology and to the meeting of East and West. The *Wake* has many meanings, among them the simple fact that in recoursing all of the human pasts our age has the distinction of doing it in increasing wakefulness.

> Joyce was probably the only man ever to discover that all social changes are the effect of new technologies (self-amputations of our own being) on the order of our sensory lives. It is the shift in this order, altering the image that we make of ourselves around the world, that guarantees that every major technical innovation will so disturb our sensory lives that wars necessarily result as misbegotten efforts to recover old images.

> There are ten thunders in the *Wake*. Each is a cryptogram or codified explanation of the thundering and reverberating consequences of the major technological changes in all human history. When a tribal man hears thunder, he says, "What did he say that time?," as automatically as we say "Gesundheit."

> Joyce was not only the greatest behavioural engineer who ever lived, he was one of the funniest men, rearranging the most commonplace items to produce hilarity and insight: "where the hand of man never set foot." (pp. 4–5)

War and Peace in the Global Village blossoms with marginalia taken from *Finnegans Wake*, so that Joyce can comment in person from the sidelines. By 1938, Joyce was tinkering with the idea of a global village. He condensed it in two remarks in *Finnegans Wake*: "the urb, it orbs" and "urban and orbal." Both echo *Urbi et Orbi*, the title of the Pope's annual Easter message to the city (urbi) of Rome and to the world (orbi). The Introduction to *War and Peace* also includes (pp. 46–48) a brief résumé of the themes (explored in detail in the book on Joyce and Menippism) in the ten hundred-letter "thunders" of the *Wake*.

It was, in fact, about 1965 or 1966, a couple of years before the writing of *War and Peace in the Global Village*, when we first tackled together the ten "thunderclaps." By then, we had been reading the *Wake* off and on together for a year or two, for sheer delight in playing with language and as a way to stay sharp. Joyce was exercise.

We had developed the habit, that summer, of sitting in the back yard of our house on Wells Hill Avenue in Toronto, and reading aloud together every day "a page" of the *Wake*. The "page" often extended to five or six, and our beginning point was usually chosen at random. That is, we never set out to read systematically from one end of the book to the other. "A page" may not seem like a lot, but a page from the *Wake* is like no ordinary page. It demands the closest attention with all your senses operating at once, or as many as you can muster. And with two minds alert for nuance and reference, sometimes a couple of lines would occupy ten or twenty minutes of intense work, shuttling back and forth in the text and making links with other passages and entering marginal references. (Once in a rare while we would knuckle down and read an entire chapter over the course of just a few days. We did so with the first chapter, because it is so dense—it contains two thunders—and so tightly woven, and with a few others, e.g., the chapter devoted to HCE, or to ALP.) The *Wake* is not, like a novel, to be read all at one go; it needs to be sampled and sipped and relished in bits. And used.

Of course, now and then we would stumble across a "thunder," and wonder what in blazes Joyce was doing there. Eventually, our curiosity piqued, we wrote to ask a friend, Ivan Kramoris at Buffalo's Lockwood Memorial Library, to send us page-references to all ten thunders. He did, a few days later. After we received his reply, we spent the next several days reading the thunders and puzzling over them. First we noted the obvious, that the thunders differed from each other; they made different kinds of sounds. We noticed that they were generally associated with episodes in the book or set-pieces. Then we noticed that, like the rest of *Wake*-ese, they burgeoned with other words—and suddenly the dam burst. It might have been as we read the "episode" of Belinda and The Letter (both letter of the alphabet, and the letter as symbolizing repeatability and reproduction). Or it might have been while reading the "tale" of Kersse and the Captain, interspersed with and surrounded by a multiplicity of radio references. Or while reading Joyce's allegory of the Charge of the Light Brigade, the charged beam shot at the screen of the television tube. Whatever; we made the basic identifications in the thunder we were working on in a matter of a few hours, by following our habit of relating the present word to the larger context of the page and the episode. I remember that day, more than thirty years ago now, as a long day heady with excitement. We couldn't bear to stop until we had "cracked the code" of three or four of the thunders and by then the time for dinner was long past. Over the next few days, we sorted out the other six or seven. Several years later, those identifications appeared, vastly abbreviated, as three pages in *War and Peace in the Global Village*. It took months of concerted effort to begin to winkle out the thousands of words *in* the thunders; now, several of them have yielded thirty or more pages of words, each word denoting or alluding to a theme in the episode or an associated technology. Prior to our discovery of the thunders and their significance, Marshall McLuhan looked up to Joyce as a writer and artist of encyclopedic wisdom and eloquence unparalleled in our time, as the first two "snapshots," above, declare. After, he recognized in Joyce the prescient explorer, one who used patterns of linguistic energy to descry the patterns of culture and society and technology. Joyce was the perfect *doctus grammaticus,* expert in writing and reading both the written book and the book of nature, and in using each to interpret the other. (He pointed out that he had written *Finnegans Wake* "after the style of television.")

A final note: Marshall McLuhan regarded Joyce as a colleague, and used him that way. Whenever he made a discovery about technology and culture, he would open the *Wake* and read for a bit, and there, sure enough, he would find that Joyce had already been over the ground years earlier. Joyce followed the lines of force in the language and read and recorded what was registered there about the convolutions and disturbances of human experience and perception. Often, too, McLuhan would find a pregnant allusion or turn of phrase in the *Wake* that would set off a chain reaction of associations about some matter under discussion. He did not simply use Joyce to confirm an insight—he did that to whatever extent the text allows (some critics have charged that McLuhan used Joyce's page as an ink-blot into which to project his own fantasies)—he also used Joyce to stimulate fresh awareness of the present moment. In the same spirit, Joyce recommended using Vico "for all he was worth." Even today, Joyce gladly performs the same service for anyone willing to rise (or, as some insist, sink) to his level of play. It is a commonplace that all great art has the same invigorative and illuminative power; in particular, that power defines and characterises "low and motley" Menippean satire.

CHAPTER TEN

Introduction
Paradox in Chesterton

MARSHALL MCLUHAN

To-day the Chesterton public remains very much the public that read his books as they appeared. And for these readers he inevitably represents a variety of literary attitudes and manners which have begun to "date" in a way which bars many younger readers from approaching him. So that, for example, even in Catholic colleges books by Chesterton are not commonly on the reading-lists, nor do many of the present crop of students read anything more by him than an occasional "Father Brown."

The present book strikes out a line of radical evaluation which should do much to save Chesterton from this growing indifference. For in presenting him as a master of analogical perception and argument, Mr. Kenner at once divorces the Toby-jug Chesterton of a particular literary epoch from the central and important Chesterton who had an unwavering and metaphysical intuition of being. The specific contemporary relevance of Chesterton is this, that his metaphysical intuition of being was always in the service of the search for moral and political order in the current chaos. He was a Thomist by connaturality with being, not by study of St. Thomas. And unlike the neo-Thomists his unfailing sense of the relevance of the analogy of being directed his intellectual gaze not to the schoolmen but to the heart of the chaos of our time.

The point of the comparison may be made plain in this way. St. Thomas carried on his systematic speculation in the thirteenth century. Behind that century there lay fifteen centuries of encyclopædic irrationalism. From the decline of the briefly-achieved Greek order in politics and morals the West was dominated not by rationalism but by psychologism. That is, the cosmologies which were held up for the contemplation of men, whether Stoic or Epicurean, Divine Logos or concourse of atoms, were not philosophies but psychologies. They were strategies of a moral kind evolved as a practical means of bearing up against the universal confusion.

When the Church Fathers adapted the neo-Platonic and Stoic concept of the Logos to Christian Revelation, they committed the Church to many centuries of symbolism and allegory. The result was that for a very long time the outer world was seen as a net-work of analogies which richly exemplified and sustained the psychological and moral structure of man's inner world. Both inner and outer worlds were mirrors in which to contemplate the Divine Wisdom. Society, national and international, grew up once more. And it was an organic and closely-knit society in which the individual enjoyed a very high degree of psychological if not physical security, because of the universal acceptance of the moral and social implications of the Divine order mirrored simultaneously in physical nature, human nature, and political organization. Shakespeare is never more medieval than when he is stating this view of man and society. It is one of his favorite themes, as when his Ulysses says,

> The heavens themselves, the planets and this centre
>
> Observe degree, priority, and place,
>
> Insisture, course, proportion, season, form,
>
> Office and custom in all line of order.
>
> . . . . O! When degree is shak'd,
>
> Which is the ladder to all high designs,
>
> The enterprise is sick. How could communities,
>
> Degrees in schools, and brotherhood in cities,
>
> Peaceful commerce from dividable shores,
>
> The primogeniture and due of birth,
>
> Prerogative of age, crowns, sceptres, laurels,
>
> But by degree, stand in authentic place?
>
> Take but degree away, untune that string, . . .
>
> Then everything includes itself in power,
>
> Power into will, will into appetite;
>
> And appetite, an universal wolf,
>
> So doubly seconded with will and power,

Must make perforce an universal prey

And last eat up itself.

That is already a rather rationalistic and mechanical formulation, because Shakespeare wrote when this great symbolic and psychological synthesis was really destroyed. But in the thirteenth century St. Thomas was situated in the midst of a world in which psychological and symbolic awareness of order was almost the only awareness. His great rational synthesis represented a maximum degree of abstraction and withdrawal from that psychological plane of symbolic perception. But it should be emphasized that St. Thomas never rejected that psychological order. He took it for granted. He was sustained and nourished by it. And he never questioned or denied its value. In fact, the degree and scope of his rational synthesis is inconceivable without it.

But St. Thomas was followed by a host of rationalizers who were not so much nourished by the great symbolic cultural unity of the previous centuries as irritated by some contemporary rationalizer. St. Thomas had restored the anti-symbolic Aristotle to his proper role in systematic thought. But for every schoolman who understood the due relation between Aristotle and Plato or between Aristotle and the Church Fathers there were hundreds of noisy disputants who had their way to make in the world. By the early seventeenth century Descartes could rally enthusiastic support for the proposition that since no philosopher had ever been convinced by the dialectical or metaphysical proofs of other philosophers for the truth of anything, therefore the time had come to introduce a kind of proof which all men could accept—namely, mathematical proof.

What Descartes really did was to make explicit the fact which had been prepared by centuries of decadent scholastic rationalism: the fact that a complete divorce had been achieved between abstract intellectual and specifically psychological order. Henceforth men would seek intellectually only for the kind of order they could readily achieve by rationalistic means: a mathematical and mechanistic order which precludes a human and psychological order. Ethics and politics were abandoned as much as metaphysics. But both society and philosophy were in a state of great confusion by the time this desperate strategy was adopted.

Since the time of Descartes the strategy has been followed consistently. A high degree of abstract mechanical order has been achieved. Great discoveries of a potentially benign sort have been made. And human moral, psychological, and political chaos has steadily developed, with its concurrent crop of fear and anger and hate. The rational efforts of men have been wholly diverted from the ordering of appetite and emotion, so that any effort to introduce or to discover order in man's psychological life has been left entirely to the artist. Whereas the medieval artist was a relatively anonymous person whose function was not to discover order but to represent an already achieved unity, the modern artist is regarded as a pioneer:

His sail-broad vans

He spreads for flight, and in the surging smoke

Uplifted spurns the ground; thence many a league

As in a cloudy chair ascending rides

Audacious.

As the contemporary artist attempts to chart the psychological chaos created in the heart of man by a mechanistic society his activity is scanned with the utmost concern. A Blake, a Wordsworth, a Baudelaire, a Rimbaud, a Picasso, or a Rouault is regarded as a major source of hope and discovery. The disproportionate burden placed on the artist is the measure of the failure of the philosophy.

The point of the preceding diagnosis is this: that whereas St. Thomas was a great abstract synthesizer facing a unified psychological world, the modern Thomist has an abstract synthesis of human knowledge with which to face a psychological chaos. Who then is the true Thomist? The man who contemplates an already achieved intellectual synthesis, or the man who, sustained by that synthesis, plunges into the heart of the chaos? I say "sustained," not guided by, that synthesis; because the Catholic Thomist does not know the answers to contemporary problems in social and political ethics. He knows only when a particular line of action is promising and analogically consistent, whether it will tend to support a valid solution, and whether it is in conformity with reason and being. But he is the reverse of fecund in such proposals.

Let us remember that St. Thomas was sustained by a great psychological and social order in an age of dialectical confusion. We can be similarly sustained and nourished in an organic way by his speculative synthesis while we face the problem of creating a practical moral and social order. The main problem for Thomists to-day, therefore, is not speculation but action. And this necessarily means an action which co-operates in multiple ways with the numerous hopeful features of the contemporary world.

To take an example. Catholics have failed to understand or utilize Vico. Vico's great discovery of a psychological method for interpreting historical periods and cultural patterns is rooted in his perception that the condition of man is never the same but his nature is unchanging. For two centuries the Viconian method has been used by those who denied the rational form of man and who had only the desire to destroy rather than to perfect social order. Spengler finally perverted it to the point of paranoic rationalism. On the other hand, the first strikingly valid use of the Viconian method occurs in Gilson's *Unity of Philosophical Experience*. Vico was not a Thomist, and so he has been abandoned to the sceptics [*sic*]; but he invented an instrument of historical and cultural analysis of the utmost use for the discovery of psychological and moral unity in the practical order: something which St. Thomas was not interested in because such unity did, by and large, exist in his world.

Another example. The Catholic teaching of philosophy and the arts tends to be catechetical. It seeks precisely that Cartesian pseudo-certitude which it officially deplores, and divorces itself from the complex life of philosophy and the arts. This is only to say that the Catholic colleges are just like non-Catholic colleges: reflections of a mechanized world. The genuine critical discoveries, on the other hand, made by T. S. Eliot and F. R. Leavis, about how to train, simultaneously, esthetic and moral perceptions in acts of unified awareness and judgment: these major discoveries are ignored by Catholic educators. Rather in the rationalistic patterns of Buchanan and Adler they imagine that there is some Thomistic residue which is to be trusted.

This is where Chesterton comes in. His unfailing sense of relevance and of the location of the heart of the contemporary chaos carried him at all times to attack the problem of morals and psychology. He was always in the practical order. It is important, therefore, that a Chesterton anthology should be made along the lines indicated by Mr. Kenner. Not an anthology which preserves the Victorian flavor of his journalism by extensive quotation, but one of short excerpts which would permit the reader to feel Chesterton's powerful intrusion into every kind of confused moral and psychological issue of our time. For he seems never to have reached any position by dialectic or doctrine, but to have enjoyed a kind of connaturality with every kind of reasonableness.

So very impressive is this metaphysical side of Chesterton that it is always embarrassing to encounter the Chesterton fan who is keen about *The Ballad of the White Horse* or the hyperbolic descriptive parts of Chesterton's prose. In fact, it might be the kindest possible service to the essential Chesterton to decry all that part of him which derives so obviously from his time. Thus it is absurd to value Chesterton for that large and unassimilated heritage he got from William Morris—the big, epic, dramaturgic gestures, riotous colour, medieval trappings, ballad themes and banal rhythms. Morris manages these things better than Chesterton ever did: and nobody wants to preserve William Morris.

There is also a lot of irrelevant pre-Raphaelite rhetoric in Chesterton. From Rossetti came those pale auburn-haired beauties who invariably haunt his stories. The tiresome alliteration is from Swinburne. From Edward Lear came the vein of anarchic nursery wisdom which served the Victorians as a strategy for keeping sane. By acting insane in a childish way, a kind of temporary equilibrium was maintained: but it was also an evasion of that world of adult horror into which Baudelaire gazed with intense suffering and humility. For the Victorians the nursery was the only taproot connecting them with psychological reality. But for Chesterton the rhetoric and dimensions of childhood had also their true Christian vigor and scope. He was never tempted into the *cul-de-sac* in which the *faux-naïf* of the Christopher Robin variety invariably winds up.

Nevertheless, there is in Chesterton a considerable aroma of the desperate jauntiness and pseudo-energy of the world of Stevensonian romance: enough to make it desirable to give back to Stevenson the things that are Stevenson's rather than to try to make this dubious adolescent rhetoric appear to be of equal value with Chesterton's metaphysical intuition of being. From Stevenson's master Henley, Chesterton adopted the note of professional heartiness—a journalist's strategy for debunking the esthetish despair of the eighties and nineties. It has led to Kipling and Bulldog Drummond. Henley fathered the optimistic reaction to the intellectual languor of the later Victorians, and *Wine, Water and Song* is typical of Chesterton's sympathy with that sort of lugubriously self-conscious jollity. But just how unessential it was to him is plain from the fact that Chesterton really was happy. Henley and Kipling never were.

One Victorian feature of Chesterton's which is more closely allied to his real strength he got from Oscar Wilde: rhetorical paradox and epigram. Pater's Marius the Epicurean awoke to "that poetic and, as it were, moral significance which surely belongs to all the means of daily life, could we but break through the veil of our familiarity of things by no means vulgar in themselves." Wilde made much of this basic paradox in his life and art, as when in *The Decay of Lying* he proved that social and artificial things are more exciting than the "nature" of the romantic poets, and that "Life imitates Art far more than Art imitates Life."

The way in which Whitman and Browning and others appear in Chesterton is even more obvious. But the conclusion which it seems necessary to draw from these Victorian aspects of Chesterton is simply that he was not sufficiently interested in them to make a genuinely personal fusion of them. Had they been necessary to his primary awareness of things, he would have been obsessively limited by them in that drastic way in which a Stevenson or a Pater is limited and "dated."

In a word, Chesterton was not a poet. The superstition that he was is based on the vaguely uplifting connotations of "the poetic" prevalent until recently. He was a metaphysical moralist. Thus he had no difficulty in imagining what sort of psychological pressures would occur in the mind of a fourth-century Egyptian, or a Highland clansman, or a modern Californian, popping himself inside of them and seeing with their eyes in the way that makes Father Brown unique among detectives. But he was not engaged in rendering his own age in terms of such varied experience, as the artist typically is. The artist offers us not a system but a world. An inner world is explored and developed and then projected as an object. But that was never Chesterton's way. "All my mental doors open outwards into a world I have not made," he said in a basic formulation. And this distinction must always remain between the artist who is engaged in making a world and the metaphysician who is occupied in contemplating a world. It should also relieve the minds of those who from a sense of loyalty to Chesterton's philosophical power have felt obliged to defend his rhetoric and his verses as well.

It is time to abandon the literary and journalistic Chesterton to such critical fate as may await him from future appraisers. And it is also time to see him freed from the accidental accretions of ephemeral literary mannerisms. That means to see him as a master of analogical perception and argument who never failed to focus a high degree of moral wisdom on the most confused issues of our age.

CHAPTER ELEVEN

Introduction to *The Bias of Communication*

MARSHALL MCLUHAN

For anyone acquainted with poetry since Baudelaire and with painting since Cézanne, the later world of Harold A. Innis is quite readily intelligible. He brought their kinds of contemporary awareness of the electric age to organize the data of the historian and the social scientist. Without having studied modern art and poetry, he yet discovered how to arrange his insights in patterns that nearly resemble the art forms of our time. Innis presents his insights in a mosaic structure of seemingly unrelated and disproportioned sentences and aphorisms. Such is page 108 for example with its scholarly footnote that will certainly bear looking into. Anybody who has looked up the reference material that Innis cites so frequently will be struck by the skill with which he has extracted exciting facts from dull expositions. He explored his source material with a "Geiger counter," as it were. In turn, he presents his finds in a pattern of insights that are not packaged for the consumer palate. He expects the reader to make discovery after discovery that he himself has missed. His view of the departmentalized specialisms of our Universities as ignoble monopolies of knowledge is expressed on page 194: "Finally we must keep in mind the limited role of Universities and recall the comment that 'the whole external history of science is a history of the resistance of academies and Universities to the progress of knowledge.'"

One can say of Innis what Bertrand Russell said of Einstein on the first page of his *A B C of Relativity* (1925): "Many of the new ideas can be expressed in non-mathematical language, but they are none the less difficult on that account. What is demanded is a change in our imaginative picture of the world." The "later Innis" who dominates *The Bias of Communication* had set out on a quest for the causes of change. The "early Innis" of *The History of the Fur Trade* had conformed a good deal to the conventional patterns of merely reporting and narrating change. Only at the conclusion of *The Fur Trade* study did he venture to interlace or link complex events in a way that reveals the causal processes of change. His insight that the American Revolution was in large part due to a clash between the interests of the settlers on one hand, and the interests of the fur traders on the other, is the sort of vision that becomes typical of the later Innis. He changed his procedure from working with a "point of view" to that of the generating of insights by the method of "interface" as it is named in chemistry. "Interface" refers to the interaction of substances in a kind of mutual irritation. In art and poetry this is precisely the technique of "symbolism" (Greek, *symballein*—to throw together) with its paratactic procedure of juxtaposing without connectives. It is the natural form of conversation or dialogue rather than of written discourse. In writing, the tendency is to isolate an aspect of some matter and to direct steady attention upon that aspect. In dialogue there is an equally natural interplay of multiple aspects of any matter. This interplay of aspects can generate insights or discovery. By contrast, a point of view is merely a way of *looking at* something. But an insight is a sudden awareness of a complex process of interaction. An insight is a contact with the life of forms. Students of computer programming have had to learn how to approach all knowledge structurally. In order to transfer any kind of knowledge to tapes it is necessary to understand the form of that knowledge. This has led to the discovery of the basic difference between classified knowledge and pattern recognition. It is a helpful distinction to keep in mind when reading Innis since he is above all a recognizer of patterns. Dr. Kenneth Sayre explains the matter as follows in his *The Modelling of Mind* (University of Notre Dame Press, 1963, page 17): "Classification is a *process*, something which takes up one's time, which one might do reluctantly, unwillingly, or unenthusiastically, which can be done with more or less success, done very well or done very poorly. Recognition, in sharp contrast, is not time-consuming. A person may spend a long while looking before recognition occurs, but when it occurs it is 'instantaneous.' When recognition occurs, it is not an act which would be said to be performed either reluctantly or enthusiastically, compliantly or under protest. However, the notion of recognition being unsuccessful, or having been done very poorly, seems to make no sense at all."

In this book, Innis has much to say about the oral as opposed to the written methods of approaching the learning process. In the paper titled "A Critical Review," he explains: "My bias is with the oral tradition, particularly as reflected in Greek civilization, and with the necessity of recapturing something of its spirit." (p. 190) E. A. Havelock, a former colleague of Innis, has recently devoted an entire study to the clash of the old oral and the new written culture of Greece. His *Preface to Plato* (Harvard, 1963) would have delighted Innis, and there are very many sentences in Innis which should become the subject of full investigations.

I am pleased to think of my own book *The Gutenberg Galaxy* (University of Toronto Press, 1962) as a footnote to the observations of Innis on the subject of the psychic and social consequences, first of writing then of printing. Flattered by the attention that Innis had directed to some work of mine, I turned for the first time to his work. It was my good fortune to begin with the first essay in this book: "Minerva's Owl." How exciting it was to encounter a writer whose every phrase invited prolonged meditation and exploration: "Alexandria broke the link between science and philosophy. The library was an imperial instrument to offset the influence of Egyptian priesthood." (p. 10)

Innis takes much time to read if he is read on his own terms. That he deserves to be read on his own terms becomes obvious as soon as that experiment is tried even once. So read, he takes time but he also saves time. Each sentence is a compressed monograph. He includes a small library on each page, and often incorporates a small library of references on the same page in addition. If the business of the teacher is to save the student's time, Innis is one of the greatest teachers on record. The two sentences just quoted imply and invite an awareness of the specific structural forms of science and philosophy as well as the structural nature and functions of Empires, libraries and priesthoods. Most writers are occupied in providing accounts of the contents of philosophy, science, libraries, Empires and religions. Innis invites us instead to consider the formalities of power exerted by these structures in their mutual interaction. He approaches each of these forms of organized power as exercising a particular kind of force upon each of the other components in the complex. All of the components exist by virtue of processes going on within each and among them all. Just what "science" or "philosophy" was at this time will be manifested by what each does to the other in their encounter in the social and historic process. And so with the other components. They explain themselves by their behaviour in an historic action. Innis had hit upon the means of using history as the physicist uses the cloud chamber. By bouncing the unknown form against known forms, he discovered the nature of the new or little known form.

This use of history as a scientific laboratory, as a set of controlled conditions within which to study the life and nature of forms, is very far removed from the conventional narrative of a Toynbee. Toynbee is like the announcer of a sporting event. He tells a good deal about what is happening. His tone of earnest concern indicates to the reader or listener that the events have some significance. In the same situation Innis would have observed that the form of the sporting event was an interesting model of perception, giving us an immediate image of the motives and patterns of the society that had invented this corporate extension of itself. He would then explain that his role of announcer, like that of the audience at the sporting event, was part of the structure of the game, having a distorting bias of perception and amplification that gave the game in question a great deal of political and commercial force.

As soon as the reader grasps that Innis is concerned with the unique power of each form to alter the action of other forms it encounters, he will be able to proceed as Innis did. He can begin to observe and indicate the action and counteraction of forms past and present. He will discover that Innis never repeats himself, but that he never ceases to test the action of oral forms of knowledge and social organization in different social contexts. Innis tests the oral form as it reacts in many different written cultures, just as he tests the effects of time-structured institutions in their varieties of contact with space-oriented societies.

It would be a mistake to suppose that Innis had garnered most of the available insights from any given historical test that he happens to run. In the same way, he is quite capable of inaccurate observation during the running of his tests of the interactions of social forms, though this in no way impairs the validity of his way of testing the structural properties of social forms. For example, he notes that "The Greeks took over the alphabet and made it a flexible instrument suited to the demands of a flexible oral tradition by the creation of words." (p. 7) The alphabet is a technology of visual fragmentation and specialism, and it led the Greeks quickly to the discovery of classsifiable data. Havelock clarifies this at length in his *Preface to Plato*. As long as the oral culture was not overpowered by the technological extension of the visual power in the alphabet, there was a very rich cultural result from the interplay of the oral and written forms. The revival of oral culture in our own electric age now exists in a similar fecund relation with the still powerful written and visual culture. We are in our century "winding the tape backwards." The Greeks went from oral to written even as we are moving from written to oral. They "ended" in a desert of classified data even as we could "end" in a new tribal encyclopedia of auditory incantation.

Innis sometimes mistook the interplay of written and oral forms, ascribing to the written form itself what was a hybrid product of its interaction with oral culture: "The alphabet borrowed from the Phoenicians was given vowels and adapted to the demands of speech. The ear replaced the eye. With the spread of writing the oral tradition developed fresh powers of resistance evident in the flowering of Greek culture in the sixth and fifth centuries." (p. 136) Had Innis made a more intense analysis of the visual modalities inherent in the phonetic alphabet, or a more thorough study of the dynamics of oral forms, he would have avoided some of these slips. But the method he discovered remains. He had discovered a means of using historical situations as a lab in which to test the character of technology in the shaping of culture.

Innis taught us how to use the bias of culture and communication as an instrument of research. By directing attention to the bias or distorting power of the dominant imagery and technology of any culture, he showed us how to understand cultures. Many scholars have made us aware of the "difficulty of assessing the quality of a culture of which we are a part or of assessing the quality of a culture of which we are not a part." (p. 132) Innis was perhaps the first to make of this vulnerable fact of all scholarly outlook the prime opportunity for research and discovery. Peter F. Drucker in *Managing for Results* (Harper & Row, 1964) has shown how in any human organization or situation 90 per cent of the events are caused by 10 per cent. Most human attention is allocated to the 90 per cent area which is the area of problems. The 10 per cent area is the area of irritation and also of opportunity. It was the genius of Harold Innis that he refused to be distracted by the 90 per cent area of problems. He went straight to the 10 per cent core of opportunity and sought insight into the causes that underlay the whole situation. For example, he writes: "We are perhaps too much a part of the civilization which followed the spread of the printing industry to be able to detect its characteristics. Education in the words of Laski became the art of teaching men to be deceived by the printed word." (p. 139)

Once Innis had ascertained the dominant technology of a culture he could be sure that this was the cause and shaping force of the entire structure. He could also be sure that this dominant form and all its causal powers were necessarily masked from the attention of that culture by a psychic mechanism of "protective inhibition," as it were. At a stroke he had solved two major problems that are forever beyond the power of the "nose-counters" and of statistical researchers. First, he knew what the pattern of any culture had to be, both physically and socially, as soon as he had identified its major technological achievements. Second, he knew exactly what the members of that culture would be ignorant of in their daily lives. What has been called "the nemesis of creativity" is precisely a blindness to the effects of one's most significant form of invention. A good example of this technological blindness in Innis himself was his mistake in regarding radio and electric technology as a further extension of the patterns of mechanical technology: "The radio appealed to vast areas, overcame the division between classes in its escape from literacy, and favoured centralization and bureaucracy. (p. 82) Again: "Competition from the new medium, the radio, involved an appeal to the ear rather than to the eye and consequently an emphasis on centralization." (p. 188) This is an example of Innis failing to be true to his own method. After many historical demonstrations of the space-binding power of the eye and the time-binding power of the ear, Innis refrains from applying these structural principles to the action of radio. Suddenly, he shifts the ear world of radio into the visual orbit, attributing to radio all the centralizing powers of the eye and of visual culture. Here Innis was misled by the ordinary consensus of his time. Electric light and power, like all electric media, are profoundly decen-tralizing and separatist in their psychic and social consequences. Had he not been hypnotized by his respect for the pervasive conventional view on this question, Innis could have worked out the new electric pattern of culture quite easily.

What is rare in Innis occurs in his mention of the views of Wyndham Lewis: "Wyndham Lewis has argued that the fashionable mind is the time-denying mind." He is referring to *Time and Western Man*, which is devoted to a denunciation of the obsession with time as a religious mystique in the work of Bergson, Alexander, Whitehead and others. Because of his own deep concern with the values of tradi-tion and temporal continuity, Innis has managed to misread Wyndham Lewis rad-ically. Earlier in the same essay, "A Plea for Time," he raises an issue that may bear on the occasional miscarriage of his own structural method of analysis. Speaking of the unfortunate effects of the extreme development of print on our twentieth cen-tury culture, he observes: "Communication based on the eye in terms of printing and photography had developed a monopoly which threatened to destroy Western civilization first in war and then in peace." (p. 80) Innis did not like monopolies in any form. He saw that they bred violent reactions: "The disastrous effect of the monopoly of communication based on the eye hastened the development of a competitive type of communication based on the ear, in the radio and in the link-ing of sound to the cinema and to television. Printed material gave way in effective-ness to the broadcast and to the loud speaker." (p. 81) What Innis has failed to do in this part of his essay is to make a structural analysis of the modalities of the visu-al and the audible. He is merely assuming that an extension of information in space has a centralizing power regardless of the human faculty that is amplified and extended. But whereas the visual power extended by print does indeed extend the power to organize a spatial continuum the auditory power extended electrically does in effect abolish space and time alike. Visual technology creates a centre-margin pat-tern of organization whether by literacy or by industry and a price system. But elec-tric technology is instant and omnipresent and creates multiple centres-without-margins. Visual technology whether by literacy or by industry creates nations as spatially uniform and homogeneous and connected. But electric technology creates not the nation but the tribe—not the superficial association of equals but the cohesive depth pattern of the totally involved kinship groups. Visual technologies, whether based on papyrus or paper, foster fragmentation and special-ism, armies and empires. Electric technology favours not the fragmentary but the integral, not the mechanical but the organic. It had not occurred to Innis that elec-tricity is in effect an extension of the nervous system as a kind of global membrane. As an economic historian he had such a rich experience of the technological exten-sions of the bodily powers that it is not surprising that he failed to note the char-acter of this most recent and surprising of human extensions.

There is one department in which Innis never fails, and in which the flavour of Innisence is never lacking—his humour. Humour is of the essence of his aphoristic association of incongruities. His technique of discovery by the juxtaposition of forms lends itself everywhere to a series of dramatic surprises. On page 77 in the midst of considering the revolt of the American colonies and nineteenth-century wars he suddenly observes a parallel with the press wars of Hearst and Pulitzer as related to the emergence of the comic strip. He is unrivalled in his power to discover choice items in contemporary history to illuminate grave matters of archaeology. Referring to the neglect of the horse as a factor in military history, he recalls that "E. J. Dillon remarked concerning a mounted policeman that he was always surprised by the look of intelligence on the horse's face." (p. 95) The mosaic structure of insights employed in the work of the later Innis is never far removed from the comic irony of Abraham Lincoln. Innis found that his technique of insight engendered a perpetual entertainment of surprises and of intellectual comedy.

To record the intellectual influences that shaped the work of Innis would be a large, if rewarding, task. His studies at the University of Chicago after the First World War occurred at a most favorable time. The work of Emile Durkheim and Max Weber had fecundated a new group of economic and social studies that flowered in the writings of Thorstein Veblen, John Dewey, George Herbert Mead and Robert Ezra Park. These men created an atmosphere at Chicago in the 1920s that attracted and inspired many able students. Most of these men had, like Innis, spent their youth in small towns. The speedy growth of the metropolis after the first war presented an inexhaustible subject for these sociologists, and much of their work was directed to urban study and analysis, using the small town as a basis for comparison and contrast. Innis tended to follow another pattern, though, as we shall see, he was deeply in debt to Robert Ezra Park. Durkheim, the late-nineteenth-century founder of analytic sociology dealt with whole populations. The Chicago school dealt with local communities. Innis is European rather than American in his choice of the larger themes. From Park, however, he learned how to identify the control mechanisms by which a heterogeneous community yet manages to arrange its affairs with some degree of uniformity. Perhaps Innis was aided in this choice by his familiarity with the staple economy of Canada. A semi-industrialized country, rich in major resources like wheat, lumber, minerals, fur, fish, and wood pulp has a peculiar economic and social life compared to a more diversified and developed economy. Innis seized the opportunity to deal with this unique pattern of a staple economy and was not led to follow the popular pattern of urban studies that was being pursued by the exciting and productive Chicago group. I suggest that Innis made the further transition from the history of staples to the history of media of communication quite naturally. Media are major resources like economic staples. In fact, without railways, the staples of wheat and lumber can scarcely be said to exist. Without the press and the magazine, wood pulp could not exist as a staple either.

In May, 1940, the Canadian *Journal of Economics and Political Science* published an article by Robert Park entitled "Physics and Society" [reprinted in *Society* by Robert E. Park (Glencoe, Illinois: The Free Press, 1955), pp. 301–321.) Park began by citing Walter Bagehot to the effect that society is a social organism maintained by a social process. The theme of his essay is recapitulated this way: "I have gone into some detail in my description of the role and function of communication because it is so obviously fundamental to the social process, and because extensions and improvements which the physical sciences have made to the means of communication are so vital to the existence of society and particularly to that more rationally organized form of society we call civilization." (*Society*, p. 314)

The ideas of Park seem to have appealed more to the mind of Harold Innis than to that of any other student of Robert Park. Anybody can hear the Innis note in such observations by Park as the following: "Technological devices have naturally changed men's habits and in doing so, they have necessarily modified the structure and functions of society." (p. 308) Again: "From this point of view it seems that every technical device, from the wheelbarrow to the airplane, in so far as it provided a new and more effective means of locomotion, has, or should have, marked an epoch in society. This is so far true as most other important changes in the means of transportation and communication. It is said likewise that every civilization carries in itself the seeds of its own destruction. Such seeds are likely to be the technical devices that introduce a new social order and usher out the old." (*Society*, pp. 309–310) In the same year as his "Physics and Society" article, Park published "News as a Form of Knowledge": "I have indicated the role which news plays in the world of politics in so far as it provides the basis for the discussions in which public opinion is formed. The news plays quite as important a role in the world of economic relations, since the price of commodities, including money and securities, as registered in the world market and in every local market dependent upon it, is based on the news." (p. 80)

These ideas were not lost on Harold Innis. Indeed, Innis developed them much further than Park did, and needs to be considered as the most eminent of the Chicago group headed by Robert Park.

CHAPTER TWELVE

Media Ad-Vice
An Introduction

MARSHALL MCLUHAN

> All of my recommendations, therefore, can be reduced to this one: study the modes of the media, in order to hoick all assumptions out of the subliminal nonverbal realm for scrutiny and for prediction and control of human purposes.
>
> —Marshall McLuhan

Customer in an antique shop: "What's new?"

Professor Key has helped to show how the deceits of subliminal advertising can be a means of revealing unexpected truth: the childlike faith of the ad agencies in four-letter words points to our obsession with infantile bathroom images as the chemical bond between commercial society and the universal archetypes.

The old journalism had aimed at objectivity by giving "both sides at once," as it were, the pro and con, the light and shade in full perspective. The "new journalism," on the other hand, eagerly seeks subjectivity and involvement in a resonant environment of events: Norman Mailer at the Chicago convention, or Truman Capote writing *In Cold Blood.*

In the same way, the old history—as Michel Foucault explains in *The Archaeology of Knowledge* (Pantheon Books, New York, 1972)—sought to show "how a single pattern is formed and preserved. How for so many different successive minds there is a single horizon." But now the problem of the "new history" is "no longer one of tradition, of tracing a line, but one of division, of limits. It is no longer one of lasting foundations, but one of transformations that serve as new foundations. . . ."

The study of advertising as contemporary cultural history, or history on the hop and in the hopper, of history as process rather than as a product, such is the investigation of Professor Key. Advertising is an environmental striptease for a world of abundance. But environments as such have a way of being inaccessible to inspection. Environments by reason of their total character are mostly subliminal to ordinary experience. Indeed, the amount of any situation, private or social, verbal or geographic, that can be raised and held to the conscious level of attention is almost insignificant. Yet ads demand a lot of attention in our environmental lives. Ads are focal points for the entire range of twentieth-century knowledge, skills, and technologies. Psychologists and anthropologists toil for the agencies. So, Professor Key has drawn our attention to the use made in many ads of the highly developed arts of camouflage.

T. S. Eliot long ago pointed out that the camouflage function of "meaning" in a poem was like the juicy piece of meat carried by the burglar to distract the housedog of the mind so that the poem could do its work. Professor Key explains that the proclaimed purpose of the ad may, at one level, be just such a decoy so that the ad may do its work at another level of consciousness.

Secrets Within Banality

Today many people feel uneasy when serious attention is paid to objects and subjects that they are accustomed to classify as "trash." They feel that the base commercial operation of ads is beneath any claim to their awareness or analysis.

Such people, on the one hand, have little heeded the lessons of history and archaeology which reveal how the midden-heaps of the ages provide the wisdom and riches of the present. And yet, on the other hand, they know how their snobbish "freeze" (or surrender) in the presence of the horrid vulgarities of commerce is exactly what is needed to render them the cooperative puppets of ad manipulation. The ad as camouflage often uses the blatant appeal to hide more subtle and powerful motivations than appear on the surface.

Shakespeare's oft-misquoted remark about "one touch of nature" that "makes the whole world kin" really concerns the eagerness of men to swallow a flattering bait. He is not suggesting that natural beauty is a social bond!

One touch of nature makes the whole world kin:

That all with one consent praise new-born gawds

Though they are made and moulded of things past,

And give to dust that is a little gilt

More laud than gilt o'erdusted.

Men are united only in their eagerness to be deceived by appearances.

> The wise gods seal our eyes;
>
> In our own filth drop our clear judgments; make us
>
> Adore our errors; laugh at us while we strut
>
> To our confusion

Thus part of the business of the ad is to seem frank, open, hearty, and direct. The business establishment long ago founded itself on ebullient attitudes of trust and confidence which were part of the discovery that "Honesty is the best policy" and "Crime doesn't pay." "Policy," of course, is the Machiavellian term for "deceit," so immediate and overt honesty can be camouflage for ultimate exploitation, in ads as in politics. However, we live today in the first age of the electric information environment, and there is now a sense in which we are the first generation that can say, "There is nothing old under the sun."

Since Sputnik (October 17, 1957), the planet Earth went inside a man-made environment and Nature yielded its ancient reign to Art and Ecology. Ecology was born with Sputnik, for in an electric information environment all events become clamorous and simultaneous. An old adage at IBM is: "Information overload equals pattern recognition." At instant speed the hidden becomes plain to see.

Minds Are Quicker Than Eyes

Since the Mind is very much faster than light (it can go to Mars and back in an instant, whereas light takes minutes), the hidden structure of many old things can now become apparent. With the new information surround, not only specialisms and monopolies of knowledge become less useful, but the world of the subliminal is greatly reduced. Whatever the practical uses and expediency of the subliminal may have been in the past, they are not as they were. Even the future is not what it used to be. For at electric speeds, it is necessary to anticipate the future in order to live in the present, and vice versa.

Necessarily, the age of instant information prompts men to new kinds of research and development. It is, above all, an age of investigation and of espionage. For in the total information environment, man the hunter and scanner of environments returns to supervise the inner as well as the outer worlds, and nothing is now unrelated or irrelevant.

T. S. Eliot had two statements that directly concern our now simultaneous world of "auditory" or "acoustic" space in which electric man now dwells on the "wired planet." The first passage is from his discussion of "Tradition and the Individual Talent," explaining that "the whole of the literature of Europe from Homer and within it the whole of the literature of his own country has a simultaneous existence and composes a simultaneous order." It is the character of auditory space, which we make in the act of hearing, to be a sphere whose centre is everywhere and whose margin is nowhere, for we hear from all directions at once.

In the magnetic city of the new electric environment we receive data from all directions simultaneously, and thus we exist in a world sphere of resonant information that is structured and which acts upon us in the auditory pattern. Eliot had regard to the individual talent faced by this new kind of richness and experience. So it is not strange that our time should witness a revival of many forms of oral culture and group performance, any more than it is strange that we should see on all hands the awakening and cultivation of occult traditions, and new concern with inner life and visionary experience.

For these are resonant things hidden from the eye. The wide interest in every kind of structuralism in language and art and science is direct testimony to the new dominance of the nonvisual values of audile-tactile involvement and group participation. In fact, it could be said that there is there is very little in the new electric technology to sustain the visual values of civilized detachment and rational analysis.

Mr. Eliot's second statement on the world of the simultaneous concerns the "auditory imagination":

> What I call "auditory imagination" is the feeling for syllable and rhythm, penetrating far below the conscious levels of thought and feeling, invigorating every word: sinking to the most primitive and forgotten, returning to the origin and bringing something back, seeking the beginning and the end. It works through meanings, certainly, or not without meanings in the ordinary sense, and fuses the old and obliterated, and the trite, the current, and the new and the surprising, the most ancient and the most civilized mentality.

Eliot here speaks of the mind's ear, the subliminal depths and reach of the corporate tongue bridging countless generations and cultures in an eternal present. Eliot and Joyce accepted language as the great corporate medium that encodes and environs the countless dramas and transactions of man. Their raids on this vast inarticulate resource have made literary history on a massive scale.

Meantime the enormous new environment of advertising has sprung up as a service for the consumer who hardly knows what to think of his newly bought cars and swimming pools. It is well known to the frogmen of Madison Avenue that those who read or hear the ads are mostly those who have already bought one of the objects displayed. "Ask the man who owns one," or "You feel better satisfied when you use a well-known brand." The fact is that the ad world is a colossal *put-on* as much as the world of fashion or art or politics or entertainment. The stripper puts on her audience by taking off her clothes, and the poet puts on his public by stripping or dislocating the familiar rhythms and habits of expression.

How about the adman's rip-off? He must move on more than one level in order to obtain the interplay that involves the public. The poet lets us look at the world through the mask of his poem while wearing us as his mask: "hypocrite lecteur, mon semblable, mon frère," said Baudelaire to his reader. The adman shows us the world through the mesh or mask of his product while playfully putting on our cash and credit as his own motley. But that there may be another level of reinforcement, the ads sometimes provide a barrage of optimistic innocence along with an undercurrent of guilty joys and fears upon which the blatant, gesticulating commercial rides piggyback. It is the quest of Professor Key to unconceal this hidden ground of the ad as figure, and to reveal the conflict between them.

Scuba Diving into Hidden Backgrounds

It may be that the impulse of the admen to use the hidden ground of our lives in a furtive way in their ads is no mere surrender to base impulse and greed for power. By replaying the hot glamorous images in a cool scatological pattern, the subliminal message becomes a dramatic irony of the superficial and conscious one.

The subliminal replay of the open appeal thus offers an offbeat jazz quality of quarter notes sourly commenting on the full notes, by way of a wry twist. It is the role Freud himself played as diver into the dirty unhygienic depth beneath the dewy Romantic sentiment. At the extreme point, Freud the diver got a signal: "Surface at once. Ship is sinking." When he came up for air he wrote about "Civilization and Its Discontents." After a long session in the dark unconscious, Freud recognized the visual and literate world as the location of civilized values and awareness. The dark within is the world of tribal or acoustic man who resists civilization as do our dropouts. Professor Key brings out the struggle between these worlds as inherent in the very structure of the not-so-humble ads that provide the directives and the competitive taste patterns of our commerce and our entertainment.

Bugging and Sleuthing have become a universal Business, like education. The electric age is the age of the hunter. It is the age of simultaneous information. The simultaneous ends the subliminal by making it as much a structural part of consciousness as former specialism or monopoly or secrecy. The age just behind us was just the opposite of the electric age. The mechanical and industrial society was the age of steam and hardware and highway and monopoly and specialism. It was a visual world.

The age of the electrical and simultaneous is the age of environmental and ecological awareness. Structurally speaking, the simultaneous is acoustic rather than visual. We hear from all directions at once and that is why the reign of the subliminal is ending. The subliminal or the hidden can be present to the hearing when it is not accessible to the eye.

It makes much sense when N. F. Dixon writes *in Subliminal Perception* that experienced psychologists of our sense lives have bypassed the subliminal and the auditory in favor of visual investigation. For the psychological, as much as for any other establishment, the commitments are to the preceding age of the visual. However, the new age is also subliminal to its predecessor. It is, therefore, easy to know that the eye may be solicited by lines it cannot see, and our judgments warped by motives that are not in consciousness nor in the habitual patterns of our nervous systems, "for the whole environment is full of subliminal influences which experienced psychologists have systematically neglected."

It is only fair to add that the electric environment is man-made and new; and experienced psychologists, quite as much as the rest of the population, continue to adhere to the older and familiar and visually structured world of the hardware age in which they invested all they had. For the visual is the world of the continuous and the connected and the rational and the stable.

Since we have now put an electrical environment of resonant information around the old visual one, our daily adaptations and responses are made at least as much to the new acoustic environment as to the old visual world. If one were to ask, "Which is the better world?" it would be necessary to explain that the values of an acoustical and musically oriented society are not those of the classically visual and civilized society.

Predictions of the Past

For good or ill, we have phased ourselves out of the older visual society by our electric technology that is as instant as light. If we want to get back into a visually ordered world, we shall have to recreate the conditions of that world. Meantime we have a new environment of instant information that upsets and "pollutes" all the patterns of the old visual sequences. Nothing is "in concatenation accordingly" in the simultaneous world of sound. Effects now easily and naturally precede causes, and we can freely predict the past.

At the speed of light our space-time coexistence tends to give us the whimsical manners of the girl in Professor Butler's limerick:

There was a young lady named Bright

Who moved with the quickness of light;

She went out one day

In a relative way,

And returned the previous night.

At electric speed, the goals and objectives of the old sequential and visual world are irrelevant. Either they are attained before we start or we are out of date before we arrive. All forms of specialist training suffer especially. Engineers and doctors cannot graduate in time to be relevant to the innovations that occur during their training period.

Change itself becomes the only constant. We seem to live in a world of deceits and fake values where, for example, those engaged in news coverage are often more numerous than those making the news. But the creation of a total field of world information returns man to the state of the hunter, the hunter of data.

To the sleuth, to Sherlock Holmes, nothing is quite what it seems. He lives, like us, in two worlds at once, having small benefit of either. Caught between visual and acoustic worlds, physicist Werner Heisenberg enunciated the "Uncertainty Principle." You can never perform the same experiment twice. Heraclitus, living in the old acoustic world before Greek literacy, said, "You can't step in the same river twice." And today, in the electric world we say, "You can't step in the same river," period.

In the Renaissance, when the old acoustic world of medieval and feudal order was quickly being overlaid by the visual order of the printed word, there was an epidemic concern about deceit and imposture. Machiavelli invented a new art of lying by stressing an extrovert mask of bluff, hearty sincerity. Iago tells us that he will wear his heart on his sleeve for daws to peck at. Othello demands "ocular proof" of his wife's infidelity, and is deceived by the same "proof." Shakespeare's great plays are devoted to the theme of the deceits of power. Hamlet is caught out of role. He is a medieval prince adapted to the medieval world of acoustic involvement and personal loyalty. His world of ideal musical harmony collapses into one of visual distraction and mere appearance:

> Now see that noble and most sovereign reason
>
> Like sweet bells jangled out of tune and harsh

His dilemma is stated also by Ulysses in *Troilus and Cressida*:

> Take but degree away, untune that string
>
> And, hark! What discord follows; each thing meets
>
> In mere oppugnancy: the bounded waters
>
> Should lift their bosoms higher than the shores,
>
> And make a sop of all this solid globe.

Other Side of the Looking Glass

The auditory man is an ecologist because he imagines everything affecting everything, because all happens at once as in a resonating sphere. The clash between the medieval ecologist and the Renaissance man of private aims and goals is playing in reverse today. The new technology is acoustic and total. The old establishment is visual and fragmentary. All this concerns Professor Key's studies of the deceits of the admen.

These admen teams operate on the frontier between the worlds of eye and ear, of old and new. They are trying to have the best of both worlds by wearing both masks. Ben Jonson, Shakespeare's great contemporary, devoted much of his work to the presentation of the deceiver and the deceived, stressing the inherent appetite of most people to wallow in deceit as a delectable diet:

Still to be neat, still to be drest,

As you were going to a feast;

Still to be powdered, still perfumed

Lady, it is to be presumed,

Though art's hid causes are not found,

All is not sweet, all is not sound.

This could be an anti-advertisement today if equal time were allowed to query the counsel of each ad. Saving the appearances mattered more and more during the Renaissance and after. Molière's *Misanthrope* and *Tartuffe* are built on the assumption that truth is a matching of inner state and outer behaviour. The fact that truth is making not matching, process not product, can never satisfy the visual man with his mirror held up to nature.

By contrast, Walter Pater plunged his readers into the forbidden world of the unconscious when he presented them with the image of Da Vinci's "Mona Lisa." He sought the truth on the other side of the looking-glass:

The presence that thus rose so strangely beside the waters, is expressive of what in the ways of a thousand years men had come to desire. Hers is the head upon which all "the ends of the world are come," and the eyelids are a little weary. . . . Set it for a moment beside one of those white Greek goddesses or beautiful women of antiquity, and how would they be troubled by this beauty, into which the soul with all its maladies has passed?
(*The Renaissance*)

Pater is fascinated by his image of a sick "soul with all its maladies" spurning the slick white Greek goddesses of rationality. Pater has flipped, fashionably, out of the visual and back into the medieval acoustic world. "All art," he said, "constantly aspires toward the condition of music."

It is this music that began to be heard in the Romantic depths of the starved and rationalistic psyche of the visual cultures that reached from the Renaissance to the Victorian age. Pater's pen portrait of "Mona Lisa" continues in a plangent tone that might win the applause of any ad copy-writer:

She is older than the rocks among which she sits; like the vampire, she has been dead many times, and learned the secrets of the grave; and has been a diver in deep seas, and keeps their fallen day about her; and trafficked for strange webs with Eastern merchants: and, as Leda, was the mother of Helen of Troy, and, as Saint Anne, the mother of Mary; and all this has been to her but as the sound of lyres and flutes, and lives only in the delicacy with which it has moulded the changing lineaments, and tinged the eyelids and the hands.

This passage is a striking description of the Western subconscious with all its evocations of the occult and of delirious vices.

Subliminal Graffiti

It is plain that the subconscious is a wicked witch's brew of superhuman interest for all boys and girls. This *Mona Lisa* affair raises a major aspect of Professor Key's study. *Does the discovery of graffiti in the deodorants and aids to glamor threaten the public of consumers, or does it merely reveal the childish itch of the admen themselves?* For example, the title *Gentlemen Prefer Blondes* may be both immoral and immortal because it links hair and gold, faces and feces. For gold and dung have always had affinities, even as the greatest perfumes include a subtle ingredient of excrement.

There is the further fetching factor of the author's name, Anita Loos. It doesn't suggest the prim Puritan altogether. Since the world of dung and excrement is quite near to the daily conscious level, are we to panic when the admen put these at the bottom of the big hamper of goodies that they proffer the affluent?

Will the graffiti hidden under the lush appeal expedite sales or merely impede the maturity quotient of the buyers? Will the graffiti lurking in the glamor crevices set up a resonant interval of revulsion against the consumer appeals, or will the confrontation of fur and feces in the ads merely sadden and deepen and mature the childish consumer world? It is a strange and tricky game to mount the sweet enticing figure on a rotten ground.

To use, on the other hand, four-letter words in the libretto of the siren's song may prove to be a metaphysical discovery. The poet W. B. Yeats meditated in anguish over the light of man:

Love has pitched his mansion in

The place of excrement;

For nothing can be sole or whole

That has not been rent.

He, too, is desperate over the appearances.

Just how precarious a boundary Yeats provides can be noted in his nervous betrayal in the ambiguous words "pitch" and "rent." "Pitch" is filth and "rent" is venal.

In a word, the "Love" of Yeats can no more be trusted to present a clean slate than the overeager admen with their subliminal reinforcement of glamor by graffiti. The passionately embracing young man asks his partner, "Why speak of love at a time like this?" The remark serves as a corollary to the moan of Yeats. But it also opens up the *Playboy* world where girls are playmates.

The Playboy's Plaything

Things have changed electrically since I published *The Mechanical Bride* in 1951. The assembly-line love goddess, abstract and austere and inhuman, has been succeeded by hula-hooping, mini-skirted, tribally anonymous jujubes. Utterly embracable, consumable, and expendable, they expect little, for they know that the fragile ego of the playboy cannot endure the threat of any strain or commitment.

Thanks to color photography, and then to color TV, the magnetic city has become a single erogenous zone. At every turn there is an immediate encounter with extremely erotic situations which exactly correspond to the media "coverage" of violence. "Bad news" has long been the hard core of the press, indispensable for the moving of the mass of "good news" which is advertising. These forms of sex and violence are complementary and inseparable. Just what would be the fate of wars and disasters without "coverage" could be considered a meaningless question, since the coverage itself is not only an increase of the violence but an incentive to the same.

The power-starved person can easily see himself getting top coverage if he is involved in a sufficiently outrageous act of hijacking or mayhem. The older pattern of success story by achievement simply takes too long to be practical at electric speeds. Why not make the news instead of a life?

The close relation between sex and violence, between good news and bad news, helps to explain the compulsion of the admen to dunk all their products in sex by erogenizing every contour of every bottle or cigarette. Having reached this happy state where the good news is fairly popping, the admen say, as it were: "Better add a bit of the bad news now to take the hex off all that bonanza stuff." Let's remind them that LOVE, replayed in reverse, is EVOL—transposing into EVIL and VILE. LIVE spells backward into EVIL, while EROS reverses into SORE. And we should never forget the SIN in SINCERE or the CON in CONFIDENCE.

Let's tighten up the slack sentimentality of this goo with something gutsy and grim.

As Zeus said to Narcissus:

"Watch yourself."

CHAPTER THIRTEEN

The Emperor's Old Clothes

MARSHALL MCLUHAN

The natural effect of any new technology is to create a new environment for itself. In effect, an environment is a special organization of available energies. As an energy system, an environment is a process. It reprocesses the earlier environments. Old environments are the nutriment of new ones. As they are assimilated by the new energy system, the older systems are transformed into art forms. From the cliché environment to the archetypal content, the new environmental system turns the old environments into anti-environments. That is one way of perceiving what a work of art is. Art as an anti-environment is an indispensable means of perception. For environments, as such, are imperceptible. Their power to impose their ground rules on our perceptual life is so complete that there is no scope for dialogue or interface. Hence the need for art or anti-environments.

Indeed, the power of the environment to be invisible and to condition, or to brainwash subjects, was what Pavlov stressed in his work, according to the recent investigations of Erwin Straus.[1] The message of Pavlov was that the stimulus cannot be a conditioner. Only a totally controlled environment affects conditioning. Such is also the message of Jacques Ellul in his book, *Propaganda*.[2] Ideology, he says, is not propaganda. Only the simultaneous use of all the available environmental technologies is propaganda. The Western world, locked in habits of fragmented and specialized perception, ignores both the meaning of Pavlov and of Ellul by insisting on translating their vision into the terms of the old technologies. From the time that Neolithic man-the-planter began to create environments one at a time by specialist extensions of his hands and arms and feet, men have always looked at a new environment as if it were the old one. We can never see the Emperor's new clothes. But we are staunch admirers of his old garb. Only small children and artists are sensuously apt to perceive the new environment. Small children and artists are antisocial beings who are as little impressed by the established mores as they are conditioned by the new.

In his *Uncommon Law*, Alan P. Herbert records a British legal case that concerned the publication of Sunday newspapers. Evidence was brought that "what is called 'news' is always an anti-social and disturbing act; that 'news' consists, as to ninety percent, of the records of human misfortunes, unhappiness and wrongdoing, as to nine per cent of personal advertisement. . . ."[3]

It has often mystified readers of the press that real news is bad news. Good news is simply not news. The ads are full of good news. Good news is a repeat of the old environment, while bad news is a probe into the new environment. Bad news reveals the lines of force in an environment, while good news tends merely to picture the situation passively. Thus the Nielsen ratings in press stories are even more whimsically destructive and sudden than those in entertainment.

It does help to look at the newspaper as a direct, exploratory probe into the environment. Seen in this light, there is more meaning in the aesthetic bonds between the poet, the sleuth, and even the criminal. For James Bond, Humphrey Bogart, Rimbaud, and Hemingway are all figures who explore the shifting frontiers of morals and society. They are engaged in detecting the social environment by probing and transgression. For to probe is to cross boundaries of many kinds; to discover the patterns of new environments requires a rigorous study and inventory of sensuous effects. The components of new environments cannot be discovered directly. Edgar Allan Poe's detective, Dupin, is an aesthete. The aesthetes were the first to use the senses consciously and systematically as probes into the environment. Walter Pater's injunction, "To burn always with a hard gemlike flame," referred to the action of the plumber's blowtorch, a technical invention of his day.

As the visual gradient built up in the culture and technology of the seventeenth and eighteenth centuries, much accelerated by the printing press, man lost much of the power to deal with the non-visual factors in experience.[4] The visual bias of our culture even today is such as to create a great gap between literary and scientific sectors. For the world of electric circuitry is only incidentally related to visual factors. And *The Philosophical Impact of Contemporary Physics* by Mili_ _apek[5] reveals the handicaps confronting even the Einsteins in their unconscious commitments to visual culture.

The eighteenth century went so far in developing the visual gradient of its culture that realism became acceptable. The putting of the ordinary outer environment inside books and theatres for inspection and enjoyment was to go even further in the nineteenth century. But in the middle of the nineteenth century the birth of modern art occurred in several arts at once. Whereas the Romantics had developed outer landscape in poetry and painting as a means of defining and controlling inner mental states, the symbolists, by fragmenting the realistic Romantic landscapes, were able to use the pieces as heuristic probes. The probes were used to explore and define the inner landscapes that had eluded merely visual organization and detection. A similar reversal from outer to inner modalities occurred in the rise of the stream-of-consciousness technique in poetry and fiction alike. Paradoxically, stream of consciousness offered the reader a means of making rather than of matching. By pushing cinematic and photographic imagery flow to an extreme, the poets discovered a means of making a world in which all the senses participated at once. Such had been the earlier vision of the "Romantic Image," as Frank Kermode has shown in his book of that title.[6] It is a vision that is fully realized in "Among School Children" by W. B. Yeats. As the visual gradient of the Renaissance reached its ultimate development, the poets, from Blake and Coleridge to Hopkins and Yeats, strove to restore the unity of the imaginative life by creating a multisensuous interplay. Yeats wrote:

> I have spent my life in clearing out of poetry every phrase written for the eye, and bringing all back to syntax that is for the ear alone. . . ."Write for the ear," I thought, so that you may be instantly understood as when actor or folk singer stands before an audience.[7]

If poets and artists began to revolt a century ago against the merely visual and pictorial organization of space and experience, it is notable that the camera has revolted likewise. Cinema is not merely visual, being the joining of eye and foot. In *Our World from the Air*, E. A. Gutkind[8] has revealed the entirely structural and nonobjective qualities that are released from the terrestrial surface when camera joins the airplane. At 35,000 feet the earth belongs to Picasso, and abstract *making*. At 12,000 feet, it is still in the hands of representational art, or the modes of matching. At night the urban landscape belongs to Seurat and Rouault. It is a world of light *through* rather than of light *on*. It is the world of TV and reverse perspective in which the viewer is the vanishing point.

Such extensions of our faculties have immediate effects on our habits of perception. This is called "negative feedback," or learned responses to new situations. The photograph revolutionized the human image as much as it changed the patterns and spaces of our cities. Indeed, the photograph gave us a push in the direction of the programmed environment. As our data become more inclusive and ecological, we naturally begin to look at the environment as a huge teaching machine that can translate us out of the human dimension altogether. It then occurs to us that we might be able to translate, or program, the environment before it translates us. Oceanographers, confronting the extravagant life of the sea, are yet mindful of the equilibrium among its creatures and components. It is the maintenance of this equilibrium that initiates trains of actions and effects of "mindless ferocity." Such had been the first theories of political economy when human factors were subordinated to the Newtonian image of Nature. As we approach the stage of programming the environment itself, it becomes natural to interrupt and suspend the "mindless ferocity" of Nature by anticipating causes with consequences. It is a revolution well under way, and it is parallel to a similar revolution in education. A great shift from instruction to discovery is beginning in education. It is the shift from matching to making, from blueprint to heuristic probe. It is based on the same kind of knowledge that earlier had enabled the engineer to predict the behaviour of skyscrapers, bombs, and rockets. We can begin to program the planet itself by understanding the actions under and above its mantle.

So little did the ancients know of the make-up of their terrestrial environment that they misnamed the planet. Had they been able to perceive the extent of the waters on the earth (70.8 per cent of its surface) they might well have called it Oceanus. But their perceptions of their earthly environment were no more inadequate or deluded than the perceptions of men in other ages and cultures. It might be well to consider briefly the role of the artist in correcting the bias of environmental perception.

If we note the artistic response of the Romantics to the first mechanical and industrial age, it will help to explain the artistic response to the first electric age. For with electric circuitry we may have come to the end of the Neolithic time of the Planter and the Wheel. The electronic age is again the age of the hunter, the non-specialist, who can probe the entire environment. New data-retrieval systems make this total probing more and more natural.

James Joyce published *Finnegans Wake* in 1939, revealing the return of the tribal cycle for electronic man and opening the entire world of language as a Phoenix Playhouse of dramatic metamorphoses. The artistic response to the age of circuitry has been to portray new dimensions of human interdependence and new patterns of human identity. The unconscious that had long been the environment of consciousness has become the content of modern artistic awareness. The Romantics, on the other hand, had responded to the first mechanical environment of railways and factories by a nostalgic dream of the preceding agrarian technology. Has it always occurred this way? Does the content of each new environment have to be the old environment? Does the new organization of energy that is a new environment automatically process the old environment into an archetypal ideal of art? The television environment has steadily upgraded the old movie forms into sentimentally valued art forms. The medieval world got the same treatment from the

Gutenberg technology. If technological changes create new environments, or new processes of energy organization, what is to be the process of the new satellite environments on our perception and experience?

It is a common observation that in the space age we do much of our lab work outside the planet. That is just a way of looking at the new environment in terms of the old one. For radio, telescopes, and space capsules are not new content for the old situation. In the same way, the computer is not a new mechanical gadget for pepping up the old mechanical environment. The computer is not mechanical at all. Electric circuitry is an organic thing, an extension of our nervous system. Our natural impulse is to ignore the environmental aspects and to try to fit it into the old situation in the style of "horseless carriage" and "wireless." But our natural response is quite helpless and irrelevant, as the history of technology testifies.

The capsule and the satellite have created a new environment for our planet. The planet is now the content of the new spaces created by the new technology. Instead of being an environment in time, the earth itself has become a probe in space. That is, the planet has become an anti-environment, an art form, an extension of consciousness, yielding new perception of the new man-made environment. Whereas the mechanical environment turned the old agrarian world into an art form, the electric technology enables us to mime or simulate the old planetary environment in our capsules. As Buckminster Fuller has pointed out, "the rocket capsule that will keep man living successfully in space for protracted periods . . . will be the first 'scientific dwelling' in history."[9] Science, quite as much as art, is concerned with the construction of anti-environments. In the electric age the anti-environments of science incorporate the nervous system. They become "responsive environments," or probes. With electric circuitry we can not only program the entire environment responsively as a work of art, we can include the learning process in the environment itself.

In his *Poetics* (Chapter IV, 1448b), Aristotle reminded us that mimesis is the process by which all men learn. He alluded to the process of making by which our perceptions simulate within us the environment that we encounter outside ourselves. It is this learning and making process that, by electric circuitry, is being extended beyond our central nervous system. The next phase of this extension will naturally concern the action of making consciousness technologically. What we have called education in recent centuries has consisted in visiting or in simulating as many earlier environments and cultures as possible. Language is unrivalled in providing the actual sensuous modalities of other environments, with their unique ground rules. Electric circuitry can become a means to bypass language and plug directly into other modes of consciousness. Already the artists have shown us the means to this end with their strategy of the "objective correlative," or an inclusive experiential control. It is a method for anticipating the effects of a contrived situation that

Edgar Allan Poe previewed in his essay, "The Philosophy of Composition." Instead of being concerned with the content of the work, Poe's method points to our own time when it is possible to include the environment in the content.

With electric circuitry, all of the mechanical enterprises of mankind tend to acquire reverse characteristics. Just as the educational establishment tends to shift its stress from instruction to discovery with the audience directly involved in the learning process, so all mechanical industry tends to abandon packaging in favor of the tailor-made or custom-built service for the individual. This pattern begins to emerge in computer design procedures in architecture. It appears quite spectacularly in the world of the book and of publishing with the advent of xerography. The book was the first mass-produced object. It was the first repeatable and uniform product. The process by which this kind of product was achieved was a process soon extended to many other forms of making. The process consists in the extreme fragmentation of the ancient craft of the scribe. Printing from moveable type is not only an analytic procedure of fragmentation, but it fathered similar fragmentation in many areas of human perception and human action.

It is precisely on this process of analytic fragmentation that all the fabrics of modern production, marketing, and pricing were built. It is a process that dissolves with the advent of electric circuitry. The dissolution of this process can be illustrated from the effects of xerography on book publication. Xerography makes the reader both author and publisher in tendency. The highly centralized activity of publishing naturally breaks down into extreme decentralism when anybody can, by means of xerography, assemble printed, or written, or photographic materials which can be supplied with sound tracks.

There are many electric information services at present that permit individuals to phone for printed data on any subject whatever. Computers are ready to go to work on their specific problem, or interest. Bibliographies and printed materials from many parts of the world can be made available to the individual in a few hours. The whole tendency of xerography is to transform the book into a tailor-made, custom-built service. The way in which the book is ceasing to be a mass-produced object or commodity provides a very good index to the changing aspect of the world itself as it becomes a responsive information environment. As the specific individual needs to become paramount in the new book-making, the public is drawn into the book-making process. Artists have, during the past century, been vividly aware of the ever increasing measure in which the audience shares in the creative process. This is an aspect of the "mass audience" that is frequently deplored and misunderstood by the representatives of the old mechanical culture and environment. Such people tend to see the mass audience as the mere obliteration of old landmarks, and of individual differences. They pay no attention to the increasingly creative awareness of people who are deeply involved in one another by means of electric circuitry. They are engaged in the ancient routine of regarding the patterns of the previous environment with nostalgic reverence.

The individualism of the mechanical culture and environment was paid for at the cost of much alienation from man, and work, and society. It was also accompanied by an almost total denial of participation in the creative process on the part of the public. The mechanical culture and environment produced the spectator and the consumer instead of the participant and the co-creator. Mechanized specialism permitted high virtuosity in the shaping of the art object, but such objects were denied any real role in the social life. They were classified as "art" and made peripheral to society and to individual consciousness alike. "We have no art," say the Balinese; "We do everything as well as possible." In the same way, art as a classified activity dissolves with the advent of electric circuitry. The art object is replaced by participation in the art process. This is the essential meaning of electric circuitry and responsive environments. The artist leaves the Ivory Tower for the Control Tower, and abandons the shaping of art objects in order to program the environment itself as a work of art.

It is human consciousness itself that is the great artifact of man. The making and shaping of consciousness from moment to moment is the supreme artistic task of all individuals. To qualify and to perfect this process on a world environmental scale is the inherent potential of each new technology.

CHAPTER FOURTEEN

The Emperor's New Clothes

MARSHALL MCLUHAN AND HARLEY PARK

In his poem "Esthétique du Mal" Wallace Stevens writes:

> This is the thesis scrivened in delight,
>
> The reverberating psalm, the right chorale.
>
> One might have thought of sight, but who could think
>
> Of what it sees, for all the ill it sees?
>
> Speech found the ear, for all the evil sound,
>
> But the dark italics it could not propound.
>
> And out of what one sees and hears and out
>
> Of what one feels, who could have thought to make
>
> So many selves, so many sensuous worlds,
>
> As if the air, the mid-day air, was swarming
>
> With the metaphysical changes that occur,
>
> Merely in living as and where we live.

He indicates that the slightest shift in the level of visual intensity produces a subtle modulation in our sense of ourselves, both private and corporate. Since technologies are extensions of our own physiology, they result in new programs of an environmental kind. Such pervasive experiences as those deriving from the encounter with environments almost inevitably escape perception. When two or more environments encounter one another by direct interface, they tend to manifest their distinctive qualities. Comparison and contrast have always been a means of sharpening perception in the arts as well as in general experience. Indeed, it is upon this pattern that all the structures of art have been reared. Any artistic endeavor includes the preparing of an environment for human attention. A poem or a painting is in every sense a teaching machine for the training of perception and judgment. The artist is a person who is especially aware of the challenge and dangers of new environments presented to human sensibility. Whereas the ordinary person seeks security by numbing his perception against the impact of new experience, the artist delights in this novelty and instinctively creates situations that both reveal it and compensate for it. The artist studies the distortion of sensory life produced by new environmental programming and tends to create artistic situations that correct the sensory bias and derangement brought about by the new form. In social terms the artist can be regarded as a navigator who gives adequate compass bearings in spite of magnetic deflection of the needle by the changing play of forces. So understood, the artist is not a peddler of new ideals or lofty experiences. He is rather the indispensable aid to action and reflection alike.

Therefore the question of whether art should be taught in our schools can easily be answered: of course it should be taught, but not as a subject. To teach art as a subject is to ensure that it will exist in a state of classification serving only to separate art off from the other activities of man. As Adolf Hildebrand points out in *The Problem of Form*, "Deflected thus from his natural course, the child develops his artificial rather than his natural resources and it is only when he reaches full maturity that the artist learns to think again in terms of the natural forces and ideas which in his childhood were his happiest possession." In the space age of information environments, art necessarily takes on new meaning and new functions. All previous classifications of these matters lose their interest and relevance.

In his *Approach to Art* E. H. Gombrich notes the extraordinary shift from making to matching that began for Western art in fifth-century Athens. In discovering the joys of matching or of realistic representation, the Greeks were not behaving like free men, but like robots. In the representation of reality stress is laid upon the visual sense usually at the expense of all the other senses. Such representation began with the rise of literacy and cannot occur at any time or at any place without the presence of a technology that favors the visual sense at the expense of all the other senses. For many people it is one of the horrors of our present age that we must live amidst the effects of technologies that do not favor the visual sense in anything like the degree that phonetic literacy does. The phonetic alphabet, as explained *in The Gutenberg Galaxy*, is the only form of writing that abstracts sight and sound from meaning. This fact is stressed by David Diringer in *The Alphabet*. By contrast, pictographic writing tends to unite the senses and semantics in a kind of gestalt. When the visual sense is played up above the other senses, it creates a new kind of space and order that we often call "rational" or pictorial space and form. Only the visual sense has the properties of continuity, uniformity and connectedness that are assumed in Euclidean space. Only the visual sense can create the impression of a continuum. Alex Leighton has said, "To the blind all things are sudden." To touch and hearing each moment is unique, but to the sense of sight the world is uniform and continuous and connected. These are the properties of pictorial space which we often confuse with rationality itself.

Perhaps the most precious possession of man is his abiding awareness of the analogy of proper proportionality, the key to all metaphysical insight and perhaps the very condition of consciousness itself. This analogical awareness is constituted of a perpetual play of ratios among ratios: A is to B what C is to D, which is to say that the ratio between A and B is proportioned to the ratio between C and D, there being a ratio between these ratios as well. This lively awareness of the most exquisite delicacy depends upon there being no connection whatever between the components. If A were linked to B, or C to D, mere logic would take the place of analogical perception. Thus one of the penalties paid for literacy and a high visual culture is a strong tendency to encounter all things through a rigorous story line, as it were. Paradoxically, connected spaces and situations exclude participation whereas discontinuity affords room for involvement. Visual space is connected and creates detachment or noninvolvement. It also tends to exclude the participation of the other senses. Thus the New York World's Fair defeated itself by imposing a visual order and story line that offered little opportunity for participation by the viewer. In contrast, Expo Canada presented not a story line but a mosaic of many cultures and environments. Mosaic form is almost like an X-ray compared to pictorial form with its connections. The Canadian mosaic aroused extraordinary enthusiasm and participation, mystifying many people.

The same difference exists between movie and TV. The movie is highly pictorial, but kinematically it is discontinuous and nonvisual, and thus demands participation. This discontinuous quality has been very much played up in such movies as *The Seventh Seal* and *Blow-Up*, to name only two in a rapidly developing métier. A movie is a succession of discrete images which are separated by extremely small spans of time. Because of their rapid succession, the images are fused in the conscious mind and appear connected. Our relatively recent insights into the power of the preconscious in both the creation and the apprehension of works of art indicate that the subliminal is in fact a strong force in psychic reorganization. It is in this sense that the movie form can be described as a medium which deals in disconnected spaces.

TV, on the other hand, is a kind of X-ray. Any new technology, any extension or amplification of human faculties, when given material embodiment, tends to create a new environment. This is as true of clothing as of speech, or script, or wheel. This process is more easily observed in our own time when several new environments have been created. In the latest one, TV, we find a handful of engineers and technicians in the 10 percent area, as it were, creating a set of radical changes in the 90 percent area of daily life. The new TV environment is an electric circuit that takes as its content the earlier environment, the photograph and the movie in particular. The interplay between the old and the new environments generates an innumerable series of problems and confusions which extend all the way from how to allocate the viewing time of children and adults to pay-TV and TV in the classroom. The new medium of TV as an environment creates new occupations. As an environment, it is imperceptible except in terms of its content. That is, all that is seen or noticed is the old environment, the movie. But even the effects of TV on the movie go unnoticed, and the effects of the TV environment in altering the entire character of human sensibility and sensory ratio are completely ignored. The viewer is in the situation of being X-rayed by the image. Typically, therefore, the young viewer acquires a habit of depth involvement which alienates him from the existing arrangements of space and organized knowledge, whether at home or in the classroom. However, this condition of alienation extends to the entire situation of Western man today.

The function of the artist in correcting the unconscious bias of perception in any given culture can be betrayed if he merely repeats the bias of the culture instead of readjusting it. In fact, it can be said that any culture which feeds merely on its direct antecedents is dying. In this sense the role of art is to create the means of perception by creating counterenvironments that open the door of perception to people otherwise numbed in a nonperceivable situation. In Françoise Gilot's book *Life with Picasso* the painter notes that: "When I paint, I always try to give an image people are not expecting and, beyond that, one they reject. That's what interests me. It's in this sense that I mean I always try to be subversive. That is, I give a man an image of himself whose elements are collected from among the usual way of seeing things in traditional painting and then reassembled in a fashion that is unexpected and disturbing enough to make it impossible for him to escape the questions it raises."

Under the heading "What exists is likely to be misallocated" Peter Drucker in *Managing for Results* discusses the structure of social situations: "Business enterprise is not a phenomenon of nature but one of society. In a social situation, however, events are not distributed according to the 'normal distribution' of a natural universe (that is they are not distributed according to the bell-shaped Gaussian curve). In a social situation a very small number of events at one extreme—the first 10 per cent to 20 per cent at most—account for 90 per cent of all results." What Drucker is presenting here is the environment as it presents itself for human attention and action. He is confronting the phenomenon of the imperceptibility of the environment as such. Edward T. Hall tackles this same factor in *The Silent Language*. The ground rules, the pervasive structure, the over-all pattern elude perception except insofar as an antienvironment or a countersituation is constructed to provide a means of direct attention. Paradoxically, the 10 percent of the typical situation that Drucker designates as the area of effective cause and the area of opportunity, this small factor, is the environment. The other 90 percent is the area of problems generated by the active power of the 10 percent environment. For the environment is an active process pervading and impinging upon all the components of the situation. It is easy to illustrate this.

The content of any system or organization naturally consists of the preceding system or organization, and in that degree the old environment acts as a control on the new. It is useful to notice that the arts and sciences serve as antienvironments that enable us to perceive the environment. In a business civilization we have long considered liberal study as providing necessary means of orientation and perception. When the arts and sciences themselves become environments under conditions of electric circuitry, conventional liberal studies, whether in the arts or sciences, will no longer serve as an antienvironment. When we live in a museum without walls, or have music as a structural part of our sensory environment, new strategies of attention and perception have to be created. When the highest scientific knowledge creates the environment of the atom bomb, new controls for the scientific environment have to be discovered, if only in the interest of survival.

The structural examples of the relation of environment to antienvironment need to be multiplied in order to understand the principles of perception and activity involved. The Balinese, who have no word for art, say, "We do everything as well as possible." This is not an ironic but a factual remark. In a preliterate society art serves as a means of merging the individual and the environment, not as a means of training perception of the environment. Archaic or primitive art looks to us like a magical control built into the environment. Thus to put the artifacts from such a culture into a museum or antienvironment is an act of nullification rather than of revelation. Today what is called "Pop Art" is the use of some object from our own daily environment as if it were antienvironmental. Pop Art serves to remind us, however, that we have fashioned for ourselves a world of artifacts and images that are intended not to train perception or awareness but to insist that we merge with them as the primitive man merges with his environment. Therefore, under the terms of our definition of art as antienvironmental, this is nonart except insofar as the illumination of the interior environment of the human mind can be regarded as an artistic stance.

The world of modern advertising is a magical environment constructed to maintain the economy, not to increase human awareness. We have designed schools as antienvironments to develop the perception and judgment of the printed word, but we have provided no training to develop similar perception and judgment of any of the new environments created by electric circuitry. This is not accidental. From the development of phonetic script until the invention of the electric telegraph, human technology has tended strongly toward the furtherance of detachment and objectivity, detribalization and individuality. Electric circuitry has quite the contrary effect. It involves in depth. It merges the individual and the mass environment. To create an antienvironment for such electric technology would seem to require a technological extension of both private and corporate consciousness. The awareness and opposition of the individual are in these circumstances as irrelevant as they are futile.

The structural features of environment and antienvironment appear in the age-old clash between professionalism and amateurism, whether in sport or in studies. Professional sport fosters the merging of the individual in the mass and in the patterns of the total environment. Amateur sport seeks rather the development of critical awareness of the individual and, most of all, critical awareness of the ground rules of the society as such. The same contrast exists for studies. The professional tends to specialize and to merge his being uncritically in the mass. The ground rules provided by the mass response of his colleagues serve as a pervasive environment of which he is uncritical and unaware,

The party system of government affords a familiar image of the relations of environment and antienvironment. The government as environment needs the opposition as antienvironment in order to be aware of itself. The role of the opposition seems to be, as in the arts and sciences, that of creating perception. As the government environment becomes more cohesively involved in a world of instant information, opposition would seem to become increasingly necessary but also intolerable. It begins to assume the rancorous and hostile character of a DEW Line, or a Distant Early Warning System. It is important, however, to consider the role of the arts and sciences as Early Warning Systems in the social environment. The models of perception they provide can give indispensable orientation to future problems well before they become troublesome.

The legend of Humpty Dumpty suggests a parallel to the 10–90 percent distribution of causes and effects. His fall brought into play a massive response from the social bureaucracy. But all the King's horses and all the King's men could not put Humpty-Dumpty back together again. They could not re-create the old environment; they could only create a new one. Our typical response to a disrupting new technology is to re-create the old environment instead of heeding the new opportunities of the new environment. Failure to notice the new opportunities is also failure to understand the new powers. This means that we fail to develop the necessary controls or antienvironments for the new environment. This failure leaves us in the role of mere automata.

W. T. Easterbrook has done extensive exploration of the relations of bureaucracy and enterprise, discovering that as soon as one becomes the environment, the other becomes an antienvironment. They seem to bicycle along through history alternating their roles with all the dash and vigor of Tweedledum and Tweedledee. In the eighteenth century when *realism* became a new method in literature, what happened was that the external environment was put in the place of antienvironment. The ordinary world was given the role of art object by Daniel Defoe and others. The environment began to be used as a perceptual probe. It became self-conscious. It became an "anxious object" instead of being an unperceived and pervasive pattern. Environment used as probe or art object is satirical because it draws attention to itself. The Romantic poets extended this technique to external nature, transforming nature into an art object. Beginning with Baudelaire and Rimbaud and continuing in Hopkins and Eliot and James Joyce, the poets turned their attention to language as a probe. Long used as an experiment, language became an instrument of exploration and research. It became an antienvironment. It became Pop Art along with the graphic probes of Larry Rivers, Rauschenberg and many others.

The artist as a maker of antienvironments permits us to perceive that much is newly environmental and therefore most active in transforming situations. This would seem to be why the artist has in many circles in the past century been called the enemy, the criminal.

Pablo shook his head. "Kahnweiler's right," he said. "The point is, art is something subversive. It's something that should *not* be free. Art and liberty, like the fire of Prometheus, are things one must steal, to be used against the established order. Once art becomes official and open to everyone, then it becomes the new academicism." He tossed the cablegram down onto the table. "How can I support an idea like that? If art is ever given the keys to the city, it will be because it's been so watered down, rendered so impotent, that it's not worth fighting for."

I reminded him that Malherbe had said a poet is of no more use to the state than a man who spends his time playing ninepins. "Of course," Pablo said. "And why did Plato say poets should be chased out of the republic? Precisely because every poet and every artist is an antisocial being. He's not that way because he wants to be; he can't be any other way. Of *course* the state has the right to chase him away—from *its* point of view—and if he is really an artist it is in his nature not to want to be admitted, because if he is admitted it can only mean he is doing something which is understood, approved, and therefore old hat—worthless. Anything new, anything worth doing, can't be recognized. People just don't have that much vision." (Françoise Gilot and Carlton Lake, *Life with Picasso*)

It helps to explain why news has a natural bias toward crime and bad news. It is this kind of news that enables us to perceive our world. The detective since Poe's Dupin has tended to be a probe, an artist of the big town, an artist-enemy, as it were. Conventionally, society is always one phase back, is never environmental. Paradoxically, it is the antecedent environment that is always being upgraded for our attention. The new environment always uses the old environment as its material.

In the Spring, 1965 issue of the *Varsity Graduate* of the University of Toronto, Glenn Gould discussed the effects of recorded music on performance and composition. This is a reversal or chiasmus of form that occurs in any situation where an environment is pushed up into high intensity or high definition by technological change. A reversal of characteristics occurs, as in the case of bureaucracy and enterprise. An environment is naturally of low intensity or low definition. That is why it escapes observation. Anything that raises the environment to high intensity, whether it be a storm in nature or violent change resulting from a new technology, turns the environment into an object of attention. When it becomes an object of attention, it assumes the character of an antienvironment or an art object. When the social environment is stirred up to exceptional intensity by technological change and becomes a focus of much attention, we apply the terms "war" and "revolution." All the components of "war" are present in any environment whatsoever. The recognition of war depends upon their being stepped up to high definition.

Under electric conditions of instant information movement, both the concept and the reality of war become manifest in many situations of daily life. We have long been accustomed to war as that which goes on between publics or nations. Publics and nations were the creation of print technology. With electric circuitry publics and nations became the content of the new technology: "The mass audience is not a public as environment but a public as content of a new electric environment." And whereas "the public" as an environment created by print technology consisted of separate individuals with varying points of view, the mass audience consists of the same individuals involved in depth in one another and involved in the creative process of the art or educational situation that is presented to them. Art and education were presented to the *public* as consumer packages for their instruction and edification. The members of the mass audience are immediately involved in art and education as participants and co-creators rather than as consumers. Art and education become new forms of experience, new environments, rather than new antienvironments. Preelectric art and education were antienvironments in the sense that they were the content of various environments. Under electric conditions the content tends, however, toward becoming environmental itself. This was the paradox that Malraux found in *The Museum Without Walls*, and that Glenn Gould finds in recorded music. Music in the concert hall had been an antienvironment. The same music when recorded is *music without halls*, as it were.

Another paradoxical aspect of this change is that when music becomes environmental by electric means, it becomes more and more the concern of the private individual. By the same token and complementary to the same paradox, the pre-electric music of the concert hall (the music made for a public rather than a mass audience) was a corporate ritual for the group rather than the individual. This paradox extends to all electric technology. The same means which permit a universal and centralized thermostat in effect encourage a private thermostat for individual manipulation. The age of the mass audience is thus far more individualistic than the preceding age of the *public*. It is this paradoxical dynamic that confuses every issue about "conformity," "separatism" and "integration" today. Profoundly contradictory actions and directions prevail in all these situations. This is not surprising in an age of circuitry succeeding the age of the wheel. The feedback loop plays all sorts of tricks to confound the single-plane and one-way direction of thought and action as they had been constituted in the pre-electric age of the machine.

Applying the foregoing to the Negro question, one could say that the agrarian South has long tended to regard the Negro as environment. As such, the Negro is a challenge, a threat, a burden. The very phrase, "white supremacy," quite as much as the phrase "white trash," registers this environmental attitude. The environment is the enemy that must be subdued. To the rural man, the conquest of nature is an unceasing challenge. It is the southerner who contributed the cowboy to the frontier. The Virginian, the archetypal cowboy, as it were, confronts the environment as a hostile, natural force. To the man on the frontier, other men are environmental and hostile. By contrast, to the townsmen, men appear not as environmental but as content of the urban environment.

Parallel to the Negro question is the problem of French Canada. The English Canadians have been the environment of French Canada since the railway and Confederation. However, since the telegraph and radio and television, French Canada and English Canada alike have become the content of this new technology. Electric technology is totally environmental for all human communities today. Hence the great confusion arising from the transformation of environments into antienvironments, as it were. All the earlier groupings that had constituted separate environments before electricity have now become antienvironments or the content of the new technology. Awareness of the old unconscious environments therefore becomes increasingly acute. The content of any new environment is just as unperceived as that of the old one had been initially. As a merely automatic sequence, the succession of environments and the dramatics accompanying them tend to be rather tiresome, if only because the audience is very prone to participate in the dramatics with an enthusiasm proportionate to its lack of awareness. In the electric age all former environments whatever become antienvironments. As such the old environments are transformed into areas of self-awareness and self-assertion, guaranteeing a very lively interplay of forces.

The visual sense, alone of our senses, creates the forms of space and time that are uniform, continuous and connected. Euclidean space is the prerogative of visual and literate man. With the advent of electric circuitry and the instant movement of information, Euclidean space recedes and the non-Euclidean geometries emerge. Lewis Carroll, the Oxford mathematician, was perfectly aware of this change in our world when he took Alice through the looking-glass into the world where each object creates its own space and conditions. To the visual or Euclidean man, objects do not create time and space. They are merely fitted into time and space. The idea of the world as an environment that is more or less fixed is very much the product of literacy and visual assumptions. In his book *The Philosophical Impact of Contemporary Physics* Milič Čapek explains some of the strange confusions in the scientific mind that result from the encounter of the old non-Euclidean spaces of preliterate man with the Euclidean and Newtonian spaces of literate man. The scientists of our time are just as confused as the philosophers, or the teachers, and it is for the reason that Whitehead assigned: they still have the illusion that the new developments are to be fitted into the old space or environment.

One of the most obvious changes in the arts of our time has been the dropping not only of representation, but also of the story line. In poetry, in the novel, in the movie, narrative continuity has yielded to thematic variation. Such variation in place of story line or melodic line has always been the norm in native societies. It is now becoming the norm in our own society and for the same reason, namely, that we are becoming a nonvisual society.

In the age of circuitry, or feedback, fragmentation and specialism tend to yield to integral forms of organization. Humpty-Dumpty tends to go back together again. The bureaucratic efforts of all the King's horses and all the King's men were naturally calculated to keep Humpty-Dumpty from ever getting together again. The Neolithic age, the age of the planter after the age of the hunter, was an age of specialism and division of labor. It has reached a somewhat startling terminus with the advent of electric circuitry. Circuitry is a profoundly decentralizing process. Paradoxically, it was the wheel and mechanical innovation that created centralism. The circuit reverses the characteristics of the wheel, just as Xerography reverses the characteristics of the printing press. Before printing, the scribe, the author and the reader tended to merge. With printing, author and publisher become highly specialized and centralized forms of action. With Xerography, author and publisher and reader tend to merge once more. Whereas the printed book had been the first mass-produced product, creating uniform prices and markets, Xerography tends to restore the custom-made book. Writing and publishing tend to become services of a corporate and inclusive kind. The printed word created the Public. The Public consists of separate individuals, each with his own point of view. Electric circuitry does not create a Public. It creates the Mass. The mass does not consist of separate individuals, but of individuals profoundly involved in one another. This involvement is a function not of numbers but of speed.

The daily newspaper is an interesting example of this fact. The items in the daily press are totally discontinuous and totally unconnected. The only unifying feature of the press is the date line. Through that date line the reader must go, as Alice went, "through the looking glass." If it is not today's date line, he cannot get in. Once he goes through the date line, he is involved in a world of items for which he, the reader, must write a story line. He makes the news, as the reader of a detective story makes the plot. In the same way, the relatively open-ended movie at the Czech pavilion at Expo allowed for intense audience participation through the easy availability of the consensus.

Just as the printing press created the Public as a new environment, so does each new technology or extension of our physical powers tend to create new environments. In the age of information, it is information itself that becomes environmental. The satellites and antennae projected from our planet, for example, have transformed the planet from being an environment into being a probe. This is a transformation which the artists of the past century have been explaining to us in their endless experimental models. Modern art, whether in painting or poetry or music, began as a probe and not as a package. The Symbolists literally broke up the old packages and put them into our hands as probes. And whereas the package belongs to a consumer age, the probe belongs to an age of experimenters.

One of the peculiarities of art is to serve as an antienvironment, a probe that makes the environment visible. It is a form of symbolic, or parabolic, action. Parable comes from a word that means literally "to throw against," just as symbol comes from one meaning "to throw together." As we equip the planet with satellites and antennae, we tend to create new environments of which the planet is itself the content. It is peculiar to environments that they are complex processes which transform their content into archetypal forms. As the planet becomes the content of a new information environment, it also tends to become a work of art. Where railway and machine created a new environment for agrarian man, the old agrarian world became an art form. Nature became a work of art. The Romantic movement was born. When the electric circuit enveloped the mechanical environment, the machine itself became a work of art. Abstract art was born.

As information becomes our environment, it becomes mandatory to program the environment itself as a work of art. The parallel to this appears in Jacques Ellul's *Propaganda*, where he sees propaganda not as an ideology or content of any medium, but as the operation of all the media at once. The mother tongue is propaganda because it exercises an effect on all the senses at once. It shapes our entire outlook and all our ways of feeling. Like any other environment, its operation is imperceptible. When an environment is new, we perceive the old one for the first time. What we see on the *Late Show* is not TV, but old movies. When the Emperor appeared in his new clothes, his courtiers did not see his nudity, they saw his old clothes. Only the small child and the artist have the immediacy of approach that permits perception of the environmental. The artist provides us with antienvironments that enable us to see the environment. Such antienvironmental means of perception must constantly be renewed in order to be efficacious. That basic aspect of the human condition by which we are rendered incapable of perceiving the environment is one to which psychologists have not even referred. In an age of accelerated change, the need to perceive the environment becomes urgent. Acceleration also makes such perception of the environment more possible. Was it not Bertrand Russell who said that if the bath water got only half a degree warmer every hour, we would never know when to scream? New environments reset our sensory thresholds. These, in turn, alter our outlook and expectations.

The need of our time is for a means of measuring sensory thresholds and a means of discovering exactly what changes occur in these thresholds as a result of the advent of any particular technology. With such knowledge in hand, it would be possible to program a reasonable and orderly future for any human community. Such knowledge would be the equivalent of a thermostatic control of room temperatures. It would seem only reasonable to extend such controls to all the sensory thresholds of our being. We have no reason to be grateful to those who haphazardly juggle the thresholds in the name of innovation.

Redesign of the so-called "light shows" so that they cease to be merely bombardment and become probes into the environment would be most beneficial in an educational sense.

The Two Cultures by C. P. Snow is a handy instance of our contemporary dilemma between visual and nonvisual methods of codifying and processing reality (C. P. Snow seems to be blowing both horns of the dilemma). The dilemma is the same as that which confronted Alice in *Through the Looking Glass*. Before she went through the looking glass she was in a visual world of continuity and connected space where the appearance of things matched the reality. When she went through the looking glass, she found herself in a nonvisual world where nothing matched and everything seemed to have been made on a unique pattern. (As a matter of fact, because of electric technology we do have two cultures. They are the culture of our children and that of ourselves; we don't dialogue.) The work of Robert Ardrey in *The Territorial Imperative* is a kind of report from Alice after she had gone through the looking glass. Territoriality is the power of things to impose their own assumptions of time and space by means of our sensory involvement in them. Again, it is a world of making rather than of matching. Modern physics in general carries us into an unvisualizable territory. The speeds as well as the submicroscopic character of its particles are beyond visual representation. John R. Platt in *The Step to Man* explains how it would be possible to incorporate the twenty million books in the world today into an electronic library no larger than the head of a pin.

The present concern with the "death of God" is very much related to the decline in visual culture. The theologian Altizer tells us that the death of God happened roughly two hundred years ago "when the understanding of history grew to supplant an old God concept. The Christ preserved by the Church has been so progressively dissolved and the God it preached so far decomposed that it is not possible to begin to see Jesus as the core of faith and as incarnate in humanity wherever there is life, and to see God as the opposite of humanity, life, progress—that is, death." (James Heisig, *The Wake of God*, Divine Seminary, 1967.) In a visual sense God is no longer "up there" and "out there" any more than twenty million books in a pinhead could be said to be "in there." Visual orientation has simply become irrelevant. Some feel that Christianity's existence must always stand in the tension between being in the world and standing outside it. Kierkegaard was keenly aware of this, as were St. Paul and, later, Martin Luther. But the tension between inner and outer is a merely visual guideline, and in the age of the X-ray inner and outer are simultaneous events.

As the Western world goes Oriental in its inner trip with electric circuitry, it is not only the conventional image of God that is deposed: the whole nature of self-identity enters a state of crisis. God the clockmaker and engineer of the universe is no more an essential visual image to the West than is the identity card or the visual classification as an image of private personal status. The problem of personal identity first arose in the West with King Oedipus, who went through the crisis of detribalization, the loss of corporate involvement in the tribal group. To an ancient Greek the discovery of private identity was a terrifying and horrible thing that came about with the discovery of visual space and fragmentary classification. Twentieth-century man is travelling the reverse course, from an extreme individual fragmentary state back into a condition of corporate involvement with all mankind. Paradoxically, this new involvement is experienced as alienation and loss of private selfhood. It began with Ibsen and the Russian writers like Dostoevsky, for whom there remained a much larger degree of awareness of the old tribal and corporate life than anything available to other European writers in the nineteenth century. The novelists and dramatists who began the quest to discover "Who am I?" have been succeeded by the existentialist philosophers, who meditate upon the meaninglessness of private lives in the contemporary world:

One can say, in short, that meaninglessness is spreading before our eyes. A strange inner mutation is thereby produced which takes on the aspect of a genuine uprooting. Entirely new questions are being asked. They insist on being asked, where one hitherto seemed to be in an order which contained its own justification; it is the very order to which the barracks man belonged in the days when he was still a living being, when he was in the present.

He for whom reflection has become a need, a primordial necessity, becomes aware of the precarious and contingent character of the conditions which constitute the very framework of his existence. The word "normal" which he once made use of in a way which now seems to him so imprudent, is emptied of its significance—let us say at least that it is suddenly, as it were, marked by a sign which makes it appear in a new and disturbing light. (Gabriel Marcel, *Problematic Man*, Herder and Herder, 1967)

Marcel is quite aware that there are no concepts or categories that can resolve this crisis:

Let us now go back to the questions which the barracks man was asking himself: *Who am I? What sense does my life have?* It is obvious that one does not resolve these questions by saying to this man (or to myself if I ask them of myself): You are a rational animal. An answer of this kind is beside the point. I said earlier that meaninglessness was spreading: that is to say that I, who have a profession, a country, means of existence, etc., cannot help but turn these questions somehow towards myself. Why is this so? Let us reason *a contrario*, and suppose that I shut myself up prudently, jealously, in that favored category where these questions do not arise. But if I have really managed, by an effort of imagination, to put myself in the place of the barracks man, it is through his eyes that I will be brought to consider the step by which I placed myself once and for all in the category of the privileged, who know who they are, and what they are living for. In other words, by the combined action of imagination and reflection, I have been able to bring about a change which bears not only upon the object, but upon the subject himself, the subject who questions.

However, he seems to favor the illusion that these dilemmas are ideological in origin rather than a consequence of a re-programming of the human environment in its sensory modes. The rear-view mirror is the favorite instrument of the philosophical historian:

In particular, one can hardly contest the fact that nationalism in its modern, post-revolutionary form, is the product of an ideology that developed in the eighteenth century and combined, under conditions very difficult to state precisely, with a pre-romanticism whose origins seem to be found in Rousseau. Abandoned to its own inclination, this ideology led to a kind of cosmopolitanism of reason. The nationalism which issued from the French Revolution built itself to a large extent upon the ruins of the basic communities which had persisted until the end of the *ancien régime*, but which the individualism of the philosophy of the Enlightenment inevitably helped to dissolve. One cannot deny, on the other hand, that there was a close connection between this fact and the devitalization of religion which occurred in the same period. But the industrial revolution, at least during the first part of the nineteenth century, was destined to play a part in considerably aggravating this tendency—to a large extent, moreover, under the influence of a liberalism which on the economic plane (as we know all too well) was destined to engender the most inhuman consequences, the individual being reduced to a more and more fragmentary condition, under the cover of an optimism which seems to us today to have been the height of hypocrisy.

Marcel occasionally entertains the possibility of considering existence not as a classification or category, but as a total environment:

> The profound justification of the philosophers of existence has perhaps consisted above all in the fact that they have brought out the impossibility of considering an existent being without taking into consideration his existence, his mode of existence. But regarding this very existence, the words *rational animal* furnish us no genuine enlightenment.

But in general he is aware of the futility of history. In the electric age, however, history no longer presents itself as a perspective of continuous visual space, but as an all-at-once and simultaneous presence of all facets of the past. This is what T. S. Eliot calls "tradition" in his celebrated essay, "Tradition and the Individual Talent." Eliot's concept seemed quite revolutionary in 1917, but it was in fact a report of an immediate and present reality. Awareness of all-at-once history or tradition goes with a correlative awareness of the present as modifying the entire past. It is this vision that is characteristic of the artistic perception which is necessarily concerned with making and change rather than with any point of view or any static position.

The bourgeois nineteenth century referred only to those faces and features which were most strikingly visual in their tidiness and order. That world now persists in some degree in suburbia with the Educational Establishment as its sustaining bulwark. Antithetic to suburbia is the beatnik world, which in the nineteenth century was Bohemia. This is a world in which visual values play a very minor role. One hippie was heard to say, "I have no use for this Cromwell character. I'm a Cavalier!" Cromwell was a sort of *avant-garde* program of visual values. His "Ironsides" were an advance image of industrial production and weaponry. Their "Roundheads" are now the "square" citizens of the upper executive world. "Square," of course, simply means visual and uninvolved.

The transition between worlds may have occurred at the moment of the hula hoop. Mysteriously, people were fascinated by hula hoops as an invitation to involvement and gyration, but nobody was ever seen rolling one in the approved style of the hoop and stick of yesteryear. When exhorted by their elders to roll these hoops down a walk, children simply ignored the request. An equivalent situation today is the disappearance of the word "escapism" in favor of the word "involvement." In the twenties, all popular art, whether written or photographed for the movies, was branded as pure escapism. It has not occurred to anybody to call TV viewing escapist any more than it had occurred to anybody to roll the hula hoop as though it were a wheel. Today popular art is intensely involving, and it contains none of the visual values that characterized respectable art a century ago. Popular art has indeed swamped Bohemia and enlarged its territories many times. The aesthete, 1967 model, does not affect any nineteenth-century elegance, but in the interest of involvement presents a shaggy and multisensuous image. Upon meeting him we may well be inclined to say, "You're putting me on!" This is indeed the case. The image to which both beatnik and Beatle aspire is that of "putting on" the corporate audience. It is not a private need of expression that motivates them, but a corporate need of involvement in the total audience. This is humanism in reverse, instead of the corporate image of an integral society.

> The revolt against the exclusively humanistic conception of art has been long in gestation, but it first comes into visible existence in the painting of Cézanne, and Cézanne's fundamental importance in the history of this revolution is due precisely to the fact that he was the first who dared assert that the purpose of art is not to express an ideal, whether religious or moral or humanistic, but simply to be humble before nature, and to render the forms which close observation could disentangle from vague visual impressions. The consequences of this peculiar kind of honesty were hardly such as Cézanne himself would have expected. First came cubism, and then a gradual purification of form which reached its logical conclusion in the abstract or nonfigurative art of Piet Mondrian or Ben Nicholson. This formalist type of art is now widespread among artists in every medium, and whether you like it or not, like technology it has come to stay. (Herbert Read, *The Redemption of the Robot*, Trident Press, 1966)

A somewhat different approach to the problem of the transforming action of new environments upon older ones can be taken by the study of cliché and archetype. The world of the cliché is itself environmental since nothing can become a cliché until it has pervaded some world or other. It is at the moment of pervasiveness that the cliché becomes invisible. In their study of *The Popular Arts* Stuart Hall and Paddy Whannel have provided many illustrations of the principle by which a world of cliché, by the art of enveloping an older cliché, seems to turn the older cliché into an archetype or art form. They point to the verbal world of Mickey Spillane, in which the free-lance avenger saves the law by working outside it. Raymond Chandler is much more sophisticated:

> As Chandler's work develops, his themes emerge with greater clarity. When he died he was still at work on *The Poodle Springs Story*. This was to be only incidentally a thriller.

Marlowe, married to a wealthy girl, is in danger of becoming her "poodle," confined to the empty round of California cocktail parties. "The contest between what she wants Marlowe to do and what he will insist on doing will make a good sub-plot. I don't know how it will turn out, but she'll never tame him. Perhaps the marriage won't last, or she might even learn to respect his integrity," Chandler wrote, " . . . a struggle of personalities and ideas of life": the thriller becoming the novel of manners.

It is not only that a new medium creates a new environment, which acts upon the sensory life of its inhabitants. The same new environment acts upon the older literary and artistic forms as well:

As these various satirical modes are more fully employed we begin to understand Chandler's real achievement. Like the true satirist, his gift lies in a disenchanted view of life, and depends upon a highly artificial style. Like the mock-heroic writers and poets, who made play with "heroism," Chandler makes play with the notion of "toughness." He inverts the thriller conventions, draws attention to their artificiality. A hard, polished prose surface permits his wit to play freely. Where the lesser practitioners in the field break their necks to build up the arch-hero, the superman, at the centre of their work, Chandler sets out to portray the most practised of anti-heroes. Apart from Marlowe, who is keeper of both conscience and consciousness in the novel, and through whose elliptical eye every detail is observed and placed, few of the other characters have true "depth." They are consciously two-dimensional, like the characters in a Ben Jonson play or in Restoration comedy. Perhaps, like the latter, a Chandler novel is a decadent work of art, and there are signs of this in the language (for one thing the similes tend to be over-elaborate and ornate or bizarre). But his use of the witticism or the wisecrack has the same pointed "surface" effect as the rhymed couplet or the epigram in Restoration comedy. There are countless effects of a literary kind which lesser novelists, practicing in the more major literary genres, are able to achieve, but which escaped Chandler. But there are many compensating pleasures which are not to be found in their work. Few writers have so compromised and over-worked a popular literary form with such skill, craftsmanship and tact.

The hero of the modern thriller puts on the audience, as it were, in a typical gesture of total involvement, whereas the hero of the older adventure story was an aristocratic individual. The new hero is a corporate rather than a private individual figure:

As Orwell showed in his comparison between Raffles and Miss Blandish, the modern thriller-hero can no longer afford to stand aside from the action in his story with that aristocratic detachment which was possible in his immediate predecessors. Unlike Sherlock Holmes or Lord Peter Wimsey or that miraculous *deus ex machina* Hercule Poirot, the thriller-hero must finally enter the action as the main protagonist. The omniscience of the earlier detective-heroes provided some distance between them and the mere mortals caught up in the drama and confusion of the crime. But now this hero, of all the figures in the novel, must be the *most* exposed to the play of passion and violence, the one most intimately caught up with the actual experience of punishment. And if we ask why this change has come about we are forced to give a complex set of reasons, all of which suggest how deeply rooted the literature is in the social imagination. Perhaps it is because we can no longer accept the figure who stands outside the action and yet knows all the answers: we demand greater verisimilitude today. Perhaps it is because these impersonal figures seem now too superhumanly remote: since the revolution in our thinking by Freud and psychoanalysis, we take a different view of crime, punishment and violence which the thriller reflects. We cannot believe in the hero who is himself wholly free from the inner compulsions of violence and lawlessness—we demand that he should stand closer to the villain, exposed to the very evils he is dedicated to remove: "there, but for the grace of God . . ." Certainly, the philosopher would argue that the thriller also shows a collapse in the belief in an abstract and incorruptible justice.

What Hall and Whannel are saying is that the new hero is constituted differently by virtue of being representative of the entire reading public.

The Mike Hammer and James Bond stories are, of course, fantasies—but fantasies which communicate a graphic and heightened realism. Characters may be overdrawn, situations stereo-typed, resolutions predictable. But the fictional life of these stories is convincing at the very level at which the modern reader, especially the young reader, is likely to find himself most under pressure: at the level of the sensations. In a quite precise sense, the thriller novel is a novel of the sensations. Its power lies in its experiential quality, in the absence of relieving factors and the starkness of the action, and in the image of human behavior which it offers.

In exactly the same way the modern painting does not allow for the single point of view or the dispassionate survey. The modern painter offers an opportunity for dialogue within the parameters inherent in an art form which is moving away from the rational-visual and into the total world of man's sensory involvement.

APPENDICES

I. a note on tactility

In a visual culture it sounds quite paradoxical to say that sculpture is primarily tactile and only incidentally visual. In fact, tactility is a matter that has scarcely been discussed, and yet it is crucial in the world of the arts. There are occasional passages on the subject, like Ortega y Gasset's in *Man and People* (Norton):

And it is true that the visible and the act of seeing afford greater clarity as examples in a first approach to our doctrine, it would be a grave mistake to suppose that sight is the most important "sense." Even from the psycho-physiological point of view, which is ancillary, it seems more and more probable that touch was the original sense from which the others were gradually differentiated. From our more radical point of view it is clear that the decisive form of our intercourse with things is in fact touch. And if this is so, touch and contact are necessarily the most conclusive factor in determining the structure of our world.

Yet Ortega y Gasset scarcely develops this theme and when he does illustrate it, it is without any reference whatever to tactility. For example, when he is discussing Herbert Spencer and his doctrine of the handshake, he is in the very center of tactility. Tactility is the world of the interval, not of the connection, and that is why it is antithetic to the visual world. For the visual is above all the world of the continuous and the connected. For visual or civilized man, the handshake has reversed its original function and meaning of stressing the cultural interval or division between peoples. An analogue to the handshake as tactile and as stressing interval exists in the Oriental world, where, as Ortega y Gasset writes:

> Courtesy, as we shall later see, is a social technique that eases the collision and strife and friction that sociality is. Around each individual it creates a series of tiny buffers that lessen the other's bump against us and ours against the other. The best proof that this is so lies in the fact that courtesy was able to attain its most perfect, richest, and most refined forms in countries whose population density was very great. Hence, it reached its maximum where that is highest—namely, in the Far East, in China and Japan, where men have to live too close to one another, almost on top of one another. Without all those little buffers, living together would be impossible. It is well known that the European in China produces the impression of a rude, crass, and thoroughly ill-educated being. So it is not surprising that the Japanese language has succeeded in suppressing those two slightly and sometimes more than slightly impertinent pistol-shots, the *you* and the *I*, in which, whether I want to or not, I inject my personality into my neighbor and my idea of his personality into the *You*.

The strategy of courtesy as a means of maintaining social interval is of the very essence of tactility.

In music, however, it receives even more notable stress. Both upbeat and downbeat are tactile modes that create the separation whose closure makes a unique rhythm. The matter is at least alluded to in Harold Schonberg's *The Great Conductors* (Simon & Schuster), when he cites the observation of Richard Strauss:

> In fifty years of practice, I have discovered how unimportant it is to beat each quarter note or eighth note. What is decisive is that the upbeat, which contains the whole of the tempo that follows, should be rhythmically exact and that the downbeat should be

extremely precise. The second half of the bar is immaterial. I frequently conduct it like an *alla breve* (i.e., in twos). Always conduct in periods, never bars. . . . Second rate conductors are frequently inclined to pay too much attention to the elaborations of rhythmic detail, thus overlooking the proper shaping of a phrase as a whole. . . . Any modification of tempo made necessary by the character of the piece should be carried out imperceptibly, so that the unity of tempo remains intact.

The social, the political and the artistic implications of tactility could only have been lost to human awareness in a visual or civilized culture which is now dissolving under the impact of electric circuitry. The Japanese sense of the importance of touch as interval is sufficiently indicated in *The Book of Tea* by Okakura-Kakuzo (Kenkyusha):

We must know the whole play in order to properly act our parts; the conception of totality must never be lost in that of the individual. This Laotse illustrates by his favorite metaphor of the Vacuum. He claimed that only in vacuum lay the truly essential. The reality of a room, for instance, was to be found in the vacant space enclosed by the roof and walls, not in the roof and walls themselves. The usefulness of a water pitcher dwelt in the emptiness where water might be put, not in the form of the pitcher or in the material of which it was made. Vacuum is all potent because all containing. In vacuum alone motion becomes possible. One who could make of himself a vacuum into which others might freely enter would become master of all situations. The whole can always dominate the part.

The author continues his discussion in a passage that is perhaps better accommodated to Western perception:

In art the importance of the same principle is illustrated by the value of suggestion. In leaving something unsaid the beholder is given a chance to complete the idea and thus a great masterpiece irresistibly rivets your attention until you seem to become actually a part of it. A vacuum is there for you to enter and fill up to the full measure of your aesthetic emotion.

II. a note on color tv

Neither black and white nor color television is a picture. It is an X-ray. Light comes through the image at the viewer; the viewer is not a camera but a screen. The TV camera has no shutter but works like a shifting mosaic. Totally different from photographs and movies, the TV image is discontinuous and flat. That is, it is a world of intervals. It is extremely tactile and participant.

The current phrase "living color" is self-contradictory since the TV industry takes "living" to mean realistic and representational. A similar mistake was made by the movie industry when it pushed toward photographic realism rather than realism of process, as in the Chaplin pictures. Chaplin was so conscious of this aspect of film that he frequently acted his scenes backward, although they were projected to run forward. Tony Schwartz has a tape on which Chaplin is speaking phrases backward, analytically and anatomically. Yet when played, they sound like normal speech. This is similar to the Stratton glasses which make us see the world upside down. The fact is that we do see the world upside down, righting it mentally for reasons that are totally unknown. The movie, because of its movement, strongly favors this awareness of processes in or out of nature. Photographic realism nullifies this aspect of the movie altogether. The talkie bypassed process in favor of simple narrative. TV is at present trying to recap all the worst mistakes in the history of movies. Since there are very few color experts in the world, there is very little hope of their having any influence on the television industry. In any event, color TV demands a considerable educational effort in perception.

We could say that the TV generation of teen-agers is, of course, getting the two-dimensional message of TV with all the force that the Negro community got the message of radio in the twenties. Naturally, the industry will continue to ignore the two-dimensional aspect of TV, and anyone over thirty is certainly not going to feel the new habit of perception latent in the TV image. It is precisely here that the artist has a crucial role to play in alerting human awareness to the meaning of technology.

The center or macula lutea of the eye is responsive to hue and variations in hue and texture. The periphery, on the other hand, is concerned with darkness and lightness and also with movement. Although the eye can eliminate any consideration of hue (for example, in scotoptic or twilight vision), when the macula is involved, it is inevitable that the periphery be involved as well. In other words, the macula and periphery work in tandem. However, peripheral vision can exist by itself. While color vision is inclusive, black and white is partial. Black and white TV is automatically inclined toward movement just as surely as color TV is inclined toward stasis and iconic values.

The potential of any technology is always dissipated by its users' involvement in its predecessor. The iconic thrust of color TV will be buried under mountains of old pictorial space.

CHAPTER FIFTEEN

Culture and Communication
The Two Hemispheres

MARSHALL MCLUHAN AND ERIC MCLUHAN

To the Inuit, truth is given, not by "seeing is believing," but through oral tradition, mysticism, intuition, all cognition—in other words, not simply by observation and measurement of physical phenomena. To the Inuit, the ocularly visible apparition is not clearly so common as the purely auditory one; "hearer" would be a better name than "seer" for their holy men.

Robert J. Trotter, writing on "The Other Hemisphere" *in Science News*,[1] reports an investigation of brain-hemisphere dominance and patterns of behaviour "among the Inuit or Eskimo people of Baffin Island in northeastern Canada." The project discovered, among the Inuit people, a language that reflected "a high degree of spatial, right-hemispheric orientation. Linguistic studies rate it as being the most synthetic of languages. American English is at the other end of the same scale, and is rated as the most analytic (left-hemisphere)." Inuit sculptures, lithographs, and tapestries are "without apparent linear or three-dimensional analytic orientation." That is, they have never developed any measure of visual bias such as is normal in Western culture.

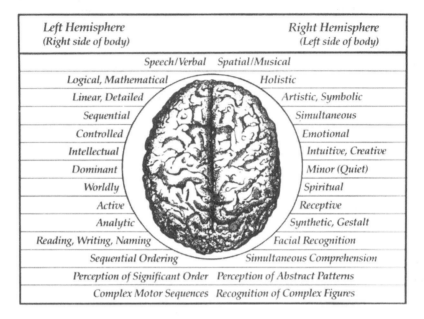

Left Hemisphere (Right side of body)	Right Hemisphere (Left side of body)
Speech/Verbal	Spatial/Musical
Logical, Mathematical	Holistic
Linear, Detailed	Artistic, Symbolic
Sequential	Simultaneous
Controlled	Emotional
Intellectual	Intuitive, Creative
Dominant	Minor (Quiet)
Worldly	Spiritual
Active	Receptive
Analytic	Synthetic, Gestalt
Reading, Writing, Naming	Facial Recognition
Sequential Ordering	Simultaneous Comprehension
Perception of Significant Order	Perception of Abstract Patterns
Complex Motor Sequences	Recognition of Complex Figures

Reproduced courtesy of R. H. Trotter

To the Inuit, nature's forms "lie hidden" until man reveals them one by one. Their language makes little distinction between "nouns" and "verbs"; rather, all words are forms of the verb "to be," which is itself lacking in Eskimo. "Eskimo isn't a nominal language; it doesn't name things which already exist, but brings things/action (nouns/verbs) into being as it goes along . . . when the mother is in labor, an old woman stands around and says as many different eligible names as she can think of. The child comes out of the womb when its name is called." (Edmund Carpenter, *Eskimo Realities*, 39).

In the beginning was the word. The primitive is a phenomenologist who equates reading aloud the Book of Nature with the making process. As a man speaks, his language is in a state of birth, as is also the thing about which he is talking. Such parentage confers responsibilities. In this sense, every man is an artist. Primitives have no need, as we have, of a special and unique group (artists) that uses special processes and perceptions. Carvings are often discarded after being made, just as "words fade away." "When Orpingalic says, 'And we will fear to use words,' he doesn't mean he's afraid of the words themselves. He means he's in awe of their power to bring the universe into existence. Words must 'shoot up of themselves.' They must arise naturally out of experience. To impose words of his own would be sacrilegious. 'Many are the words that rush over me, like the wings of birds out of darkness.'" (*Eskimo Realities*, 52).

Prior to writing and to print, words and utterances were still endowed with the magical power to form and transform existence. The difference between the two states is clearly reflected in the hemispheric differences in the brain. Trotter's chart of the characteristics of the left and right hemispheres presents a pattern of basic contrasts.[2] Because the dominant feature of the left hemisphere is linearity and sequentiality, there are good reasons for calling it the "visual" (quantitative) side of the brain; and because the dominant features of the right hemisphere are the simultaneous, holistic and synthetic, there are good reasons for indicating it as the "acoustic" (qualitative) side of the brain.

We are not Argus-eyed but Argus-eared.

Visual space is the result of left-hemisphere dominance in a culture, and its use is restricted to those cultures that have immersed themselves in the phonetic alphabet and thereby suppressed the activity of the right hemisphere.

Since, as Jeremy Campbell points out in *Grammatical Man*,[3] alphabetic consonants and much of syntax are products of the left hemisphere, visual space is an extrapolation into the environment of the left brain in high definition—abstract, structured as a figure minus a ground. Acoustic space has the basic character of a dynamic sphere whose focus or centre is simultaneously everywhere and whose margin or periphery is nowhere. As it is multisensory, involving both the interval of tactility and kinetic equilibrium-pressure, it is one of the many figure/ground right-hemisphere forms of space. Ordinarily, the two hemispheres are in constant dialogue through the *corpus callosum*, and each hemisphere uses the other as its ground except when one (i.e., the left) is habitually dominant. Each hemisphere, as it were, provides a particular type of information processing less available to the other. As Dr. J. E. Bogen notes, "The type of cognition proper to the right hemisphere has been called *appositional*, a usage common to the parallel use by neurologists of *propositional* to encompass the left hemisphere's dominance for speaking, writing, calculation and related tasks.[4]

The individual features of the face, as isolated figures, are easily noted by the left hemisphere, which cannot handle them together as a pattern. It is the "acoustic" power of simultaneous comprehension that gives the right hemisphere the ability to recognize faces. By the same token, the sense of touch creates the space of the "resonant interval": interval defines the relation of figure to ground and provides the structure, the con-figuration of ground. Synesthetic interplay among all the senses would seem to relate mainly to the right hemisphere. That Trotter, in "The Other Hemisphere," selects a Third World or non-literate society for observation and illustration points to the fact that societies that have not developed the use of the phonetic alphabet tend to adopt the same Third World posture. While the Third World is mainly oral/aural, even when it cultivates some non-phonetic form of writing such as Sanskrit, the First World (Western) countries tend to be visual (left hemisphere), even when most of their population is declining into a semi-literate state via the information environment of electronic technologies.

Technologies themselves regardless of content, produce a hemispheric bias in the users.

Herbert Krugman performed brain-wave studies, comparing the response of subjects to print and television. One subject was reading a book as the TV came on. As soon as she looked up her brain waves slowed significantly. In less than two minutes, she was in a predominantly alpha state—relaxed, passive, unfocused. Her brain wave response to three different types of TV content was basically the same, even though she told Krugman she "liked" one, "disliked" another, and "was bored by" the third. As a result of a series of such experiments, Krugman argues that this predominantly alpha state is characteristic of how people respond to TV—any TV. He recently remarked, "the ability of respondents to show high right brain response to even familiar logos, their right brain response to stories even before the idea content has been added to them, the predominantly right brain response to TV, and perhaps even to what we call print advertising—all suggests that in contrast to teaching, the unique power of the electronic media is to *shape* the content of people's imagery, and in that particular way determine their behaviour and their views."[5]

Krugman's investigations were, he admitted, initially undertaken to disprove that "the medium is the message." His quantitative results point to the massive and subliminal erosion of our culture through right-hemisphere indoctrination by TV in all its forms, including VCRs, video games, computer monitors and word-processors. In a wider sense, all electric media, as a new ground, give salience only to the right hemisphere. There is no way to quantify the right hemisphere, which emphasizes inner and qualitative aspects of experience.

How paradoxical that the hardware channels of radio and telephonic communication contribute to an extraordinary software effect. Nathaniel Hawthorne was particularly sensitive to the implications of electric information and not infrequently remarked on them, as in *The House of the Seven Gables*: "Is it a fact that . . . by means of electricity the world of matter has become a great nerve, vibrating thousands of miles in a breathless point of time? Rather, the round globe is a vast head, a brain, instinct with intelligence! Or, shall we say, it is itself a thought, and no longer the substance which we deemed it!" When people are on the telephone or on the air, they have no physical bodies but are translated into abstract images. Their old physical beings are entirely irrelevant to the new situations. The discarnate user of electric media bypasses all former spatial restrictions and is present in many places simultaneously as a disembodied intelligence. This puts him one step above angels, who can only be in one place at a time. Since, however, discarnate man has no relation to natural law (or to Western lineality), his impulse is towards anarchy and lawlessness. Minus his body, the user of telephone or radio or TV also is minus his private identity, an effect that is becoming increasingly evident.

In another experiment, an audience was equally divided, with each half seated facing a translucent-opaque screen placed in the middle of a room. A movie was shown and then the audience was asked to write a brief response. One group saw light reflected from the screen in the usual manner; the other group saw light passing through the screen, as with television. In their remarks, the "light-on" group adopted an objective, detached tone and was analytic as to narrative, continuity, cinematography, editing and workmanship, and so on. Whereas they reported "how the movie looked," by contrast, the "light-through" group was mainly concerned with "how the movie felt." Their responses were subjective and emotional: they discussed themselves, how they felt, and the mystical or archetypal significance of characters or actions. The differences between the light-on and light-through situations (immediate ground) were sufficiently potent to cause one group to have a right-hemispheric experience and the other to have a left-hemispheric experience. With the low-intensity mosaic TV image, this effect is greatly amplified.

Cultural dominance by either the left or the right hemisphere is largely dependent upon environmental factors.

The lineality of the left hemisphere is supported by an alphabet-based service environment of roads and transportation, and by logical or rational activities in social and legal administration. Dominance of the right hemisphere, however, depends upon a cultural milieu or environment of a simultaneous or resonating character. Such dominance is normal in oral societies, and today our universal environment of simultaneous electric information has entirely subverted the dominance of the left hemisphere. By tuning in on the new audile-tactile awareness made available by our electric ground, Fritjof Capra found that modern physics was, unwittingly, retrieving a worldview harmonious with ancient Eastern wisdom. His problems in reconciling the two were entirely those of the hemispheres:

I had just gone through a long training in theoretical physics and had done several years of research. At the same time, I had become very interested in eastern mysticism and had begun to see the parallels to modern physics. I was particularly attracted to the puzzling aspects of Zen, which reminded me of the puzzles in quantum theory. At first, however, relating the two was a purely intellectual exercise. To overcome the gap between rational, analytical thinking and the meditation experience of mystical truth, was, and still is, very difficult for me. (*The Tao of Physics*, 9–10)

The alphabet created visual space, and with it a lineal and visual "outer world" environment of services and experiences (everything from architecture and highways to representational art), which contributed to the ascendancy or dominance of the left, or lineal, hemisphere. This observation is consistent with the findings of the Russian neurophysiologist A. K. Luria, who found that the area of the brain which controls linear sequencing, and, hence, mathematical and scientific thinking, is located in the pre-frontal region of the left hemisphere. "The mental process for writing a word entails still another specialization: putting the letters in the proper sequence to form the word. Lashley discovered many years ago that sequence analysis involved a zone of the brain different from that employed for spatial analysis. In the course of our extensive studies we have located the region responsible for sequential analysis in the anterior regions of the left hemisphere" ("The Functional Organization of the Brain," 71–2). Luria's results show that the expression "linear thinking" is not merely a figure of speech, but a mode of activity peculiar to the left hemisphere of the brain. His results support the observation that the use of the alphabet, with its emphasis on linear sequence, stimulates dominance of this area of the brain in cultural patterns.

Luria's observations provide an understanding of how the written alphabet, with its lineal structure, was able to create conditions conducive to the development of Western science, technology, and rationality. Many left-hemisphere stroke patients become aphasic, losing some or all of their ability to speak or to write, in some cases also losing the capacity for sustained (sequential) thought. They seem to become "astonied" (fifteenth-century English), or "stunned"—the experience is not unlike being "stoned" on drugs. In part, this may be the result of a loss of muscular motor control. But much of it is directly related to the inner-outer split between the hemispheres and to linearity as a feature of the left side of the brain. Speech and writing have to be *uttered*, in a sequence. Just as all forms of sequential activity (as contrasted to configuration or pattern) are functions of the left hemisphere, so too all forms of utterances (and artefacts), whether technological or verbal or written, are functions of the left hemisphere. This extends to private identity—uttering the self as fragmented and abstracted from the group—and to entrepreneurial aggression of all kinds. Conversely, all technologies that emphasize the outer or the abstract or sequentiality in organizing experience, contribute to left-hemisphere dominance in a culture. Harold Innis remarked on the Oriental (right-hemisphere) antipathy to sequence and abstraction and our sort of precision:

> Social time, for example, has been described as qualitatively differentiated according to the beliefs and customs common to a group and as not continuous but as subject to interruption of actual dates. It is influenced by language which constrains and fixes prevalent concepts and modes of thought. It has been argued by Marcel Granet that the Chinese are not equipped to note concepts or to present doctrines discursively. The Word does not fix a notion with a definite degree of abstraction or generality but evokes an indefinite complex of particular images. It is completely unsuited to formal precision. Neither time nor space is abstractly conceived; time proceeds by cycles and is round. (*The Bias of Communication*, 62)

Dr. Bogen noted, appositely, "what may well be the most important distinction between the left and the right hemisphere modes is the extent to which a linear concept of time participates in the ordering of thought." (*The Human Brain*, 141)

The visual power of the phonetic alphabet to translate other languages into itself is part of its power to invade right hemisphere (oral) cultures.

Tribal, right-hemisphere "closed" cultures are holistic and entire and resistant to penetration by other preliterate cultures. But the specialist qualities of the left-hemisphere phonetic alphabet have long provided the only means of invading and taking over oral societies. "Propaganda cannot succeed where people have no trace of Western culture." These words of Jacques Ellul in *Propaganda* draw attention to one of the crucial features of Western history. It is no accident that the Christian church, dedicated to propaganda and propagation, adopted Graeco-Roman phonetic literacy from the earliest days. The impact of alphabetic literacy is strong enough not only to break the tribal bond, but to create individualized (left-hemisphere) consciousness as well. Phonetic literacy—our alphabet—alone has this power.

The spread of Graeco-Roman literacy and civilization became inseparable from Christian missionary and educational activity. Paradoxically, people are not only unable to receive, but are unable to retain doctrinal teaching without a minimum of phonetic or Western culture. Here is the observation of Ellul on this matter:

> In addition to a certain living standard, another condition must be met: if a man is to be successfully propagandized, he needs at least a minimum of culture. Propaganda cannot succeed where people have no trace of Western culture. We are not speaking here

of intelligence; some primitive tribes are surely intelligent, but have an intelligence foreign to our concepts and customs. A base is needed—for example, education; a man who cannot read will escape propaganda, as will a man who is not interested in reading. People used to think that learning to read evidenced human progress; they still celebrate the decline of illiteracy as a great victory: they condemn countries with a large proportion of illiterates: they think that reading is a road to freedom. All this is debatable, for the important thing is not to be able to read but to understand what one reads, to reflect on and judge what one reads. Outside of that, reading has no meaning (and even destroys certain automatic qualities of memory and observation). But to talk about critical faculties and discernment is to talk about something far above primary education and to consider a very small minority. The vast majority of people, perhaps 90 percent, know how to read, but they do not exercise their intelligence beyond this. They attribute authority and eminent value to the printed word or, conversely, reject it altogether. As these people do not possess enough knowledge to reflect and discern, they believe—or disbelieve—*in toto* what they read. And as such people, moreover, will select the easiest, not the hardest, reading matter, they are precisely on the level at which the printed word can seize and convince them without opposition. They are perfectly adapted to propaganda.[6]

The dominance of the left hemisphere (analytic and quantitative) entails the submission or suppression of the right hemisphere; and so, for example, our intelligence tests exist only for measuring left-hemisphere achievement, and take no cognizance of the existence of the (qualitative) right hemisphere.

The dyslexic: Everyman as cubist.

The present electronic age, in its inescapable evocation of simultaneity, presents the first serious threat to the 2500-year dominance of the left hemisphere. It is no surprise that students whose right brains have had eighteen years' education by TV have problems with left-brain curricula and SAT tests.

The current spate of dyslexia and other reading difficulties—some 90 percent of the victims are males—is a direct result of TV and other electric media pressuring us to return to the right hemisphere. Dyslexia is an inability to adopt a single, fixed point of view with respect to all letters and words: conversely, it consists of approaching letters and words from many points of view simultaneously (right-hemisphere fashion), minus the assumption that any one way is solely correct. As the pressure continues, so will the problems with our left-hemisphere alphabet. The cubists, as artists and "antennae of the race," detected the shift some seventy years ago, and explored the grammar of this sensory modality. If literacy is to survive for another generation in the West, our writing system will soon have to be completely recast in a mould congenial to right-hemisphere sensibility and satisfactions. We might, for example, replace it with a syllabary of fifty to seventy characters.

A variety of factors can give salience or dominance either to the right (simultaneous and acoustic) hemisphere of the brain, or to the left (lineal and visual). But no matter how extreme the dominance of either hemisphere in a particular culture, there is always some degree of interplay, thanks to the *corpus callosum*, that part of the nervous system which bridges the hemispheres. Even the Chinese with their traditionally monopolistic cultivation of the right hemisphere, which invests every aspect of their lives, their language, and their writing with artistic delicacy—even the Chinese exert much left-hemisphere stress through their practicality and their concern with moral wisdom. However, their sensory stress falls heavily on what Heisenberg calls the "resonant interval," that is, touch.

> Indeed the use of space is one of the Chinese painter's most coveted secrets, one of the first thoughts in his head when he begins to plan his composition. Almost every space in our pictures has a significance: the onlooker may fill them up with his own imagined memory or with her feeling merely. There was a Chinese poet of the Sung dynasty, Yeh Ch'ing Ch'en, who wrote the sorrows of a parting and described the scene as follows:
>
> Of the three parts Spring scene, two are sadness,
>
> And other part is nothing but wind and rain.
>
> Who would venture to paint this scenery, but yet who would deny the truth of it? This is what we leave to the well-disposed blank, more eloquent than pictorial expression. (Chiang Yee, *The Chinese Eye*, 189–90)

The Chinese, in other words, use the eye as an ear, creating the paradoxical situation that Tony Schwartz notes in *The Responsive Chord* apropos the TV image: "In watching television, our eyes function like our ears."

The interval between the wheel and the axle has long served as an example not only of "touch," but of "play." Without "play," without that figure/ground interval, there is neither wheel nor axle. The space between the wheel and the axle, which defines both, is "where the action is"; and this space is both audile and tactile.

The Chinese use the intervals between things as the primary means of getting "in touch" with situations.

Nothing could be more expressive that this statement of the properties of the right hemisphere in contrast to the left. For, to the left hemisphere, the interval is a space *logically* connected and filled and bridged. Such is the dictate of lineality and visual order in contrast to the resonating interval or gap of the simultaneous world of the right hemisphere. In *The Book of Tea*, Kakuzo Okakura explains the Japanese attitude to social relationships as a "constant readjustment to our surroundings." This is in extreme contrast to the Western or visual "point of view," which assumes a fixed position from which to examine each situation and to assert one's preference. Right-hemisphere culture has no place for the private individual, just as the left-hemisphere society regards tribal groups as sinister and threatening (remember the "Yellow Peril").

> Suzuki, the great authority on Zen Buddhism, describes muga as "ecstasy with no sense of *I am doing it*," "effortlessness." The "observing self" is eliminated, a man "loses himself," that is, he ceases to be a spectator of his acts. Suzuki says: "With the awakening of consciousness, the will is split into two: . . . actor and observer. Conflict is inevitable, for the actor (-self) wants to be free from the limitations of the observer-self. Therefore in Enlightenment the disciple discovers that there is no observer-self, "no soul entity as an unknown or unknowable quantity." Nothing remains but the goal-and-the-act that accomplishes it. (Ruth Benedict, *The Chrysanthemum and the Sword*, 247–8)

The right-hemisphere culture has a great affinity for the simultaneity of the age of electric information, as Kakuzo Okakura explains: "The present is the moving infinity, the legitimate sphere of the Relative. Relativity seeks Adjustment. Adjustment is Art. The art of life lies in a constant readjustment to our surroundings." (*The Book of Tea*, 44)

The right-hemisphere culture naturally seeks to "tune" or reconfigure intervals rather than to "connect" situations and relationships:

> The Taoists claimed that the comedy of life could be made more interesting if everyone would preserve the unities. To keep the proportion of things and give place to others without losing one's own position was the secret of success in the mundane drama. We must know the whole play in order to properly act our parts; the conception of totality must never be lost in that of the individual. This Laotse illustrates by his favourite metaphor of the Vacuum. He claimed that only in vacuum lay the truly essential. The reality of a room, for instance, was to be found in vacant space enclosed by the roof and walls, not in the roof and walls themselves. The usefulness of a water pitcher dwelt in

the emptiness where water might be put, not in the form of the pitcher or the material of which it was made. Vacuum is all potent because all containing. In vacuum alone motion becomes possible. (*The Book of Tea*, 44–5)

Kakuzo adds: "In Jiu-Jitsu one seeks to draw out and exhaust the enemy's strength by non-resistance, vacuum, while conserving one's own strength for victory in the final struggle." In Western art, however, we admire the power of statement and the "bounding line" in design, whereas the right-hemisphere culture gives play to the opposite principle; instead of statement, the stress is on "the value of suggestion": "In art the importance of the same principle is illustrated by the value of suggestion. In leaving something unsaid the beholder is given a chance to complete the idea and thus a great masterpiece irresistibly rivets your attention until you seem to become actually a part of it. A vacuum is there for you to enter and fill up to the full measure of your aesthetic emotion." (*The Book of Tea*, 46)

This is of the same order as the preliterate Greek technique of mimesis, discussed earlier. By contrast, Wyndham Lewis, in *Men without Art*, maintains that the role of the artist is to prevent our becoming adjusted, since to individualized Western society the Protean "well-adjusted man" is an impercipient robot.

Julian Jaynes proposed that the preliterate Homeric hero had "no subjective consciousness, no mind, or soul, or will":

> Iliadic man did not have subjectivity as do we; he had no awareness of his awareness. No internal mind-space to introspect upon. In distinction to our own subjective conscious minds, we can call the mentality of the Myceneans a bicameral mind. Volition, planning, initiative is organized with no consciousness whatever and then "told" to the individual in his familiar language, sometimes with the visual aura of a familiar friend or authority figure or "god," or sometimes as a voice alone. The individual obeyed these hallucinated voices because he could not "see" what to do by himself. (*The Origin of Consciousness in the Breakdown of the Bicameral Mind*, 75)

The culture-heroes of preliteracy and postliteracy alike are robots.

"Robotism" for those with writing means the suppression of the conscious "observer" self or conscience so as to remove all fear and circumspection, all encumbrances to ideal performance. Such a man "becomes as the dead, who have passed beyond the necessity of taking thought about the proper course of action. The dead are no longer returning *on*; they are free. Therefore to say "I will live as one already dead" means a supreme release from conflict."[7] The Japanese use "living as one already dead" to mean that one lives on the plane of expertness. As W. B. Yeats noted in "Sailing to Byzantium,"

> I hail the superman:
>
> I call it death-in-life and life-in-death.

It entails the extinction of the left-hemisphere detached and objective self. If the result resembles detachment, it is from pushing the right hemisphere all the way, to the point of reversal of apparent characteristics. As Ruth Benedict remarks, "it is used in common, everyday exhortation. To encourage a boy who is worrying about his final examinations from middle school, a man will say, 'Take them as one already dead, and you will pass them easily.' To encourage someone who is undertaking an important business deal, a friend will say, 'Be as one already dead.' When a man goes through a great soul crisis and cannot see his way ahead, he quite commonly emerges with the resolve to live 'as one already dead'" (page 249). She continues:

> It points up vividly the difference between Western and Eastern psychology that when we speak of a conscienceless American we mean a man who no longer feels the sense of sin which should accompany wrongdoing, but that when a Japanese uses the equivalent phrase he means a man who is no longer tense and hindered. The American means a bad man; the Japanese means a good man, a trained man, a man able to use his abilities to the utmost. He means a man who can perform the most difficult and devoted deeds of unselfishness. The great American sanction for good behaviour is guilt; a man who because of a callused conscience can no longer feel this has become antisocial. The Japanese diagram the problem differently. According to their philosophy man in his inmost soul is good. If his impulse can be directly embodied in his deed, he acts virtuously and easily. Therefore, he undergoes, in "expertness," self-training to eliminate the self-censorship of shame(haji). Only then is his "sixth sense" free of hindrance; it is his supreme release from self-consciousness and conflict. (Page 251)

The paradox today is that the ground of the latest Western technologies is electronic and simultaneous, and thus is structurally right-hemisphere and "Oriental" and oral in its nature and effects. This situation began with the telegraph more than a century ago. Still, the overwhelming pattern of procedures in the Western world remains lineal, sequential, and connected in political and legal institutions, and also in education and commerce, but not in entertainment or art. A formula for complete chaos!

The ground of the Oriental right-hemisphere world, meantime, is rapidly acquiring some of the hardware connectedness of the left-hemisphere Western world. China has recently embarked on a program of alphabetic literacy, which will result in their acquiring a completely left-hemisphere cultural bias, plunging them into a new phase of individualized enterprise and aggression, for which they are already developing a ground of industrial hardware. In general, it needs to be noted that left-hemisphere man has very little power to observe or to control environments, or to see the patterns of change.

The effects of the alphabet are well-known, and by now quite predictable as we have seen them enacted in a variety of cultures and periods. But one thing is different about the modern Chinese courtship of the alphabet: the speed. It took many centuries for the alphabet to suppress the right hemisphere and the mimetic tribal bonds of the Greeks and to release the focused energy of the visual left hemisphere, for the technology had to filter up from the merchant and working classes to the aristocracy. With the Romans, too, generally only the slaves were alphabetic, and again the outward urge and thrust took some time to gather momentum: when the time was ripe—the ground was sufficient—the Alexander or Caesar appeared. China now promises fair to accomplish the same dissemination in a generation or so. The question remains whether phonetic literacy will be powerful enough to dislodge their residue of right-brain habitude, backed as it is by the new range of electronics gimmicks and media.

Left-hemisphere industrialism has blinded the Chinese to the effects of our alphabet: pattern recognition is in the right hemisphere.

The Oriental tradition reflects a particular attunement to all facets of ground, and immediate responsiveness to changes in ground configuration. Oral peoples are notoriously conservative about new technologies because of their sensibility to the side-effects involved—the new ground they bring into play—and theirs are histories of rejections of innovations. We tend to adopt anything that promises immediate efficiency or profit, and to ignore all side-effects. We pride ourselves on our uniform consistency. It is his sensitivity to ground, plus a strong sense of decorum (propriety) and a lack of private identity that enables an Oriental to change his behaviour instantly from one pattern to another. For example, until August 1945, the "chu" code of loyalty demanded of the Japanese people that they fight to the last man against the enemy. When the emperor changed the requirements of "chu" by broadcasting Japan's capitulation, the Japanese outdid themselves in expressing their co-operation with the victors.

> Occidentals cannot easily credit the ability of the Japanese to swing from one behaviour to another without psychic cost. Such extreme possibilities are not included in our experience. Yet in Japanese life the contradictions, as they seem to us, are as deeply based

in their view of life as our uniformities are in ours. It is especially important for occidentals to recognize that the "circles" into which the Japanese divide life do not include any "circle of evil." This is not to say that the Japanese do not recognize bad behaviour, but they do not see human life as a stage on which forces of good contend with forces of evil. They see existence as a drama which calls for careful balancing of the claims of one "circle" against another, each circle and each course of procedure being in itself good. (*The Chrysanthemum and the Sword*, 197)

Instead of an abstract, uniform (visual) code of conduct applicable to all situations (as a figure minus a ground), there is rather an equilibrium of properties that requires constant attunement.

In his book, *Out of Revolution*, Eugen Rosenstock-Huessy explains how the figure of Western capitalism has persisted in a program of advance by environmental destruction, without any policy of replacement of such (environmental) ground. By contrast, the right-hemisphere man, like the primitive hunter, is always intensely aware of ground, and in fact prefers ground and the experience of participation in ground to detached contemplation of figures.

Chiang Yee points to the rejection of (visual) matching and representation in Chinese art: "Verisimilitude is never a first object; it is not the bamboo in the wind that we are representing but all the thought and emotion the painter's mind when he looked upon a bamboo spray and identified his life with it for a moment." (*The Chinese Eye*, 114) He further notes, "we try, in the steps of the sages, to lose ourselves in Great Nature, to identify ourselves with her. And so in landscapes, in the paintings of flowers and birds, we try not to imitate the form, but to extract the essential feeling of the living object, having first become engulfed in the general life Stream" (page 115). The Oriental aspires not merely to love and understand a painting itself, but to probe for a meaning far beyond its confines in a world of the spirit. On these right-hemisphere terms, figure painting is a peculiar Western preoccupation that is devoid of satisfaction: "We have never elevated figure-painting as you have in the West; some of it may have a religious significance, but it seldom reaches the depths of thought which landscape attains" (page 115). It was the dominance of the left hemisphere by means of the civilizing stream of phonetic literacy that evoked in Western man the ability to detach himself from participation in his surroundings. His program to conquer nature is but one result of the enormous psychic and cultural energy released by that ground of specialist goals.

It is always the psychic and social grounds, brought into play by each medium or technology, that readjust the balance of the hemispheres and of human sensibilities into equilibrium with those grounds.

The experience of the blind amply illustrates how the shift of any component in the sensorium creates an entirely new world:

> When I came upon the myth of objectivity in certain modern thinkers, it made me angry. So there was only one world for these people, the same for everyone. And all the other worlds were to be counted as illusions left over from the past. Or why not call them by their name—hallucinations? I had learned to my cost how wrong they were.
>
> From my own experience I knew that it was enough to take from a man a memory here, an association there, to deprive him of hearing or sight, for the world to undergo immediate transformation, and for another world, entirely different but entirely coherent, to be born. Another world? Not really. The same world, rather, but seen from another angle, and counted in entirely new measures. When this happened, all the hierarchies they called objective were turned upside down, scattered to the four winds, not even like theories but like whims. (*And There Was Light*, 143–4)

This writer, Jacques Lusseyran, was made particularly aware of the right hemisphere "inner" experience afforded by blindness, by having to live in an "objective" left-hemisphere culture. Blindness creates the *seer* as much as the ancient world conceived the *seer* as blind. "Blindness works like dope, a fact we have to reckon with. I don't believe there is a blind man alive who has not felt the danger of intoxication. Like drugs, blindness heightens certain sensations, giving sudden and often disturbing sharpness to the senses of hearing and touch. But, most of all, like a drug, it develops inner as against outer experience, and sometimes to excess" (*And There Was Light*, 49). In our culture, the parallel is the caricature of inner or right-hemisphere awareness experienced by the drug culture of hallucinogenics that provide an artificial mimesis of the electric information environment.

Francis Bacon's four idols constitute the basis for a complete theory of communication in that they account for the various forms of blindness and ignorance conferred upon self and society by technology and culture alike. Each results in a transformation of sensibility, as Lusseyran notes. For the cause (ground or formal cause) of ignorance is knowledge as that of poverty is wealth; so the form of the blindness is the form or bias of sensibility. The "myth of objectivity," a result of visual bias, belongs to the "Idols of the Theatre" or what Giambattista Vico termed "the conceit of scholars" in his fourth axiom. Vico was merely following instructions when, at the outset of his *Scienza Nuova*, he set out his "Elements" or "axioms," for Bacon had prefaced his account of his "Idols" with these words:

> The formation of ideas and axioms by true induction is no doubt the proper remedy to be applied for the keeping off and cleaning away of idols. To point them out, however, is of great use for the doctrine of idols is to the interpretation of nature what the doctrine of the refutation of sophisms is in common logic.[8]

The Idols of the Tribe, and Vico's first axiom, specify the general bias of sensibility, such as the suppression of the right hemisphere by the alphabet or that of the left by radio and TV, as a pollution of exact observation which must be allowed for.[9] The Idols of the Cave, and Vico's second axiom, pinpoint intellectual laziness and conceptual dogmatism as distorting influences.[10] The Idols of the Marketplace—Vico's "conceit of nations"—arise in the "intercourse and association of men with each other,"[11] and are rooted in social and cultural preference and in the bias imposed by languages and jargons. Cleansing these Augean stables is the special task of the poet. Fourth and last, Bacon cites the Idols of the Theatre "which have immigrated into men's minds from the various doctrines of philosophies"—Old Science. These Vico terms "conceit of scholars" whose sciences have neither real antiquity of knowledge nor knowledge of antiquity, being cut off from tradition. This conceit shores up its own narrow version of thought by claiming that what it knows is what all learning has always been about.[12]

Western Old Science approaches the study of media in terms of linear, sequential transportation of data as detached figures (content); the New Science approach is via the ground of users and of environmental media effects.

The Shannon-Weaver model of communication, the basis of all contemporary Western theories of media and of communication, typifies left-brain lineal bias.

It is a kind of pipeline model of a hardware container for software content. It stresses the idea of "inside" and "outside" and assumes that communication is a kind of matching rather than resonant making:

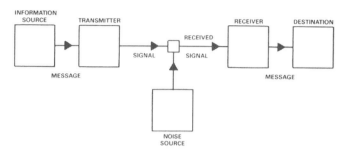

The Shannon-Weaver model of communication

The *information source* selects a desired *message* out of a set of possible messages. . . . The selected message may consist of written or spoken words, or of pictures, music, etc.

The *transmitter* changes this message into the *signal* which is actually sent over the *communication channel* from the transmitter to the *receiver*. In the case of telephony, the channel is a wire, the signal a varying electrical current on this wire; the transmitter is the site of devices (telephone transmitter, etc.) which change the sound pressure of the voice into the varying electrical current. . . . In oral speech, the information source is the brain, the transmitter is the voice mechanism producing the varying sound pressure (the signal) which is transmitted through the air (the channel). In radio, the channel is simply space (or the aether, if anyone still prefers that antiquated and misleading word), and the signal is the electromagnetic wave which is transmitted.

The *receiver* is a sort of inverse transmitter, changing the transmitted signal back into a message, and handing this message on to the destination. . . .

In the process of being transmitted, it is unfortunately characteristic that certain things are added to the signal which were not intended by the information source. These unwanted additions may be distortions of sound (in telephony, for example) or static (in radio), or distortions in shape or shading of picture (television), or errors in transmission (telegraphy or facsimile), etc. All of these changes in the transmitted signal are called *noise*. (Shannon and Weaver, *The Mathematical Theory of Communication*, 7–8)

Claude Shannon presents his theory of communication in terms of left-hemisphere verisimilitude as "first object": "The fundamental problem of communication is that of reproducing at one point either exactly or approximately a message selected at another point. Frequently the messages have *meaning*" (page 32). This is to ignore completely the ground of users and of sensibility. The Shannon-Weaver model and its descendants provide exact examples of Idols of the Theatre. In point of fact, the multiplicity of side-effects of any communication system forms an entire environment of interfacings, a kind of subculture which accompanies the central "service" or channel of communication. For example, the side-effects of the Alaska oil pipeline are the subject of a large report by the Berger Commission. The gist of this report is that the entire native population would be deprived of its environmental livelihood, were the pipeline to be built. In the same way, the side-effects of telephone or radio assume a complex system of electric technology and supporting services, the adoption of which serves as a new ground that transforms the entire user society. Equally, the system of manufacturers and roads and services that are the side-effect of the motor car alter the entire face (and odour) of any user-society.

The Shannon-Weaver model and its derivatives follow the linear pattern of efficient cause—the only sequential form of causality.

Aristotle provides the earliest systematic treatment of causes by drawing together Plato's observations. Aristotelian causality is fourfold, and is applicable both to nature and to artefacts. There are

> The material cause (the scholastic *causa materialis*), which provided the passive receptacle on which the remaining causes act—and which is anything except the matter of modern science; the formal cause (*causa formalis*), which contributed the essence, idea, or quality of the thing concerned; the motive force or efficient cause (*causa efficiens*), that is, the external compulsion that bodies had to obey; and the final cause (*causa finalis*) was the goal to which everything strove and which everything served.[13]

The first two were generally regarded as relating to *being* (right hemisphere), the last two to *becoming* (left hemisphere). As George Steiner points out, "Much of Greek drama and of the Greek theory of history is founded on the tensions which occur between realized necessity and meaningful action—that is, between Formal and Efficient Causes. Formal cause, which sends the effects ahead of the cause, found expression in Greek tragedy as Fate, or fateful necessity.[14] This doctrine of simultaneous causes lasted until the Gutenberg era when print gave complete ascendancy to visual space and modern scientific Method was born. Galileo reformulated the definition of efficient cause as the necessary and sufficient condition for the appearance of something" "that and no other is to be called cause, at the presence of which the effect always follows, and at whose removal the effect disappears."

When visual space transformed cosmology and the logos alike from resonant ground to rational figure, the mode of understanding of formal causality shifted from dynamic to abstract and ideal. Aristotle retains and confuses the oral nature of formal cause, which explains why he frequently confuses formal and final cause. Final cause, inherent in the thing from the outset, came to be misinterpreted in left-hemisphere terms as the end-point of a series of efficient causes. Bacon noted, in his *New Science*, how visual bias "interferes mischievously in the discovery of caus-es" and distorts the understanding of final causes in particular.[15] Such distortions he termed "Idols of the Tribe," and observed of sensory bias in general that "the human understanding is like a false mirror, which, receiving rays irregularly, distorts and colors the nature of things by mingling its own nature with it" (*Novum Organum*, Bk. I, xli, 34). Formal cause is usually regarded as the "defining formu-la" or definition of a thing's essence (its *form* or the "whatness" whereby we know a thing). Prior to visual space, formal cause coincided with logos as a figure/ground concern with the thing, structurally, inclusive of its whole pattern of side-effects on the ground of users.[16]

In the left hemisphere, however, formal cause is translated into a kind of Platonic abstract ideal blueprint that is never perfectly realized in any given mate-rial example. Such is the understanding of Northrop Frye, one of the principal mod-ern exponents of Platonic and Aristotelian ideas as passed through Freud and Jung. He is consistent in his left-hemisphere approach. Referring to the Jungian doc-trine of archetypes, Wimsatt and Brooks comment that "For Northrop Frye the dis-covery points to the possibility of turning literary criticism for the first time into a true science. No true science, he argues, can be content to rest in the structural analy-sis of the object with which it deals. The poet is only the *efficient* cause of the poem, but the poem, having form, has a formal cause that is to be sought. On examina-tion, Frye finds this formal cause to be the archetype."[17]

Frye is adamant on the point:

> An original painter knows, of course, that when the public demands likeness to an object, it generally wants the exact opposite, likeness to the pictorial conventions it is familiar with. Hence when he breaks with these conventions, he is often apt to assert that he is nothing but an eye, that he merely paints what he sees as he sees it, and the like. His motive in talking such nonsense is clear enough: he wishes to say that the paint-ing is not merely facile decoration, and involves a difficult conquest of some very real spatial problems. But this may be freely admitted without agreeing that the formal cause of a picture is outside the picture, an assertion which would destroy the whole art if it were taken seriously. (*Anatomy of Criticism*, 132)

There is absolutely no provision here for ground of any kind: his archetype is exactly a figure minus a ground (*vide* the discussion in *From Cliché to Archetype*). Otherwise it would be perfectly natural to observe, with the rhetoricians and gram-marians, that the formal cause of the poem, painting, or whatever is its ground: the audience (the user) and the configuration of sensibilities in the culture at the time the artefact was produced.

The four causes as a mode of exegesis of nature had been regarded as parallel to the "four levels" of interpretation of scripture by medieval grammarians (e.g., St.

Bonaventure).[18] In each case, the "fours" were simultaneous, and both systems were rendered obsolescent by the Renaissance push into visual space and left-hemisphere dominance. Figure/ground resonance and the interplay of levels and causes were eliminated, with the further advantage, from the standpoint of the *moderni*, of cutting all bondage and allegiance to the traditions. Bunge summarizes the practical left-hemisphere advantages of dumping manifold causality:

> Some of the grounds for the Renaissance reduction of causes to the *causa efficiens* were the following: (a) it was, of all the four, the sole clearly conceived one; (b) hence it was mathematically expressible; (c) it could be assigned an empirical correlate, namely, an event (usually a motion) producing another event (usually another motion) in accordance with fixed rules; the remaining causes, on the other hand, were not definable in empirical terms, hence they were not empirically testable; (d) as a consequence, the efficient cause was controllable; moreover, its control was regarded as leading to the harnessing of nature, which was the sole aim of the instrumental (pragmatic) conception of science. (*Causality*, 32–3)

All Western "scientific" models of communication are, like the Shannon-Weaver model, linear, logical, and sequential in accordance with the pattern of efficient causality.

These are all in the figure-minus-ground mode of the left hemisphere, and in contrast do not relate to the effects of simultaneity and discontinuity and resonance that typify experience in an electric culture. For use in the electric age, a right-hemisphere model of communication is necessary, both because our culture has nearly completed the process of shifting its cognitive modes from the left to the right hemisphere, and because the electronic media themselves are right-hemisphere in their patterns and operation. The problem is to discover such a model that yet is congenial to our culture with its residuum of left-hemisphere tradition. Such a model would have to take into account the apposition of both figure and ground instead of concentrating solely on an abstract sequence or movement isolated from any ground.

CHAPTER SIXTEEN

Marshall McLuhan's Theory of Communication
The Yegg[1]

ERIC MCLUHAN

Whenever provoked, Marshall McLuhan would declare, "Look, I don't have a theory of communication. I don't use theories. I just watch what people do, what *you* do." Or words to that effect. That's the short answer to our question, "What is McLuhan's Theory of Communication?" Perhaps I should end the chapter here. The long answer follows.

As he often said, Marshall McLuhan did not have A Theory of Communication. Of course, he did have definite notions about what constituted communication and what did not. He insisted regularly, though, that he didn't have A Theory of Communication, and that he didn't use theories in his work. Instead, he would aver, he "used observation"; he used "probes." It is a matter of how you begin: if you begin with theory, then one way or another your research winds up geared to making the case for or against the truth of the theory. Begin with theory, you begin with the answer; begin with observation, you begin with questions. A theory always becomes a scientific point of view and a *way of seeing* the job at hand. Begin with observation and your task is to look at things and to look at what happens. To see. That necessitates detachment, and training of critical awareness.

When McLuhan insisted that he didn't use theories, he meant that he didn't use them in the way that people expect theories to be used. "I don't have a 'theory of communication'" means "I don't work in the way of Normal Science." "I don't start with a theory to prove or disprove or submit to the torturers. I start with—

and stick with—observation." He cared less for ideas about actuality than he cared for actuality itself. This stance is also quite consistent with Francis Bacon's insistence on observation: both men were committed empiricists. At Cambridge and later, he found much to admire in Bacon's work. Observation necessitates using all points of view at once.

Commenting on something he had written or said four years earlier, McLuhan (1971) offered these remarks:

> In the four years since making the above observations I have discovered very many things about media and education. It is now perfectly plain to me that all media are environments. As environments, all media have all the effects that geographers and biologists have associated with environments in the past. Environments shape their occupants. One person, complaining about my observation that "the medium is the message," simply said: "McLuhan means that the medium has no content." This remark was extremely useful to me because it revealed the obvious, namely, the content of any medium is the user. This applies equally to electric lights, any language whatever, and, of course, housing, motor cars, and even tools of any sort. It is obvious that the user or content of any medium is completely conformed to the character of this man-made environment. His entire sensory life arranges its hierarchies and dominance in accordance with the environment in which he operates.
>
> If we say "mist on the moors tonight," we are inclined to call it poetic. When the sensory inputs are dim, the sensory response is correspondingly strong. This is why small children are always "poetic" in their responses to anything at all. A child's sensory reception is very selective, somewhat in the manner of what is offered our senses by "abstract" art. And just because the sensory offering is meagre, the sensory response is full. As we grow older, we dim down the sensory responses, and increase the sensory inputs, turning ourselves into robots. That is why art is indispensable for human survival. Art perpetually dislocates our usual sensory responses by offering a very abstract or meagre and selective input.
>
> The medium is the message because the environment transforms our perceptions governing the areas of attention and neglect alike. . . . Nearly everything that I write is concerned with areas of *exploration* in which I am actively engaged in discovery. That is why I say "I have no point of view." Anyone engaged in exploration uses every available approach, every available foothold, every accessible crevice to which to cling as he scales the unknown rock-face. The actual process of dialogue and discovery is not compatible with packaging of familiar views.
>
> A person engaged in exposition has nothing new to say, and he cannot communicate the effect of participating in the process of discovery. The TV age demands participation in this process and it is for that reason that all existing education, insofar as it is concerned with expounding what is already known, is entirely unacceptable to students. . . . [2]

What could be clearer? Under such conditions, a theory would pose a distinct liability.

When Stephen Hawking discusses his own theory of communication, it becomes immediately obvious that one function of a theory in the hands of a scientist is to prod reality into revealing itself: "we cannot distinguish what is real about the universe without a theory," he writes. A good, elegant theory will describe a wide array of observations and predict the results of new ones. "Beyond that, it makes no sense," he points out, "to ask if [a theory] corresponds to reality, because we do not know what reality is independent of a theory."[3] A theory is a way of seeing and, as such, it is a formal cause of reality.

Everywhere in his writing, whether about media or culture or poetics, McLuhan probed the nature of communication and change and perception. *Laws of Media* is an extended meditation on communication and human perception, and it comments directly on theories of communication, Eastern and Western. *Understanding Media*, *Through the Vanishing Point*, *The Gutenberg Galaxy*, and *From Cliché to Archetype*, to name a few, are extended essays on media, perception and communication. Attending to how media and environments massaged the sensibilities naturally brought into focus the function of the arts[4]—all of the arts at once, though they have tended to operate independently. These concerns prompted some seminal meditations in *Through the Vanishing Point*. Here is the opening paragraph: it is a good résumé of McLuhan's "theory" of communication, that is, of change.

> Since the advent of electric circuitry in the early nineteenth century, the need for sensory awareness has become more acute. Perhaps the mere speed-up of human events and the resulting increase of interfaces among all men and institutions ensure a multitude of innovations that upset all existing arrangements whatever.
>
> By the same token, men have groped toward the arts in hope of increased sensory awareness. The artist has the power to discern the current environment created by the latest technology. Ordinary human instinct causes people to recoil from these new environments and to rely on the rear-view mirror as a kind of repeat or ricorso of the preceding environment, thus ensuring total disorientation at all times. It is not that there is anything wrong with the old environment, but it simply will not serve as a navigational aid to the new one.[5]

The concluding essay of the book, "The Emperor's New Clothes," opens with these observations:

> In his poem "Esthétique du Mal" Wallace Stevens writes:
> This is the thesis scrivened in delight,
> The reverberating psalm, the right chorale.
> One might have thought of sight, but who could think

Of what it sees, for all the ill it sees?

Speech found the ear, for all the evil sound,

But the dark italics it could not propound.

And out of what one sees and hears and out

Of what one feels, who could have thought to make

So many selves, so many sensuous worlds,

As if the air, the mid-day air, was swarming

With the metaphysical changes that occur,
Merely in living as and where we live.

He indicates that the slightest shift in the level of visual intensity produces a subtle modulation in our sense of ourselves, both private and corporate. Since technologies are extensions of our own physiology, they result in new programs of an environmental kind. Such pervasive experiences as those deriving from the encounter with environments almost inevitably escape perception. When two or more environments encounter one another by direct interface, they tend to manifest their distinctive qualities. Comparison and contrast have always been a means of sharpening perception in the arts as well as in general experience. Indeed, it is upon this pattern that all the structures of art have been reared. Any artistic endeavor includes the preparing of an environment for human attention. A poem or a painting is in every sense a teaching machine for the training of perception and judgment. The artist is a person who is especially aware of the challenge and dangers of new environments presented to human sensibility. Whereas the ordinary person seeks security by numbing his perception against the impact of new experience, the artist delights in this novelty and instinctively creates situations that both reveal it and compensate for it. The artist studies the distortion of sensory life produced by new environmental programming and tends to create artistic situations that correct the sensory bias and derangement brought about by the new form. In social terms the artist can be regarded as a navigator who gives adequate compass bearings in spite of magnetic deflection of the needle by the changing play of forces. So understood, the artist is not a peddler of new ideals or lofty experiences. He is rather the indispensable aid to action and reflection alike.[6]

The role of the artist became a central concern in modern poetics with, first, the Symbolists, then with Wordsworth, Coleridge and Matthew Arnold, and later Eliot and Pound—all of whom contributed to McLuhan's thought on these matters. The role of the senses is fundamental to understanding how media influence culture and transform their users. *Through the Vanishing Point* counterpoints two arts simultaneously; it uses each art as a means of probing the other into revealing itself. This double-plot form McLuhan found a tremendously powerful method of investigation: counterpose two situations and use each as a means of seeing the other. Each situation consists of a figure and a ground. Several paragraphs following the words above, we find—

> Perhaps the most precious possession of man is his abiding awareness of the analogy of proper proportionality, the key to all metaphysical insight and perhaps the very condition of consciousness itself. This analogical awareness is constituted of a perpetual play of ratios among ratios: A is to B what C is to D, which is to say that the ratio between A and B is proportioned to the ratio between C and D, there being a ratio between these ratios as well. This lively awareness of the most exquisite delicacy depends upon there being no connection whatever between the components. If A were linked to B, or C to D, mere logic would take the place of analogical perception. Thus one of the penalties paid for literacy and a high visual culture is a strong tendency to encounter all things through a rigorous story line, as it were. Paradoxically, connected spaces and situations exclude participation whereas discontinuity affords room for involvement. Visual space is connected and creates detachment or noninvolvement. It also tends to exclude the participation of the other senses.[7]

The theme of analogical ratios (A is to B as C is to D) is resumed in McLuhan's last-published book, *Laws of Media: The New Science,* where it relates all of man's technologies and innovations to human speech. Analogical relations also formed a major element of *From Cliché to Archetype* (1970). I have appended the chapter on Mimesis from that study: the opening epigram alone would serve as a brief statement of McLuhan's view of communication: "The entire world of technology makes sense by miming the human body and faculties." Equally, the last sentence or two could be taken as encapsulating McLuhan's "theory":

> By way of resonance and repetition, "The soul is in a way all existing things." As the hand, with its extensions, probes and shapes the physical environment, so the soul or mind, with its extensions of speech, probes and orders and retrieves the man-made environment of artifacts and archetypes.
>
> A cliché is an act of consciousness: total consciousness is the sum of all the clichés of all the media or technologies that we probe with.

McLuhan often pointed out that the West has no theory of communication: we are denied one by our visual bias. That is to say, we have no theory of change. Communication means change: if something is communicated the recipient has changed in some manner or degree. Our "commonsense" idea of communication is merely one of transporting messages from point to point. Shannon & Weaver laid the foundation of all Western "theories of communication" with their model:

Source > Message > Channel (+ Noise)> Recipient

But it is a *transport*ation theory only, not a theory of communication.[8] They are concerned merely to get a bundle of goodies from one place to another, while keeping *Noise* to a minimum. But their "theory" contains no provision for change—except perhaps in re *Noise* (which they shun as debilitating).

Here is how McLuhan framed the idea of a series in a letter to Ralph Cohen, editor of *New Literary History*, 13 July 1973:

> The media are themselves, of course, mythic form in every sense, since they are epic enterprises involving all mankind in new environments of service and disservice. Joyce had discovered that all technologies are events of vision in human biology. Ralph Waldo Emerson wrote: "The human body is a magazine of inventions. . . . All the tools and engines on earth are only extensions of its limbs and senses." Joyce uses the "magazine" metaphor throughout the *Wake* apropos "the magazine wall where the maggies seen all", i.e. the magi, the wise people saw the entire story of human technology in the structure of the human body. Joyce proceeded to work out in detail the laws of the media which we have gradually learned to formulate as follows: that an intense impact, some shock or crisis, produces a moment of fission or abstraction of some part or function of the body and embeds it in a new material outside the body. This amounts to a new posture or situation of the old body which engenders a chain reaction both in the senses and in the environment.

Then he suggests the topic in which this book had its genesis: the idea of brief studies of the theories of communication of famous or important figures in major fields.

> I think I have already mentioned the desirability of a whole series of studies of theories of communication mounted upon all familiar figures in the arts and sciences. Since "communication" means change, any theory of communication, must naturally concentrate on the sort of public with which they felt themselves to be confronted. It is this public which always affects the structures which the performer chooses to adopt, and it is this public which he seeks to shape and alter in some way.

Although Ralph Cohen didn't leap at the suggestion, we kept the idea "on the back burner" for years. (Four of the chapters in this collection were written after this note.) The matter did arise again, a few years later, when we wrote up a proposal to make such a series (see Chapter One). Though Marshall McLuhan may not have used theories to shape or guide his own work, he did have definite ideas about what constituted communication, namely, the effect. Quite simply: no effect means no communication.

He found hundreds of passages in the work of the Moderns—Yeats, Joyce, Pound, Lewis, Eliot—where they speak frankly about their Theories of Communication and of the role of the poet or the artist in the new electric culture. Let me give three cases in point. Eliot, for one, never stops talking about communication, in his verse as well as in his prose. For example, here is a passage McLuhan flagged as "TOC" material, at the end of Eliot's meditation on "What Dante Means to Me":

> I may say that the great poet should not only perceive and distinguish more clearly than other men, the colours or sounds within the range of ordinary vision or hearing; he should perceive vibrations beyond the range of ordinary men, and be able to make men see and hear more at each end [of the spectrum] than they could ever see without his help. We have for instance in English literature great religious poets, but they are, by comparison with Dante, specialists. That is all they can do. And Dante, because he could do everything else, is for that reason the greatest 'religious' poet, though to call him a 'religious poet' would be to abate his universality.[9]

The next sentences turn from the ideal poet to the effect:

> *The Divine Comedy* expresses everything in the way of emotion, between depravity's despair and the beatific vision, that man is capable of experiencing. It is therefore a constant reminder to the poet, of the obligation to explore, to find words for the inarticulate, to capture those feelings which people can hardly even feel, because they have no words for them; and at the same time a reminder that the explorer beyond the frontiers of ordinary consciousness will only be able to return and report to his fellow-citizens, if he has all the time a firm grasp upon the realities with which they are already acquainted.

Eliot expands and clarifies this, the focus of what might be called his Theory of Communication, in the next paragraph:

> These two achievements of Dante are not to be thought of as separate or separable. The task of the poet, in making people comprehend the incomprehensible, demands immense resources of language; and in developing the language, enriching the meaning of words and showing how much words can do, he is making possible a much greater range of emotion and perception for other men, because he gives them the speech in which more can be expressed.

Join this piece to what he wrote in "Tradition and the Individual Talent"[10] (1919), another frequent McLuhan resort, and it is possible to appreciate the full outlines of Eliot's complex sense of poetry and of the poet as communicator. Everywhere he is conscious of the effect that great poetry must have, and does have.

At about the same time, Ezra Pound wrote "The Serious Artist"[11] (1913). The two essays are so complementary that Eliot must have had Pound's in mind or in front of him as he penned his own. "The Serious Artist" could equally stand as Pound's "Theory of Communication," as could any of a hundred other pieces and remarks in both his poetry and his prose. The celebrated *ABC of Reading* is an elab-

orate statement of such a Theory. Many a statement inside would provide a starting point: "Artists are the antennae of the race." "Good writers are those who keep
the language efficient. That is to say, keep it accurate, keep it clear." "Language is
the main means of human communication. If an animal's nervous system does not
transmit sensations and stimuli, the animal atrophies. If a nation's literature declines,
the nation atrophies." All of these words had been flagged by McLuhan as "TOC"
material. It becomes clear, reading both men, just how central to their enterprise is
the training of perception and of critical awareness, and not only for the poet: the
reader gets it as a side-effect of the working-over the verse gives him. *Hypocrite
lecteur*. It goes without saying that any Theory that so concentrates on effect is willy-
nilly fundamentally rhetorical. The heart of rhetoric is Decorum—a sensitive attun-
ing of audience, effect, and occasion/circumstance, at every stage of the poetic
process from invention to delivery.

Harold Bloom remarked that the popularity of Walt Whitman's poetry in
South America gives unexpected salience to the matter of effect. Having had his
impact on English verse and English-speaking consciousness in the late nineteenth century, Whitman is having exactly the effect Eliot and Pound insist it is the
poet's job to produce, but on another culture entirely and a full century later. Bloom
quotes an apposite remark by Neruda:

Pablo Neruda, by general consent Walt Whitman's truest heir, said that the
appeal of Whitman to Spanish poets "was that he taught how to see and name what
had not been seen or named before."

> Poetry in South America is a different matter altogether. You see there are in our coun-
> tries rivers which have no names, trees which nobody knows, and birds which nobody
> has described. It is easier for us to be surrealistic because everything we know is new.
> Our duty, then, as we understand it, is to express what is unheard of. Everything has
> been painted in Europe, everything has been sung in Europe, But not in America. In
> that sense, Whitman was a great teacher. Because what is Whitman? He was not only
> intensely conscious, but he was open-eyed! He had tremendous eyes to see everything—
> he taught us to see things. He was our poet.[12]

Wyndham Lewis, another of the group called the Moderns, wrote tirelessly
about matters of communication and did not shrink from giving his own thoughts
as to what constituted communication [as discussed in Chapter One, above]. Even
W. B. Yeats, though of a less analytic bent than Eliot or Pound, often meditated on
the process of communication and how to improve the effect of his sonorities on
his audience. His "The Circus Animals' Desertion," a poem about a bout of writer's
block, became a focus of *From Cliché to Archetype*; it provided a key to the processes of retrieval and archetypalization that played such a large role in McLuhan's
thinking:

Those masterful images because complete

Grew in pure mind, but out of what began?

A mound of refuse or the sweepings of a street,

Old kettles, old bottles and a broken can,

Old iron, old bones, old rags, that raving slut

Who keeps the till. Now that my ladder's gone,

I must lie down where all the ladders start,

In the foul rag-and-bone shop of the heart

In one of his late essays, Yeats wrote,

I wanted all my poetry to be spoken on a stage or sung and, because I did not understand my own instincts, gave half a dozen wrong or secondary reasons; but a month ago
I understood my reasons. I have spent my life in clearing out of poetry every phrase written for the eye, and bringing all back to syntax that is for the ear alone. Let the eye take
delight in the form of the singer and in the panorama of the stage and be content with
that.[13]

Evidently Yeats paid considerable attention to his reader and carefully adjusted his poems to secure specific effects on that sensibility. And all of these passages
had been earmarked by McLuhan as focal in each man's TOC. Perhaps they will
illustrate what he looked for in considering someone's Theory. The same annotations about "TOC" appear in every sort of book in his library.

Our question remains: How, without theories, did he himself work?

Absent a theory, the other way to work is by observation and investigative technique, like a CSI detective: first the evidence; then later, much later, the theory—
if indeed one is necessary by then. Francis Bacon, whom McLuhan greatly admired,
was not shy of pointing to the liabilities of theorizing prematurely. He would have
made a great Grissom. In the *Novum Organum*, he cautioned,

XIX

There are and can be only two ways of searching into and discovering truth. The one
flies from the senses and particulars to the most general axioms, and from these principles, the truth of which it takes for settled and immovable, proceeds to judgment and
to the discovery of middle axioms. And this way is now in fashion.[14] The other derives
axioms from the senses and particulars, rising by a gradual and unbroken ascent, so that
it arrives at the most general axioms last of all. This is the true way, but as yet untried.

A little later, speaking of the "Idols of the Market-Place," he advised, "This class
of idols is more easily expelled, because to get rid of them it is only necessary that

all theories should be steadily rejected and dismissed as obsolete."[15] Bacon had also exploited the "power of writing in aphorisms," meaning, writing discontinuous prose as a method of probing and exploration. Connected, polished prose gives the impression that all is known, all is understood. Aphorisms, or probes, by contrast, being brief, pungent, discontinuous, Bacon called "knowledge broken": because incomplete, they invite people to dig deeper and to close the gaps. The connected statement is "more fitted to win consent or belief"; the probe, "to point to action" and discovery for oneself. Bacon makes the point in *The Advancement of Learning*:

> But as young men, when they knit and shape perfectly, do seldom grow to a further stature; so knowledge, while it is in aphorisms and observations, it is in growth; but when it once is [rendered in connected prose], it may perchance be further polished and illustrate[d] and accommodated for use and practice; but it increaseth no more in bulk and substance.[16]

Bacon makes it perfectly clear that he considered his own aphoristic style an integral part of a scientific technique of keeping knowledge in a state of emergent evolution. On these same grounds, McLuhan trained himself to write discontinuously about media and environments, having found the aphoristic "probe" style preferable to that of conventional explanation. It provides a way to train sensibility and at the same time to coax experience into revealing its patterns. Bacon:

> For first, it trieth the writer, whether he be superficial or solid: for aphorisms, except they should be ridiculous, cannot be made but of the pith and heart of sciences; for discourse of illustration is cut off; recitals of examples are cut off; discourse of connexion and order is cut off; descriptions of practice are cut off. So there remaineth nothing to fill the aphorisms but some good quantity of observation: and therefore no man can suffice, nor in reason will attempt, to write aphorisms, but he that is sound and grounded.[17]

The problem faced by any explorer in our time, as McLuhan observed, is to invent tools that reveal the current situation, not to make logical connected statements:

> Connected, sequential discourse, which is thought of as rational, is really visual. It has nothing to do with reason as such. Reasoning does not occur on single planes or in a continuous, connected fashion. The mind leapfrogs. It puts things together in all sorts of proportions and ratios instantly. To put down thoughts in coded, lineal ways was a discovery of the Greek world. It is not done this way, for example, in the Chinese world. But to deny that the Chinese have access to reason would be ridiculous. They do not have rational discourse at all by Western standards. They reason by the act of interval, not by the act of connection. In the electric age we are moving into a world where not the connection but the interval becomes the crucial event in organization. [18]

In 1968, McLuhan wrote an Introduction to Harold Innis's *The Bias of Communication*.[19] It is a remarkable performance because so much of what he says about Innis's methods applies directly to his own. For example, he notes that Innis had made the same switch from connected prose to discontinuity and probing:

> [He] changed his procedure from working with a "point of view" to that of the generating of insights by the method of "interface" as it is named in chemistry. "Interface" refers to the interaction of substances in a kind of mutual irritation. In art and poetry this is precisely the technique of "symbolism" (Greek, *symballein*—to throw together) with its paratactic procedure of juxtaposing without connectives. It is the natural form of conversation or dialogue rather than of written discourse. In writing, the tendency is to isolate an aspect of some matter and to direct steady attention upon that aspect. In dialogue, there is an equally natural interplay of multiple aspects of any matter.

McLuhan had made the switch when he began to study media and environments. This interplay of aspects can generate insights or discoveries:

> By contrast, a point of view is merely a way of *looking at* something. But an insight is a sudden awareness of a complex process of interaction. An insight is a contact with the life of forms. Students of computer programming have had to learn how to approach all knowledge structurally. In order to transfer any kind of knowledge to tapes it is necessary to understand the form of that knowledge. This has led to the discovery of the basic difference between classified knowledge and pattern recognition. It is a helpful distinction to keep in mind when reading Innis since he is above all a recognizer of patterns.

It is also the basic difference between connected, rational prose and the aphoristic style. And it is a helpful distinction to keep in mind when reading McLuhan's later prose.

McLuhan's celebrated "technique of discovery" consisted in applying the Symbolist art of juxtaposing forms, which everywhere leads to a series of dramatic surprises. He applied artistic methods directly to the materials and circumstances of everyday life. He discovered that the formal sensibilities of the artist could be applied outside the realm of art as the surest way to explore environments and their effects. In "The Emperor's Old Clothes" he noted that the way a technology intrudes into a culture can suddenly illuminate relations between things normally regarded as separate:

> It does help to look at the newspaper as a direct, exploratory probe into the environment. Seen in this light, there is more meaning in the aesthetic bonds between the poet, the sleuth, and even the criminal. For James Bond, Humphrey Bogart, Rimbaud, and Hemingway are all figures who explore the shifting frontiers of morals and society. They

are engaged in detecting the social environment by probing and transgression. For to probe is to cross boundaries of many kinds; to discover the patterns of new environments requires a rigorous study and inventory of sensuous effects. The components of new environments cannot be discovered directly. Edgar Allan Poe's detective, Dupin, is an aesthete. The aesthetes were the first to use the senses consciously and systematically as probes into the environment. Walter Pater's injunction, "To burn always with a hard gem-like flame," referred to the action of the plumber's blowtorch, a technical invention of his day.

Every dominant technological or social or cultural form, together with all its causal powers, is always hidden by a process of protective inhibition: these forms are so total, so environmental as to resist every effort to notice or investigate them.

Thanks in part to the perceptual training in Practical Criticism, McLuhan had discovered a means of using historical situations to reveal the present. He reports the technique as he finds it in Innis:

Innis taught us how to use the bias of culture and communication as an instrument of research. By directing attention to the bias or distorting power of the dominant imagery and technology of any culture, he showed us how to understand cultures. Many scholars have made us aware of the "difficulty of assessing the quality of a culture of which we are a part or of assessing the quality of a culture of which we are not a part." Innis was perhaps the first to make of this vulnerable fact of all scholarly outlook the prime opportunity for research and discovery.

. . . At a stroke he had solved two major problems that are forever beyond the power of the "nose-counters" and of statistical researchers. First, he knew what the pattern of any culture had to be, both physically and socially, as soon as he had identified its major technological achievements. Second, he knew exactly what the members of that culture would be ignorant of in their daily lives. What has been called "the nemesis of creativity" is precisely a blindness to the effects of one's most significant form of invention.

Without a theory as a guide, the explorer must rely on his box of tools and his native wits. In 1967, McLuhan described his own "method" of observation this way:

Literally, *Understanding Media* is a kit of tools for analysis and perception. It is to *begin* an operation of discovery. It is not the completed work of discovery. It is intended for practical use. Most of my work in the media is like that of a safecracker. In the beginning I don't know what's inside. I just set myself down in front of the problem and begin to work. I grope, I probe, I listen, I test—until the tumblers fall and I'm in. That's the way I work with all these media.[20]

I'm perfectly prepared to scrap any statement I ever made about any subject once I find that it isn't getting me into the problem. I have no devotion to any of my probes as if they were sacred opinions. I have no proprietary interest in my ideas and no pride of authorship as such. You have to push any idea to an extreme, you have to probe.

Exaggeration, in the sense of hyperbole, is a major artistic device in all modes of art. No painter, no musician ever did anything without extreme exaggeration of a form or a mode, until he had exaggerated those qualities that interested him.[21]

The Tool Kit in *Understanding Media: The Extensions of Man* consists for the most part of the chapters in Part One. They detail, in seven essays, general principles of the functioning of media in shaping culture and society. *Understanding Media* was conceived and written as a companion to a volume that had appeared a short while earlier, *Understanding Poetry*,[22] by Cleanth Brooks and Robert Penn Warren. It was the first American text to employ techniques of Practical Criticism. McLuhan continued to insist that *Understanding Media* was not a finished product but a group of beginnings, a tool kit and some preliminary forays into new territory.

Chief among McLuhan's tools of analysis was Practical Criticism, which he picked up at Cambridge while it was still enjoying the first flush of its applications. It had been invented there in response to a scandal involving the English Department that surfaced in 1929 with the publication of *Practical Criticism; a Study of Literary Judgment*.[23] Just a few years later, McLuhan arrived to find the University still a-flutter and the English Department busy exploring and adapting the new technique.[24] Its weaknesses and its range of uses were the subject of vigorous debate. One result: the founding of a critical journal, *Scrutiny*, and the production of numerous probing books and essays. *Scrutiny* demonstrated its areas of applicability to be virtually endless: Practical Criticism worked equally incisively across all of the arts and through all areas of culture, from high-brow to low. It is a kind of critic's Swiss Army Knife.

The strengths and weaknesses McLuhan dissected in the essay, "Poetic vs. Rhetorical Exegesis" (Chapter Eight, above). Practical Criticism can tell the reader nearly everything about a poem except whether or not it is a good poem. Significantly, Practical Criticism is not theory-based: it is performance-based. It relies on observation and critical judgment—learned skills. It is a technique of interpretation that looks for four kinds of meaning in a piece of writing: the literal sense, the feeling of the speaker about the subject, the tone (attitude to reader), the intent—the effect sought. (Four-level interpretation of this sort was practiced continuously, from the Greek and Roman grammarians before Cicero and Varro throughout the Middle Ages to the eighteenth century.) The technique rests on oft-neglected oral dimensions of writing, as it is based on performance of the text. Learning this aspect takes considerable practice. The beholder must read aloud—perform—the passage or poem in a variety of ways so as to locate the right speaker's voice, the attitude, the tone to the reader (and thereby locate the reader). In this way, the critic can find his bearings in *any* prose or poetics—whatever the subject, the field, the period, the style. The same training of critical sensibility affords the user instant access to each of the arts at every level of culture and sophistication from top to bottom. Popular culture and entertainments yielded to the technique as easily as did the nobler sentiments and more refined images of classical Art. As if to prove this point, F. R. Leavis produced *Culture and Environment*, applying the technique to journalism and ads and other popular forms. A few years later, McLuhan published his first book, *The Mechanical Bride*, in the same vein.

Practical Criticism makes the ideal Grammarian's tool because of its extraordinary portability from field to field. The grammarian (from Greek, *gramma*, letters—Latin, *litera*—hence a grammarian, a literary man, a man of letters) took all written texts as his province. This purview begins with the traditional "Two Books," the man-made book and the Book of Nature. Grammarians read and interpreted each book, the writing on the page as well as the writing on the wall, with equal facility and with the same tools. (And so the true Grammarian had to be doubly encyclopedic.) The latter course leads directly to the study of media and environments. McLuhan had devoted his doctoral thesis to a close examination of the Western intellectual traditions, the Trivium and Quadrivium, long known as the seven liberal arts. They are Rhetoric, Dialectic and Grammar; and Music, Astronomy, Mathematics and Geometry. He traced the continuous line of their development from the ancient world to the Renaissance (the focus of the thesis) and indicated its further lines of development up to the present. Practical Criticism is distinctly rhetorical, both because of its structure and approach, and because of its insistence on including the audience as a factor when considering any poem. Through *mimesis*, the audience is included in the poem and can be accessed by that route. The user is the content. Grammar's twin concerns are the techniques of interpretation and etymology (the subtitle of *Understanding Media* identifies their etymologies as "*Extensions of Man*"). Grammar is necessarily encyclopedic. Media and literature, then, are not separate fields of interest: they are parallel texts that yield to parallel techniques of investigation. One job, as it were; two job sites. The ancients had two parallel systems for exegesis of their Two Books: the four causes for the Book of Nature, and the "four levels" of interpretation for either Book, sacred or profane: Holy Scripture or the man-made book. With a host of essays and *The Mechanical Bride*, McLuhan proved he was adept with Practical Criticism in the Book of the world. In 1944, he published "The Analogical Mirrors" in *The Kenyon Review*.[25] In this study, he took the other approach and performed a spectacular—and entirely traditional—four-level exegesis[26] of Gerard Manley Hopkins's poem "The Windhover."

McLuhan and Innis fell prey to the same myopia in their respective audiences. The audience for Innis's Economics writings resolutely ignored his work on media and culture (and for the most part continues to do so today); his "media audience" returned the favour and showed but passing interest in his work on economics—another condition which has not much changed with the passage of time. McLuhan's two audiences—one for his literary output, one for his media work—did the same: each ignored the work that absorbed the interest of the other. (In both cases, academic colleagues appeared to regard the bare act of paying attention to the other-worldly topic a massive intellectual blunder, made the worse by dwelling on it. Academic snobbery can be brutal.)

McLuhan referred to his procedure as starting with a problem and digging into the toolkit for something to open the matter up for elucidation. Let me give you some idea of the tools that kit held.

First, as background, a firm knowledge of the entire tradition, the *translatio studii*, from Homer to the present. Add to that a firm knowledge of the Trivium (Rhetoric, Dialectic and Grammar), an extensive knowledge of English Literature, prose and poetry, a profound knowledge of the English language, an immense vocabulary, and a deep and abiding curiosity about etymology, nourished by a knowledge of French, Latin, German, Greek, etc.

The aphoristic style, learned from Bacon and from modern ad-men, provided much more than a way of expressing things: it supplies a way of thinking in outlines and seeing whole structures.

The ability to perform traditional multi-level exegesis made short work of assessing complexity in prose and verse, old and new, and gave swift entry into a range of texts.

Equally, long practice with Practical Criticism meant a quick and sure means of entry into any human "text" product or service.

The tool kit given in *Understanding Media*, comprises the seven general principles of media in Part One:

The Medium/Environment is the Message

Hot and Cool: high and low definition

Reversal of the Overheated Medium

The Gadget Lover

Hybrid Energy

Media as Translators

Challenge and Collapse

To these, let us add the set of transformations (ongoing processes) that form the backbone of *Take Today*. Each of these is a response to pressure exerted by working at the speed of light:

Centralism yields to Decentralism

Hardware yields to Software

Jobs yield to Role-Playing

The last book, *Laws of Media: The New Science* brought to light the tetrad, the most powerful tool ever, among a number of additional observations and techniques.

Probes. A phrase, a sentence or paragraph or more could suddenly join the lists from current reading or study. These were of general use—they could clarify several matters, so tended to remain on hand for a while and find their way into many things written at the time. We'd have them in mind when working on some new project, some book or article, or a letter here or there. Anything could serve as a probe to get at the heart of something. This would encompass anything from a poet's considered observations to scraps of doggerel or prose. For example, "The Emotion of Multitude," a brief essay (2 pages) by W. B. Yeats proved especially fruitful for a period and was often quoted in full. It discusses the effect of juxtaposing two situations—the artistic effect, but we found it applies to a far broader spectrum.

Of quotes used as probes there were literally hundreds—the product of a well-stocked memory and a well-stocked library. We have seen how Yeats's remarks about "the foul rag-and-bone shop" spurred the book *From Cliché to Archetype*. T. S. Eliot's observations about "the auditory imagination," so variously useful, appears more than once in these pages. Here, from a different quarter, is Jacques Lusseyran on "the myth of objectivity":

> When I came across the myth of objectivity in certain modern thinkers, it made me angry. So there was only one world for these people, the same for everyone. And all the other worlds were to be counted as illusions left over from the past. Or why not call them by their name—hallucinations? I had learned to my cost how wrong they were.
>
> From my own experience I knew very well that it was enough to take from a man a memory here, an association there, to deprive him of hearing or sight, for the world to undergo immediate transformation, and for another world, entirely different but entirely coherent, to be born. Another world? Not really. The same world, rather, but seen from another angle, and counted in entirely new measures. When this happened, all the hierarchies they called objective were turned upside-down, scattered to the four winds, not even like theories but like whims.[27]

You can see a number of themes here that would attract McLuhan, as indeed they did. Principal among them must be the information about the senses and their effect on the imagination. Lusseyran proved a gold-mine of sensory data.

In addition to the foregoing items, the tool kit contained a rag-tag group of dozens of current working principles, processes, patterns and procedures for which we kept constant watch. Among these were the relation of environment and anti-environment, the principles of *figure* and *ground* or *figure* minus *ground*, formal causality, the various modes of space generated by sensory bias: visual space, acoustic space, tactile space, and so on. Reading afforded uncounted additional treasures, since his Grammarian's instincts taught him not to hesitate to apply things learned in one field to solving problems in any other.

Several examples: From E. H. Gombrich (*Art and Illusion*), he got the distinction between matching and making processes. From Eric Havelock, the so-essential details on the working of *mimesis* before (and now after) the onset of the alphabet. (See Appendix 3.) From Charles Baudelaire, the exquisite image, "*Hypocrite lecteur . . .*" From Jacques Ellul, a host of things, among them that real propaganda consists of the environment in action. From Elias Canetti, the dynamics of open & closed crowds.

Faced with any conundrum of modern media or culture, he would bring to bear on it every one of the tools available. Few matters could long resist such an assault.

How do you work if you can't use theories in your investigations? A little stethoscope, a pry-bar or two . . . Pass the gelignite.

Aristotle's Theory of Communication

ERIC MCLUHAN[1]

A fundamental principle of this topic is that communication entails change, that the *sine qua non* of communication is the matter of effect. If there is no effect, if there is no change in the audience, there is no communication. The approach is rhetoric to the core.

Therefore, two questions need to be asked in order to specify Aristotle's—or anyone's—theory of communication: What is his intended audience? and What effect does he aim to produce on that audience?

Aristotle was not, like Plato, or Aeschylus, a playwright so his audience was not the common (or uncommon) man: his audience may fairly be said to be a narrower group, consisting of his students and his colleagues at the Academy. As to the second question, the effect he wished to achieve is clearly evident in what is taken to be his biggest contribution to logical thought. In the *De Anima*, Aristotle says that all of the people around him think in images. He takes it for granted that his audience does so, and it is not to his liking.

> Now for the thinking soul images take the place of direct perceptions; and when it asserts or denies that they are good or bad, it avoids or pursues them. Hence the soul never thinks without a mental image.[2]

That is, he assumes this habit on the part of all or nearly all of his contemporaries, including his students and colleagues. He regards thinking in images not as a valuable faculty but rather as a *debility*, and that is why he never counts it among the main faculties of the soul. Thinking in images completely inhibits abstract reasoning, which he was wont to encourage. Since abstract thinking was fundamental to logic and philosophy (Dialectic), Aristotle absolutely *had* to find some way to circumvent that pernicious habit, image-based thought. And he found it: the syllogism. It is utterly impossible to syllogise in images: the syllogism forces the mind to think using words, to reason using the left hemisphere of the brain exclusively. But don't take my word for it. I've tried syllogising in images, and I invite you to make the experiment.

The syllogism breaks the mimetic thrall in which the poets held their Greek hearers, the same spell against which Plato inveighed in *Republic* and elsewhere and which Eric Havelock describes so eloquently. It posed a mortal threat to the new enterprise of abstract reasoning. Plato, however, never went further; at least, there is no evidence of his attempting actually to circumvent image-based thinking. Perhaps this is understandable inasmuch as Plato's background included a spell as a street-corner mime. It took his pupil, Aristotle, to undertake the challenge. Now, perhaps with great effort you, reader, can torture a few images into a semblance of a syllogism, but the result is going to be lamentable use of images and nothing like the crisp efficiency of reasoning in words. Try it yourself. Try the following, or any other, syllogism: convert each line—major premise and minor premise and conclusion—into an image. Any syllogism at all will serve the purpose. Here is the classic,

All men are mortal.

Socrates is a man.

Therefore, Socrates is mortal.

Right off, the major premise (the first line) cannot be made a single image. You might possibly imagine a picture of all men, but a real picture (would it be head-and-shoulders portraits only or full-body images?) of every human being on earth at this moment would be impossibly large, perhaps miles in width and miles in height. (Needless to say, the same would have been true of a picture of all humans on earth in Aristotle's or in Socrates' time.) But the oral man, the preliterate man, would find such a generalized image entirely too abstract for his imagination to construct. Barry Sanders has found much the same thing:

> Through his interviews, Luria could describe the broad outlines of thinking under the conditions of orality, but in the end he could learn little if anything of the native intelligence of his peasants. Any paper-test—indeed, most questions posed by a literate interviewer—strains the oral person to do something he or she seems unable to do, which

we can call by any number of different names—decontextualization, abstraction, dis-embedding, defining, describing, categorizing—things the average grammar school child does every night in homework assignments. For Luria's peasants, however, these concepts seemed foreign. They lived fully in their sensory world. They saw no reason for removing themselves from it, and they had no tools for accomplishing that task. In the end, they refused to be pulled out of their immediate situation. Categorical terms held no practical use for them. "Tree" does not exist. But that tree stands over there; it provides shade and drops fruit. The pre-literate or non-literate remains deeply situated, and confronts experience by walking right up to it and grabbing hold of it.[3]

But just for argument's sake, allow that such an image *might* be constructed. So what would such an image "say"? It actually would not "say" anything: it would simply depict all of humanity. How could anyone make it convey the notion of the statement, "all men"? Even supposing that you could overcome *that* difficulty, it is the copular verb that presents the real impossibility. A copula, as the word insists, is a joining device, a connection; images are not connected or sequential they are whole entities: there is no right place to begin or to end. How to adduce, then, in one and the same image, the notions "all men" and "mortal"? How for that matter to invent an image of "mortal" or to put a "mortal" spin on any image at all? Very well, leave *that* for the moment and pass to the minor premise (the second line): "Socrates is a man." With this statement, you encounter the same problem. You might easily give an image of Socrates, but you cannot adjoin the copular "is," or the idea "a man," because "man" by itself is too abstract. How can you be specific (Socrates) and abstract (a man) at the same time? The trouble is, both major and minor premises of a syllogism are entirely abstract, lacking *ground*; images cannot work without some sort of *ground*. And then you come to the conclusion, the third line. Even the bare idea of "therefore," presents additional impossibilities not least because it introduces sequence. As before, you encounter sheer impossibility when you try to concoct a single image that will convey the abstract idea "Socrates is mortal." Nor can you concoct even a sequence of images that make the same statement.

You simply cannot syllogise in images; it cannot be done.

Aristotle's syllogism constituted a real revolution not only in philosophy but also in making abstract thinking possible in his time and for his audience. Dialectic—logic and philosophy—requires that you develop the capacity to think in words, rather than in images. Images are entirely too illogical, too concrete; they do not provide any elbow-room in the way of abstraction. As if by magic, Aristotle's syllogism defeats thinking in images, freeing—nay, forcing—the imagination to dance with ideas and cavort with words. Our students, today, turn out to be pre-Aristotelian in their sensory lives. Almost every one of them, if questioned, will aver that he or she normally thinks in images. They are right-brain in their perceptual and cognitive bias. Teachers today, therefore confront exactly the same problems with the mental lives of their students that Aristotle faced with his, with this difference: he was aware of the nature of the problem, and we for the most part are not. Further, Aristotle decided to take action and to modify his students' modes of thought; our teachers have evidently decided that the problem lies instead with their manner and technique of teaching. The reversals and ironies accumulate.

In any event, articulating Aristotle's Theory of Communication may go some distance to helping us solve a practical and accumulating problem in classrooms today. Aristotle saw a cognitive dissonance between the new technology of the alphabet and the old mimetic potencies of the spoken word. We face a cognitive dissonance between the old technology of the printed alphabet and the new mimetic potencies of the electronic word and electronic imageries. It really is a matter of either-or. In Aristotle's time, as in our own, the tradition became counter-cultural. Which way ought we to go?

Cicero's Theory of Communication

ERIC MCLUHAN

Cicero gives his theory of communication succinctly in the end pages of *De Oratore*:

> But do not let anybody wonder how these things can possibly make any impression on the unlearned crowd when it forms the audience, because in this particular department as in every other nature has a vast and indeed incredible power. For everybody is able to discriminate between what is right and what wrong in matters of art and proportion by a sort of subconscious instinct, without having any theory of art or proportion of their own; and while they can do this in the case of pictures and statues and other works to understand which nature has given them less equipment, at the same time they display this much more in judging the rhythms and pronunciations of words, because these are rooted deep in the general sensibility, and nature has decreed that nobody shall be entirely devoid of these faculties. And consequently everybody is influenced not only by skilful arrangement of words but also by rhythms and pronunciations. For what proportion of people understands the science of rhythm and metre? Yet, all the same, if only a slight slip is made in these, making the line too short by a contraction or too long by dwelling on a vowel, the audience protests to a man. Well, does not the same thing take place in the case of pronunciation, so that if there are not only discrepancies between the members of a troupe or a chorus but even inconsistency in the pronunciation of individual actors, the ordinary public drives them off the stage? Li. It is remarkable how little difference there is between the expert and the plain man as critics, though there is a great gap between them as performers. . . nothing is so akin to our own minds as rhythms and words—these rouse us up to excitement, and smooth and calm us down, and often lead us to mirth and to sorrow; though their

extremely powerful influence is more suited for poetry and song, nor was it overlooked
by that very worthy monarch, King Numa, and by our ancestors, as is shown by the use
of the lyre and the pipes at ceremonial banquets, and by the verses of the Salii. . . .
                                                                    —*De Oratore*, III.l.195–li.197.

It is all there—a complete theory of communication, that is, of the ways in
which words communicate with us and shape our sensibilities. And this "theory"
comes straight from a virtuoso, a man hailed by all as the greatest orator of his time
and perhaps of all time. This Shakespeare of the spoken word embodied all of the
noblest ideals that were prized by the profession. In the passage above, from the closing pages of his *summa* on oratory, Cicero discusses the subconscious effect of
media: in this case, words and their attributes. Words spoken, that is, not the word
on the page or the word in silent thought. Cicero gives a good account of the transformative word: it clearly is the *logos* of rhetoric, the *logos prophorikos*. His comments
here are of a general and summary nature because they conclude the last of the three
books of *De Oratore*.

Cicero's sentiments bring to mind T. S. Eliot's observation that "genuine poetry can communicate before it is understood," meaning that the medium—the
poem—has its effect independently of the *meanings* of the words and sentences, and
independently of a reader's degree of breeding and sophistication. The function of
the poem is to reshape the reader's sensibilities, to re-trim the set of their sails; the
meanings and the ideas are there to keep the reader's mind busy, to keep the reader involved in and by the poem long enough for it to have its effect. Cicero's orator obviously had a firm grip on his audience's sensibilities and did most of his work
in the same quarter.

But these remarks betoken a shift in focus from the rest of the dialogue. Cicero
had early mastered the straightforward effects of the arguments and ideas on an
audience: these work at the levels of efficient causality and material causality. He
takes us here, however, to the subconscious level, the level of environmental activity, of formal causality.

In our time, Adolf Hildebrand asserted that the formal cause of a work of art
resided in the effect the item had on its audience. In his classic study, *The Problem
of Form in Painting and Sculpture*,[1] he wrote, "In true Art the actual form has its reality only as an effect."[2] That is, the form of a work of true art actually operates from
outside the painting or poem or piece of sculpture, and it forms **as a result of its
action** on an audience. The same rules apply to poetry and the other arts. Cicero
would find Hildebrand's conclusion entirely congenial. More recently, writing
about metrics, Paul Fussell echoes Cicero's observation:

> To do something to the reader is the end of poetry: a poem is less a notation on a page or a sequence of uttered sounds than a shaped and measured formal effect that impinges upon a reader or hearer. The reality of the poem is in its impingement. . . . The poet whose metrical effects actually work upon a reader reveals that he has attained an understanding of what man in general is like.[3]

Like Cicero, Hildebrand distinguishes two kinds of form, which he calls perceptual form and actual form. Perceptual form concerns how the thing appears or strikes the imagination; it will vary with point of view, lighting, etc. Actual form is, he says, "inferred from the appearance."[4] Like formal cause, Hildebrand's actual form is an active force, not a passive pattern or container.

The art of rhetoric had a simultaneous dimension as well as a sequential one. The sequential dimension related to the organization or disposition of the elements of a speech, how the material was parceled out for delivery to the hearers. First would come the warm-up, the exordium. Next in order would come the narration or overall statement; then, the partition, and the confirmation and refutation of arguments pro and con. Last, there might be a small digression, to relieve the pressure just before the hammer blow, the peroration. But there was also the synchronic aspect of the rhetorical logos, the five divisions. These pervaded every word, every sentence and statement, every argument, every shred of a speech from first to last. They are the anatomy of rhetoric: *inventio*, the mother-lode of material; *dispositio*, which is the diachronic aspect outlined above; *elocutio* and decorum, which is the heart of the entire business and concerns sensitivity to the effect on the audience of words and phrases and figures of speech, thought and emotion; *memory*, as a speech has to be fixed in the memory of the speaker; and *delivery* or stagecraft.[5]

Cicero used the five divisions of rhetoric—his (rhetorical) *logos*—to organize his five books on oratory. The first three are called *De Oratore*, books I–II–III. The fourth is of course the *Brutus*, Cicero's history of Roman oratory. *Orator*, the fifth in the set, is always bound with its natural companion, the *Brutus*: *Orator* is a sort of outcome of the history and the art. In *Orator*, Cicero sets out to find the ideal orator. He surveys the qualifications that the ideal man would exhibit and measures various orators of the past and present against them. Ultimately he does find the ideal: it turns out to be himself. Yet, this was no self-aggrandizement. Cicero did embody the very ideals he admired, as have agreed all critics at the time and all since then to our own time.

It is no stretch to imagine the history called *Brutus* as playing the role of Memory in Cicero's *logos*; nor is it a stretch to see the *Orator* as performing the role of Delivery in that *logos*. The first three books, those of *De Oratore*, perform the functions of the first three divisions of Rhetoric: *Inventio* (finding a topic, having a ready supply of material; the essentials of the craft) and *Dispositio* (organization) and

Elocutio (decorum: the audience; figures, ornament). These five functions are the structural essentials of the rhetorical *logos*, the *logos prophorikos*.[6]

The Romans found the Greek term *logos* untranslatable by a single Latin word so they used the hendiadys, *ratio atque oratio*—reason and speech—which they understood as pointing directly to the two main modes of language, "wisdom and eloquence." Wisdom and Eloquence was, for over 1500 years, a buzz phrase for the union of Grammar[7] and Rhetoric. The union of Rhetoric and Grammar was truly a natural and proper alignment, one that lasted for over 1500 years; it had been verily decreed in the nature of the *logos* from which they sprang. The most popular book of the Middle Ages celebrated this fact: Martianus Capella's *The Marriage of Mercury and Philology*. Mercury, the staunch messenger of the gods, stood for Rhetoric; Dame Philologia, Grammar and encyclopaedic wisdom. The seven liberal arts—the full Trivium and Quadrivium—served as the seven bridesmaids.

Mimesis, or Making Sense

MARSHALL MCLUHAN AND WILFRED WATSON

The entire world of technology makes sense by miming the human body and faculties.

Most studies of mimesis, from Plato to Auerbach and Koestler, proceed on the assumption of matching inner and outer. Notable exceptions are found in E. H. Gombrich's *Art and Illusion* and Eric Havelock's *Preface to Plato*. The technique of continuous parallel that Eliot indicates as the essential myth-making form of mimesis in his classic essay "Ulysses, Order and Myth" simply tosses aside the idea of matching in favor of interface and metamorphosis. Plato had objected to the traditional, magical idea of mimesis. E. H. Gombrich illustrates how the new Euclidean demand for matching and representational illusion began to flourish in Plato's day. Havelock explains the pre-Platonic function of mimesis:

> Plato is describing a total technology of the preserved word . . . a state of total personal involvement and therefore of emotional identification with the substance of the poetized statement. . . . A modern student thinks he does well if he diverts a tiny fraction of his psychic powers to memorize a single sonnet of Shakespeare. He is not more lazy than his Greek counterpart. He simply pours his energy into book reading and learning through the use of his eyes instead of his ears. His Greek counterpart had to mobilize the psychic resources necessary to memorize Homer and the poets. . . . You threw yourself into the situation of Achilles, you identified with his grief or his anger. You yourself became Achilles and so did the reciter to whom you listened. Thirty years later you could automatically quote what Achilles had said or what the poet had said about

him. Such enormous powers of poetic memorization could be purchased only at the cost of total loss of objectivity. . . . This then is the master clue to Plato's choice of the word *mimesis* to describe the poetic experience. It focuses initially not on the artist's creative act but on his power to make his audience identify almost pathologically and certainly sympathetically with the content if what he is saying . . . what [Plato] is saying is that any poetized statement must be designed and recited in such a way as to make it a kind of drama within the soul both of the reciter and hence also of the audience. This kind of drama, this way of reliving experience in memory instead of analyzing and understanding it, is for him the "enemy."

One of the etymologies of "matching" is "making" (mac-ian). This polarity is inherent in consciousness as such. Certainly in the cliché-to-archetype process, if cognition is matching our sensory experience with the outer world, re-cognition is a repeat of that process. We have seen how dreaming involves a *ricorso* of this waking experience of the day: "The unpurged images of day recede" (Yeats). The whole of *Finnegans Wake* is a *ricorso*, a scrubbing purgation of private and corporate experience in the collective "dreaming back." "Making sense" is a phrase that indicates repetition of some experience which yields a sudden truth or meaning. In *Le Démon de l'Analogie* Mallarmé reveals a creative process as a recap of the actual stages of apprehension. That is, creativity is the parallel of cognition, a retracking of the labyrinth of sensation. Ancient mythology is packed with examples of this awareness. Daedalus, the mightiest maker or engineer of antiquity, contrived the labyrinth that enclosed the Minotaur. The first page of *A Portrait of the Artist as a Young Man* concerns the cognitive labyrinth as it is traversed by Stephen, the artist hero, in his first encounter with the Minotaur and the other scandals (cf. Greek etymology).

Stephen's surname is not Daedalus but "Dedalus," i.e., "dead all us." Joyce's last story in *Dubliners*, "The Dead," and the last lines of the *Portrait* explain the relation of the young artist to the dead: "I go to encounter for the millionth time the reality of experience and to forge in the smithy of my soul the uncreated conscience of my race." This verbal implication of *ricorso*, the millions of repetitions of the cognitive labyrinth, which is traced on the first page of the *Portrait*, is the task of making sense, of waking the somnambulists in the labyrinth of cognition.

In recounting the making of "The Lake Isle of Innisfree," Yeats tells how he was contemplating an advertisement for soft drinks in a London shop window where a tiny ball was dancing on top of a jet of water to convey the sportive, emancipated quality of the beverage. While Yeats stood on the pavement in the eye-, ear-, and air-polluted metropolis, he proceeded to create an anti-environment, namely "Innisfree," in order to make sense of the anarchy of the world about him. In the moment of creating the artistic probe of Innisfree, Yeats tossed London on the middenheap. Art is a cliché-probe that scraps older environments in order to retrieve other clichés that have been tossed aside earlier.

Aristotelian mimesis confirms the James Joyce approach, since it is a kind of recap of natural processes, whether of making sense via cognition or of making a house by following the lines of Nature. For example, in the *Physics*, Book II, Chapter VIII, Aristotle writes: "Thus if a house, e.g., had been a thing made by Nature it would have been made in the same way as it is now by art; and if things made by Nature were made also by art, they would come to be in the same way as by Nature." Aristotle thus confirms the sacral quality of the cliché or artifact by aligning it with the cosmic forces, just as biologists say ontogeny recaps phylogeny, i.e., knowing and growing are one, which is of course the theme of *A Portrait* by Joyce.

Shakespeare repeats Aristotle in *The Winter's Tale* when he puts into the mouth of Perdita:

> For I have heard it said
>
> There is an art which in their piedness shares
>
> With great creating Nature.
>
> To which Polixenes comments:
>
> Say there be;
>
> Yet nature is made better by no mean
>
> But Nature makes that mean; so over that art,
>
> Which you say adds to Nature, is an art
>
> Which Nature makes.
>
> —*The Winter's Tale*, Act IV, Scene 3

The *Metaphysics* of Aristotle begins with the statement: "All men by Nature desire to know." An indication of this is in the delight we take in our senses; for even apart from their usefulness they are lived for themselves; biogeneticists say today that a growing organism, at every point in its growth, has to know what the whole organism is doing in order to develop. The consequences of the images are the images of the consequences. This involvement and polarity, knowing and growing, is both creative and destructive. Yeats extended this relation between art and nature in his later works, as in "Sailing to Byzantium":

> Once out of Nature I shall never take
>
> My bodily form from any natural thing,
>
> But such a form as Grecian goldsmiths make
>
> Of hammered gold and gold enamelling
>
> To keep a drowsy Emperor awake . . .

Here, once again, is the theme of art as a means of the keenest awareness, capable of giving consciousness even to a bureaucrat. Aristotle *On the Soul* (Book III, Chapter VII) points to the analogy between art and knowledge: "It is not a stone which is present in the soul but its form. It follows that the soul is analogous to the hand; for as the hand is a tool of tools, so the mind is a form of forms and sense, the form of sensible things."

By way of resonance and repetition, "The soul is in a way all existing things." As the hand, with its extensions, probes and shapes the physical environment, so the soul or mind, with its extensions of speech, probes and orders and retrieves the man-made environment of artifacts and archetypes.

A cliché is an act of consciousness: total consciousness is the sum of all the clichés of all the media or technologies that we probe with.

On Formal Cause

ERIC MCLUHAN

"Harold Innis was one of the very few people since Plato to show serious interest in formal causes and the effects that result from the formal structure of total situations." —from the interview of Marshall McLuhan by Hubert Hoskins, entitled *Electric Consciousness and the Church.*

HH: "... so what really counts is not what but how?"
McLuhan: "yes"
—*Ibid.*

... People do not want to know the cause of anything. They do not want to know why radio caused Hitler and Ghandi alike. They do not want to know that print caused anything whatever. As users of these media, they wish merely to get inside, hoping perhaps to add another layer to their environment in the manner of "The Chambered Nautilus" of Oliver Wendell Holmes.

The total non-response of hundreds of thousands of people to the suggestion that there was an actual physical environmental, man-made cause of drug addiction in our time startled me into study of the attitude of the scientific community to causation. It does not take long to discover that all of the sciences, physical and social, are interested only in describing and measuring effects while ignoring causation entirely. A *connection* is not a cause but a hang-up. This is not a matter that can be properly discussed in this [head]note, but the absence of interest in causation cannot persist in the new age of ecology. Ecology does not seek connections, but patterns. It does not seek quantities, but satisfactions and understanding. The pioneer work of Harold Innis in the study of causality relating to the material media of communication had no followers, despite his being surrounded with academic admirers. The student of media will discover that for the past 500 years Western Science has systematically excluded the study of causation by the simple process of fragmentation and quantification.[1]

Formal causality kicks in whenever "coming events cast their shadows before them." Formal cause is still hugely mysterious: the literate mind finds it is too paradoxical and irrational. It deals with environmental processes and it works outside of time. The effects—those long shadows—arrive first; the causes take a while longer.[2] Most of the effects of any medium or innovation occur before the arrival of the innovation itself. A vortex of these effects tends, in time, to become the innovation. Let us begin by looking at several examples of formal cause at work. George Steiner discusses how formal cause operates dramatically at the heart of Greek tragedy:

> We *know* what will happen to Agamemnon when he enters the house, each instant of the *agon* has been announced and prepared for. We know precisely what Oedipus will discover—in a crucial sense he too has known all along. Yet with each narration or performance of the fable our sense of shock is renewed. The tragic vision of Greek literature turns on this deep paradox: the event most expected, most consequent on the internal logic of action, is also the most surprising.[3]

Jane Jacobs approaches cities structurally, using formal cause. As she reminds us, the dogma of agricultural primacy says, agriculture first, cities later.

> Current theory in many fields—economics, history, anthropology—assumes that cities are built upon a rural economic base. If my observations and reasoning are correct, the reverse is true: that is, rural economies, including agricultural work, are directly built upon city economies and city work.[4]

In terms of efficient cause and commonsense reason, the countryside comes first and the city grows slowly out of it. But formal cause reveals that a vortex of effects comes first:

> Rural production is literally the creation of city consumption. That is to say, city economies invent the things that are to become city imports from the rural world, and then they reinvent the rural world so it can supply those imports. This, as far as I can see, is the only way in which rural economies develop at all, agricultural primacy notwithstanding.[5]

This same pattern of conformity between a *figure* and its *ground* T. S. Eliot would identify as defining a tradition and individual talent. In the electric age we can easily see that the vortex of effects of any innovation always precedes its causes. So, for example, if we see on every hand the effects of antigravity in the form of airplanes and spacecraft and submarines, then it's easy to predict that actual antigravity will soon be a feature of everyday life. And the same might be said of telepathy, since we have everywhere around us the effects of it in the form of radio, telephones, wireless computing, etc.

Aristotle, as far as I know the first to write about formal cause, never quite states right out that the formal cause of something is the *ground* that gives rise to it, though he tries to do so on many occasions. Here is the conventional view of Aristotle's system of causes:

> The production of works of art, to which Aristotle himself frequently turns for examples, most readily illustrates these four different kinds of causes. In making a shoe, the material cause is that out of which the shoe is made—the leather or hide. The efficient cause is the shoemaker, or more precisely the shoemaker's acts that transform the raw material into the finished product. The formal cause is the pattern which directs the work; it is, in a sense, the definition or type of the thing to be made, which, beginning as a plan in the artist's mind, appears at the end of the work in the transformed material as its own intrinsic form. The protection of the foot is the final cause or end—that for the sake of which the shoe was made.
>
> Two of the four causes seem to be less discernible in nature than in art. The material and efficient causes remain evident enough. The material cause can usually be identified as that which undergoes the change—the thing which grows, alters in color, or moves from place to place. The efficient cause is always that by which the change is produced. It is the moving cause working on that which is susceptible to change, e.g., the fire heating the water, the rolling stone setting another stone in motion.
>
> But the formal cause is not as apparent in nature as in art. Whereas in art it can be identified by reference to the plan in the maker's mind, it must be discovered in nature in the change itself, as that which completes the process. For example the redness which the apple takes on in ripening is the formal cause of its alteration in color. The trouble with the final cause is that it so often tends to be inseparable from the formal cause; for unless some extrinsic purpose can be found for a natural change—some end beyond itself which the change serves—the final cause, or that for the sake of which the change took place, is no other than the quality or form which the matter assumes as a result of its transformation.[6]

Formal cause is the *ground* for the material, efficient and final causes; in that sense, it "contains all the other causes." *Simile modo*, the Literal Sense contains the other Senses. See *Laws of Media*[7] (Chapter V) for other parallels to these "fours." Aristotle points out the blindness conferred by taking a moral approach (good or bad opinion) to matters of formal awareness and knowing: "it is impossible to have opinion and knowledge at the same time about the same object . . ." (οὐδέ δοξάζειν ἅμα τὸ αὐτὸ καὶ ἐπίστασθαι ἐνδέχεται).[8] In any field, analysis via the moral approach means specializing in the Moral Level of interpretation. Moralism works at the same level as efficient cause; both tend to become preoccupations and strong biases.[9] Often, the moralist approach is used as a way to evade a difficult task such as studying the object of the denouncement. This is certainly true of media study, where people will wax moralistic over the content and its effects as a means of ignoring the medium itself. Stephen Hawking found the same thing with reference to his work, much of which concerns formal causes:

> My approach has been described as naïve and simpleminded. I have been variously called a nominalist, an instrumentalist, a positivist, a realist, and several other ists. The technique seems to be refutation by denigration: If you can attach a label to my approach, you don't have to say what is wrong with it. Surely everyone knows the fatal errors of all those isms.[10]

Adolf Hildebrand asserted that the formal cause of a work of art was to be realized just as an effect of the item. In his study of *The Problem of Form in Painting and Sculpture*,[11] he wrote, "In true Art the actual form has its reality only as an effect."[12] That is, the form occurs outside the painting or piece of sculpture, and as a result of its interaction with an audience. The same rules apply to poetry and the other arts. Writing about metrics, Paul Fussell observed,

> To do something to the reader is the end of poetry: a poem is less a notation on a page or a sequence of uttered sounds than a shaped and measured formal effect that impinges upon a reader or hearer. The reality of the poem is in its impingement . . . The poet whose metrical effects actually work upon a reader reveals that he has attained an understanding of what man in general is like.[13]

Hildebrand distinguished two kinds of form, perceptual and actual. Perceptual form is how the thing appears or strikes the imagination, and it may vary with point of view, lighting, etc. Actual form is, he says, "inferred from the appearance."[14] Like formal cause, Hildebrand's actual form is an active force, not a passive pattern or container. The two kinds of form are rather close to what we used to call "structural impact" and "sensory closure." Both are structural, and neither inheres in the object or *figure*.

With formal cause, Aristotle updates the Ancients' notion of *logos*

Aristotle frequently discusses formal causality in the *Metaphysics*. In Book I Ch. 6, he makes a remarkable observation concerning Plato's relation to the Pythagoreans: in thinkers before Plato, he avers, there is to be found "no tincture of Dialectic." Aristotle offers this comment to explain why Plato chose to base the Forms in the region of his grammatical inquiries involving etymology and definitions.

> His divergence from the Pythagoreans in making the One and the Numbers separate from things, and his introduction of the Forms, were due to his inquiries in the region of definitions (for the earlier thinkers had no tincture of dialectic), and his making the other entity . . . *etc.*[15]

The word Aristotle uses for "forms" is *eidon*, and the word that is translated into English as "definitions" is *logois*:

καὶ ἡ τῶν εἰδῶν εἰσαγωγὴ διὰ τὴν ἐν τοῖσ λόγοισ ἐγένετο σκέψιν· οἱ γὰρ πρότεροι διαλεκτικῆσ οὐ μετεῖχον

Aristotle consistently equates form and definition, and definition and the *logos* of a thing.[16] He cites the antiquity of the notion as extending back at least to Empedocles:

> . . . for a thing's "nature" is much more a first principle (or "Cause") than it is matter. (Indeed, in some places even Empedocles, being led and guided by Truth herself, stumbles upon this, and is forced to assert that it is the *logos* which is a thing's essence or nature. . . .)
>
> ἀρχὴ γὰρ ἡ φύσισ μᾶλλον τῆσ ὕλησ. ἐνιαχοῦ δέ που αὐτὴ καὶ Ἐμπεδοκλῆσ περιπίπτει ἀγόμενοσ ὑπ᾽ αὐτῆσ τῆσ ἀληθείασ, καὶ τὴν οὐσίαν καὶ τὴν θύσιν ἀναγκάζεται θάναι τὸν λόγον εἶναι, οἷον ὀστοῦν ἀποδιδοὺσ τί ἐστιν.[17]

Definition and *logos* share another process, one that springs from the old idea of *logos* as "transforming word."

To the ancient understanding, the *logos* was charged with the power to bring things into being. The gods themselves spoke in thunder, and their speech could— and frequently did—alter the world and influence the course of events. Naming a thing, tantamount to defining it, meant giving it a structure and an existence. The name—*logos*—was the thing's pattern of being, its essence, its definition. In the process of choosing and uttering a thing's name, the thing itself was called into existence.[18] Naming and giving something definition was rather more than application of arbitrary labels. The name more than simply *meant* the thing, and vice-versa: the two were so closely interrelated as to be one. Name and thing embody each other. Defining and naming were each *constitutive* acts; they were equivalent: this active *logos* appears in *Genesis* as God creates the universe by means of speech. God utters the universe at the creation, by speaking its name. He, as it were, calls the universe out of non-being into being.[19] Every human act of naming echoes this act of knowing and making. A kind of replay or re-cognition, human naming demands precise perceptual knowledge of the thing and parodies the Divine act of naming and making. Here is *le mot juste* with a vengeance. So the ancients ever regarded etymology and the study of names as high science. It could provide a direct route to knowing the essential nature of things—exactly the domain of formal causality.[20] Finding the etymology meant peeling back layer after layer of concepts to expose the original perceptual configuration, where the true nature of the thing is recorded.

With these matters in mind, view Aristotle's assertion, opening the *Poetics*, that "*Mimesis* is the process by which all men learn," and, in *De Anima*, the famous passage,

> . . . the soul is in a way all existing things. . . . Within the soul, the faculties of knowledge and sensation are potentially these objects. . . . They must be either the things themselves or their forms. The former alternative is of course impossible: it is not the stone which is present in the soul but its form. It follows that the soul is analogous to the hand; for as the hand is a tool of tools, so the mind is the form of forms and sense the form of sensible things.[21]

> Oti he psyche ta ontai tos esti panta . . . he men dynamei eis ta dynamei, he d' entelecheia eis ta entelecheia. Tes de psyches to aisthetikon kai ta epistemonikon dynamei tauta esti, to men episteton to de aistheton. Anagke d' he auta he ta eide einai. Auta men gar de ou. Ou gar ho lithos en te psyche, alla to eidos. Oste he psyche hosper he cheir estin. Kai gar he cheir organon estin organon, kai nous eidos eidon kai he eisthesis eidos aistheton.[22]

In the dialogue named for Cratylus, the follower of Heraclitus, Plato has this apposite exchange between Socrates and Cratylus:

> **Socrates:** But if these things are only to be known through names, how can we suppose that the givers of names had knowledge, or were legislators before there were names at all, and therefore before they could have known them?

> **Cratylus:** I believe, Socrates, the true account of the matter to be, that a power more than human gave things their first names, and that the names which were thus given are necessarily their true names.[23]

Marshall McLuhan comments,

> Obviously, with this kind of importance associated with the names of things, and of gods, heroes, and legendary beings, etymology would be a main source of scientific and moral enlightenment. And such was the case. The prolific labors of the etymologists reflected in Plato's *Cratylus*, but begun centuries before and continued until the seventeenth century, are as much the concern of the historian of philosophy and of science as of the historian of letters and culture. Indeed, it was not only in antiquity but until the Cartesian revolution that language was viewed as simultaneously linking and harmonizing all the intellectual and physical functions of man and of the physical world as well.

At any time from Plato to Francis Bacon the statement of Cratylus would have made sense, and would have evoked respect even when its wider implications were rejected. With the opening of the Christian era, the doctrine of Cratylus gained new significance from scriptural exegesis, and especially from Genesis 2.19:

> And out of the ground the Lord God formed every beast of the field, and every fowl of the air; and brought them unto the man to see what he would call them: and whatsoever he called every living creature, that was the name thereof.

The doctrine of names is, of course, the doctrine of essence and not a naïve notion of oral terminology. The scriptural exegetists will hold, as Francis Bacon held, that Adam possessed metaphysical knowledge in a very high degree. To him the whole of nature was a book which he could read with ease. He lost his ability to read this language as a result of his fall; and Solomon alone of the sons of men has ever recovered the power to read the book of nature. The business of art is, however, to recover the knowledge of that language which once man held by nature. The problem as to which of the arts should have priority in the work of explaining man and nature had arisen among the pre-Socratic philosophers. Grammar, or allegorical exegesis of natural phenomena, as well as of folk myths and even the works of Homer and Hesiod, enjoyed many advantages for the task. In the *Cratylus*, however, Plato asserts the superior claims of dialectics for the same work, but, as a philosopher who habitually employed the grammatical modes of poetry and myth to express his own most significant and esoteric teaching, he is far from confident that grammar can be or ought to be entirely superseded. Shortly afterwards, however, Aristotle established the nature of non-grammatical scientific method in the *Posterior Analytics*.[24]

In Book V of the *Metaphysics*, Aristotle again introduces all four causes, as though for the first time:

"Cause" means (1) that from which, as imma- [25] nent material, a thing comes into being, e.g. the bronze is the cause of the statue and the silver of the saucer, and so are the classes which include these. (2) the form or pattern, i.e. the definition of the essence, and the classes which include this (e.g. the ratio 2:1 and number in general are causes of the octave), and the parts included in the definition. (3) That from which the change or the resting from change [30] first begins; e.g. the adviser is a cause of the action, and the father a cause of the child, and in general the maker a cause of the thing made and the change-producing of the changing. (4) The end, i.e. that for the sake of which a thing is. . . . [25]

Or in other words,

αἴτιον λέγεται ἕνα μὲν τρόπον ἐξ οὗ γίγνεταί τι ἐνυπάρχοντοσ,·
οἷον ὁ χαλκὸσ τοῦ ἀνδριάντοσ καὶ ὁ ἄργυροσ τῆσ φιάλησ καὶ τὰ
τούτων γένη· ἄλλον δὲ τὸ εἶδοσ καὶ τὸ παράδειγμα, τοῦτο δ' ἐστὶν ὁ
λόγοσ τοῦ τί ἦν εἶναι καὶ τὰ τούτου γένή· οἷον τοῦ διὰ πασῶν τὸ δύο
πρὸσ ἓν καὶ ὅλωσ ὁ ἀριθμόσ καὶ τὰ μέρη τὰ ἐν τῷ λόγωι. ἔτι ὅθεν ἡ
· ἀρχὴ τῆσ μεταβολῆσ ἡ πρώτη ἢ τῆσ ἠρεμήσεωσ, οἷον ὁ
Βουλεύσασ αἴτιοσ, καὶ ὁ πατὴρ τοῦ τέκνου καὶ ὅλωσ τὸ ποιοῦν τοῦ
ποιουμένου καὶ τὸ μεταβλητικὸν τοῦ μεταβάλλοντοσ. ἔτι ωσ τὸ
τέλοσ· τοῦτο δ' ἐστι τὸ οὗ ἕνεκα,

Once again, he uses *aitia* for cause in general,[26] and *eidos* for form (formal cause)—and *logos* is twice translated as "definition." The form or pattern of the thing is the *logos* of its essence. Somewhat earlier, in the first Book, Aristotle had drawn together formal cause, and *logos* ("definition") and essence (the translation may seem a bit tangled, but the Greek is clear enough):

. . . and causes are spoken of in four senses. In one of these we mean the substance, i.e. the essence (for the 'why' is reducible finally to the definition, and the ultimate 'why' is a cause and principle); in another the matter [30] . . . in a third the source of the change . . . and in a fourth . . . the purpose and the good (for this is the end of all generation and change).[27]

. . . τὰ δ' αἴτια λέγεται τετραχῶσ, ὧν μίαν μὲν αἰτίαν φαμὲν εἶναι τὴν
οὐσίαν καὶ τὸ τί ἦν εἶναί ἀνάγεται γὰρ τὸ διὰ τί εἰσ τὸν λόγον
ἔσχατον, αἴτιον δὲ καὶ ἀρχὴ τὸ διὰ τί πρῶτόν . . .

A bit later, in Book VIII, Aristotle refers to formal cause with these words:

The formal principle is the definitory formula, but this is obscure if it does not include the cause.[28]

το δ' σ εἶδοσ ὁ λόγοσ, ἀλλὰ ἄδηλοσ ἐὰν μὴ μετὰ τῆσ αἰτίασ ἦ ὁ λόγοσ.

This remark arrives a scant few lines after he had confirmed the identity of formal cause and essence, remarking as follows: τι δ' ως το ειδος; το τι ην ειναι. "What is the formal cause? His essence."[29] By the time of the *Physics,* the pairing of *logos* and *eidos* is so accustomed as to form a hendiadys. In a quick run-through of the causes he gives formal cause as "the 'form' or constituent definition"—ὡσ εἶδοσ κὰι λόγοσ τῶν πραγμάτων".[30] Near the end of *Metaphysics* Aristotle, still using *aitia* for causes in general, reprises the identity of "definition" and *logos,* with "in their universal definition they [causes] are the same"· τῷ καθόλου δὲ λόγῳ ταὐτά. . . .[31] St. Thomas Aquinas sums the matter up as follows:

> In another sense cause means the form and pattern of a thing, i.e., its exemplar. This is the formal cause, which is related to a thing in two ways. In one way it stands as the intrinsic form of a thing, and in this respect it is called the formal principle of a thing. In another way it stands as something which is extrinsic to a thing but is that in likeness to which it is made, and in this respect an exemplar is also called a thing's form. It is in this sense that Plato held the Ideas to be forms. Moreover, because it is from its form that each thing derives its nature, whether of its genus or of its species, and the nature of its genus or of its species is what is signified by the definition, which expresses its quiddity, the form of a thing is therefore the intelligible expression of its quiddity, i.e., the formula by which its quiddity is known. For even though certain material parts are given in the definition, still it is from a thing's form that the principal part of the definition comes. The reason why the form is a cause, then, is that it completes the intelligible expression of a thing's quiddity.[32]

The *logos* as constitutive utterance is the same one I wrote about in *Laws of Media*[33] and again in my study of Joyce's *Finnegans Wake, The Role of Thunder.*[34] It is the old, powerful *logos* so eloquently discussed by Eric Havelock,[35] and by Lain-Entralgo in *Therapy of the Word in Classical Antiquity.*[36] The *logos* of a thing was its essential structure or pattern, its mode of being, its definition, its entelechy.[37] Against this, in Aristotle's time, the new alphabet was exercising its influence over the imagination. A new rational mode of *logos* suddenly developed, allowing the older *logos* to come forward to serve as formal cause:

> The term *logos,* richly ambivalent, referring to discourse both as spoken and as written (argument versus treatise) and also to the mental operation (the reasoning power) required to produce it, came into its own, symbolizing the new prosaic and literate discourse (albeit still enjoying a necessary partnership with spoken dialectic). A distinction slowly formed which identified the uttered *epos* of orally-preserved speech as something different from *logos* and (to the philosophers) inferior to it. Concomitantly,

the feeling for spoken tongue as a stream flowing (as in Hesiod) was replaced by a vision of a fixed row of letters, and the single word as written, separated from the flow of the utterance that contained it, gained recognition as a separate "thing."

There is probably no attestable instance in Greek of the term *logos* as denoting a single "word," though it is often translated as though it did. The first "word for a word" in the early philosophers seems to have been *onoma*—a "name." They recognized that in the orally-preserved speech which they had to use (while striving to correct it) the subjects of significant statements were always persons, with "names," not things or ideas.

As language became separated visually from the person who uttered it, so also the person, the source of the language, came into sharper focus and the concept of selfhood was born. The history of Greek literature is often written as though the concept was already available to Homer and as though it should be taken for granted as a condition of all sophisticated discourse. The early lyric poets of Greece have been interpreted as the voice of an individualism asserting the identities of individual selves, to form a necessary condition of Greek classic culture. This in any strict sense only became true in the time of Plato.[38]

Still in Aristotle's time the mimetic power of the word, as revealed by Havelock in *Preface to Plato* and in "Prologue to Greek Literacy," was widely experienced and well known enough to be unremarkable, so the notion of verbal transformation and verbal power was equally widely acknowledged. Aristotle says in *De Anima* that we all think in images—he takes it for granted, as normal human experience.[39] In the main, comments Ross, Aristotle regards thinking in images "not as a valuable faculty but as a disability, and that is why it never figures, in the *De Anima*, among the main faculties of the soul."[40] If in his time people naturally thought in images, not in words, then an enormous leap in abstract reasoning power would accompany any successful break with image-bound thinking. The syllogism provided the answer: you cannot syllogize with images. It was a method of thinking exclusively with words. Perhaps with great effort you can torture some images into a semblance of a syllogism, but the result is lamentable use of images and nothing like the crisp efficiency of reasoning in words. Aristotle's syllogism constituted a real revolution not only in philosophy but also in making abstract thinking possible.

Dialectic—logic and philosophy—requires that you develop the capacity to think in words, rather than in images. Images are entirely too illogical, too concrete; they do not permit very much in the way of abstraction. As if by magic, Aristotle's syllogism defeats images, freeing the imagination to dance with ideas and words. Could that be a major hidden factor in its significance, to Aristotle & co., and in its essential power? Imagebuster?

When the ancient philosophers averred that the *kosmos* was "informed by" *logos*, they were making a technical statement about a formal cause. The cosmic universe was a verbal universe in which decorum played an essential and excruciatingly delicate part (this situation providing in turn a base for our meanings of "cosmetics"). Decorum is deeply Rhetorical. So the *logos* in question, governed by decorum, is not static but vibrantly active, and therefore it had to have been uttered at some time outside of time (we are in acoustic space now). Utterance presumes an utterer, and in that is matter enough for a separate disquisition: let me just remind the reader of the extensive tradition of commentary on the "Doctrine of the *Logos.*" This *logos* is also the same *logos* of creation (*inventio*) as appears in *Genesis* and in the opening of the Last Gospel: Ἐν ἀρχῇ ἦν ὁ λόγοσ, καὶ ὁ λόγοσ ἦν πρὸσ τὸν θεόν, καὶ θεὸσ ἦν ὁ λόγοσ. *In principio erat Verbum, et Verbum erat apud Deum, et Deus erat Verbum. Hoc erat in principio apud Deum . . .*

In *Physics*, Book II, Chapter 3, Aristotle uses the now-familiar formula, as he explains that the thing in question cannot be there unless the material has actually received the *form* or characteristics of the type, conformity to which brings it within the definition of the thing we say it is, whether specifically or generically.[41]

Ἄλλον δὲ τὸ εἶδοσ καὶ τὸ παράδειγμα. Τοῦτο δ' ἐστὶν ὁ λόγοσ ὁ τοῦ τί ἦν εἶναι καὶ τὰ τούτου γένε

When or how did we become estranged from what Aristotle meant by formal cause? For centuries, philosophy has translated the *logos* of formal cause by the metaphor of "blueprint." After a few moments' reflection you realize that the "blueprint" image puts all the stress on arrangement, *dispositio*. Thereby, translators & philosophers have flang one humungous and odoriferous red herring across the path, wedged it up the innocent's nose. . . ."Blueprint" is powerfully visual: such a picture-drawing of the sizes and positions of components *vis-à-vis* each other is *dispositio* in full regalia. On the surface, "blueprint," and the translation "rational plan" for *logos*, do have a little in common.[42] Marcus Long spells out the "house" illustration of the four causes:

> . . . there is a material cause for everything, in the Aristotelian sense that there is something which is potentially something else. In order to build a house we must have bricks or stones or wood. These are the house not actually but potentially, and therefore represent the *material* cause.
>
> Bricks or wood or stones have no capacity to shape themselves into houses; for this we need a carpenter or a bricklayer or a stonemason. It is through the efforts of such men that the material cause can assume a certain form. Such men, then, are the *efficient* cause or that which produces the effect, in this case a house.
>
> A bricklayer, to confine our illustration to him, does not pick up the bricks and throw them together at random, hoping for the best. He always has a plan or blueprint to guide him in the construction. This blueprint represents the form that is to be realized; it is the organizing principle. In the Aristotelian doctrine it is the form that actualizes the potentiality, making the thing the sort of thing it is. This is the *formal* cause.

We do not collect material and hire a bricklayer to build a certain type of house without some purpose in mind. We may want the house for our own dwelling, or to rent as an investment, or simply to be a garage or storehouse. It is clear that these purposes will play a large part in determining the type of material used and the sort of workmen hired. Nothing is done without a purpose. The word "purpose" comes from a Greek word *telos* meaning literally the *end* or *goal*. Insofar as we stress the purposive causes we are said to be speaking teleologically. In the pattern of the analysis of causality in Aristotle this is called the *final* cause.

There are, then, according to Aristotle, four causes involved in the explanation of the development of any object, the material, the efficient, the formal and the final. These four causes are related to Aristotle's discussion of matter and form. The material cause as potentiality is the same as matter, whereas the other causes are an expansion of the meaning of form or actuality. Of these three causes, the final cause was the most important for Aristotle, who thought of the purpose, or goal, of development as the real reason for the thing.

The expression "final cause" suggests that the present is determined by the future, in the sense that it is what a thing is to become that determines the present stage of its development. We should be misunderstanding the meaning of the term and raising unnecessary difficulties if we supposed that a nonexistent future is the cause of the existent present. There must be a meaning of final cause other than a merely temporal one. That meaning is found in the general nature of the form of the thing if considered in its timeless aspect.[43]

Aristotle, in *Metaphysics*, puts the entire matter somewhat more succinctly:

The same thing may have all the kinds of causes, e.g., the moving cause of a house is the art or the builder, the final cause is the function it fulfils, the matter is earth and stones, and the form is the definition.[44]

ἐνδέχεται γὰρ τῶι αὐτῶι πάντασ τοὺσ τρόπουσ τοὺσ τῶν αἰτίων
ὑπάρχειν, οἷον οἰκίασ ὅθεν μὲν ἡ κινησισ ἡ τέχνη καὶ ὁ οἰκοδόμοσ,
οὗ δ' ἕνεκα τὸ ἔργον, ὕλη δὲ γῆ καὶ λίθοι, τὸ δ' εἶδοσ ὁ λόγοσ.

Again the familiar pairing of form (*eidos*) and *logos*. This *logos* is clearly light-years removed from the passivity conveyed by our conventional translation: "blueprint." Marcus Long does point out, though, that "In the Aristotelian doctrine it is the form that actualizes the potentiality, making the thing the sort of thing it is." At bottom, formal cause is coercive, not passive. It *makes* the thing. It, as it were, shoves it into *being*, and it makes it be *thus*.

Etienne Gilson brought this matter clearly to view when commenting on St. Thomas's "reform of metaphysics": Thomas introduced a clear-cut distinction between the two orders of formal causality and efficient causality. Formal causality is that which makes things to be *what* they are, and, in a way, it also makes them to be, since, in order to be, each and every being has to be a *what*. But formal causality dominates the whole realm of substance, and its proper effect is substantiality, whereas efficient causality is something quite different. . . . It is, then, literally true to say that existence is a consequence which follows from the form of essence, but not as an effect follows from the efficient cause. . . . [45] In short, forms are "formal" causes of existence, to the whole extent to which they contribute to the establishment of substances which are capable of existing.[46]

Gilson emphasizes: "No point could be more clearly stated than is this one in the metaphysics of Thomas Aquinas. The form truly is 'cause of being' for that subject in which it is, and it is not such owing to another form (*forma non habet sic esse per aliam formam*)."[47] Thomas cleared up the reciprocal relation between formal and efficient causalities,[48] reflected in the ancient saw, "*causae ad invicem causae sunt, sed in diverso genere*." Causes cause causes. But the blurring remained in some minds and continued to cause trouble.

The "blueprint" metaphor gave Dialecticians—Philosophers—what they needed to make formal cause behave rationally. That powerful image immediately invests the imaginations of those who have been exposed to it, and it has related formal cause indelibly to *dispositio*. Disposition—arrangement—is perilously close to sequence and efficient cause. That blasted "blueprint" carries with it a specifically and emphatically visual bias. A blueprint details for the eye how matters are or ought to be disposed. And still, formal cause resists the pressure to turn rational and continues to live in the world of *inventio* and *elocutio* and decorum—all of them fluid and irrational.

Martin Heidegger confronted this contaminated sense of formal cause when he raised "The Question Concerning Technology,"[49] and rejected it as inadequate to his needs. In its place he posited "Enframing," as the essence of the manner in which new technologies operate on cultures. It is clear from what he says that with "Enframing" he is trying his best to convey what Aristotle meant by formal cause and *logos* (definition, essence, entelechy). He has simply found the term formal cause so polluted by usage in his time as to be nearly useless. Consider, for example, the passage,

The essence of technology lies in *Logos*. Its holding-sway belongs within destining. Since destining at any given time starts man on a way of revealing, man, thus under way, is continually approaching the brink of the possibility of pursuing and pushing forward nothing but what is revealed in ordering, and of deriving all his standards on this basis. Through this, the other possibility is blocked, that man might be admitted more and sooner and ever more primally to the essence of that which is unconcealed and to its unconcealment, in order that he might experience as his essence his needed belonging to revealing.

... Man stands so decisively in attendance on the challenging-forth of *Logos* that he does not apprehend *Logos* as a claim, that he fails to see himself as the one spoken to, and hence also fails in every way to hear in what respect he ek-sists, from out of his essence, in the realm of exhortation or address, and thus *can never* encounter only himself.

But *Logos* does not simply endanger man in his relationship to himself and to everything that is. As a destining, it banishes man into that kind of revealing which is an ordering. Where this ordering holds sway, it drives out every other possibility of revealing. Above all, Logos conceals that revealing which, in the sense of *poiēsis*, lets what presences come forth into appearance. ... Where *Logos* holds sway, regulating and securing of the standing-reserve mark all revealing. They no longer even let their own fundamental characteristic appear, namely, this revealing as such.

Thus the challenging *Logos* not only conceals a former way of revealing, bringing-forth, but it conceals revealing itself and with it that wherein unconcealment, i.e., truth, comes to pass.[50]

Had Aristotle written in modern German and been subjected to the tortures of philosophical translation, the result might very well have resembled this text. I have made just one alteration to it: I have substituted "Logos" where Heidegger has put "Enframing." By "standing reserve" he evidently means a residue of possible forms. His struggle to invent formal cause, however, illuminates one of the problems to which phenomenology as a whole is a response. For centuries since the scholastics, Dialectic has relied on the other causes and found them adequate to solving questions of figures minus grounds. But electric circuitry banishes uniformity and now we have several ground transformations per decade. This alone is enough to present philosophy with an urgent need for formal cause as a way to approach the world of electric technology.

The formal cause of a painting or a poem or an advertisement is the audience for which it was made and on which it is to operate. Northrop Frye is exactly wrong: the formal cause MUST exist outside the painting or the poem, prior to it. Here is Frye's statement in *Anatomy of Criticism*:

An original painter knows, of course, that when the public demands likeness to an object, it generally wants the exact opposite, likeness to the pictorial conventions it is familiar with. Hence when he breaks with these conventions, he is often apt to assert that he is nothing but an eye, that he merely paints what he sees as he sees it, and the like. His motive in talking such nonsense is clear enough: he wishes to say that painting is not merely facile decoration, and involves a difficult conquest of some very real spatial problems. But this may be freely admitted without agreeing that the formal cause of a picture is outside the picture, an assertion which would destroy the whole art if it were taken seriously.[51]

Frye is in trouble, and knows it: the formal cause of the poem is the reader; of the speech or the ad, the audience—and all exist "outside" the thing. Frye's remarks, somewhat later, in *Fables of Identity* help understand where he went off the rails:

> There is still before us the problem of the formal cause of the poem, a problem deeply involved with the question of genres. We cannot say much about genres, for criticism does not know much about them. A good many critical efforts to grapple with such words as "novel" or "epic" are chiefly interesting as examples of the psychology of rumor. Two conceptions of the genre, however, are obviously fallacious, and as they are opposite extremes, the truth must lie somewhere between them. One is the pseudo-Platonic conception of genres as existing prior to and independently of creation, which confuses them with mere conventions of form like the sonnet. The other is that pseudo-biological conception of them as evolving species which turns up in so many surveys of the "development" of this or that form.[52]

McLuhan responded to Frye with *From Cliché to Archetype*, a study of the dynamics of formal causes and their relation to the retrieval process. The dust jacket announces the main theme: "New Archetype is Ye Olde Cliché Writ Large." At his back, Frye has a centuries-long misunderstanding of formal cause.

Francis Bacon adamantly insisted that all study of final causes be dropped, as it was corrupting the science of his time. He turned his own attention from armchair theorizing to rooting out formal causes, based on observation and collecting empirical evidence.[53] Nature, as much as literature, constitutes an encyclopedia, so the grammarian of any age needed to bring to bear the full trivium and quadrivium as well as keen perception and critical faculties. They use the arts and sciences to penetrate the Book of Nature and recover knowledge, lost at the Fall, of the languages in which it is written. Each act of reading in either Book was therefore an act of meditation that required simultaneous awareness of all levels and causes and their interrelations.[54] Grammar brings all of her tools of etymology and formal analysis to bear on decoding and reading the Two Books.

Bacon opens Book II of his *Novum Organum* with a report on the state of understanding in each of the four departments of causality.[55]

> The unhappy state of man's actual knowledge is manifest. . . . It is rightly laid down that true knowledge is that which is deduced from causes. The division of four causes also is not amiss: matter, form, the efficient, and end or final cause. Of these, however, the latter is so far from being beneficial, that it even corrupts the sciences. . . . The discovery of form is considered desperate. As for the efficient cause and matter . . . they are but desultory and superficial, and of scarcely any avail to real and active knowledge.

The discovery of form united all labours on the Two Books; for, as held throughout the tradition, the forms manifest the Logos and provide the common language in which both Books are inscribed. They serve not as the *figure* but the *ground* of matter, and they underlie the analogical ratios between the Two Books. In this regard, etymology provides a major technique of scientific investigation. The whole aim of the arts and sciences therefore is to enable the discovery and under-standing, and ultimately the manipulation (alchemy), of forms. This constitutes media study of a high order. The great alchemists, the Paracelsans from Raymond Lully to Cornelius Agrippa, were grammarians. Bacon is perfectly aware of how the sciences and arts are united by the study of forms and formal causes:

> On a given basis of matter to impose any nature, within the limits of possibility, is the intention of human power. In like manner, to know the causes of a given effect, in what-ever subject, is the intention of human knowledge: which intentions coincide. For that which is in contemplation as a cause, is in operation as a medium. . . .
>
> He who knows the efficient and materiate causes, composes or divides things previous-ly invented, or transfers and produces them; also in matter somewhat similar, he attaineth unto new inventions; the more deeply fixed limits of things he moveth not.
>
> He who knows the forms, discloses and educes things which have not hitherto been done, such as neither the vicissitudes of nature, nor the diligence of experience might ever have brought into action, or as might not have entered into man's thoughts.[56]

Laws of Media: The New Science also concerns this area of formal causality. Our tetrad of laws[57] brings Aristotle up to date; at the same time, it provides an analyt-ic of formal cause, the first ever proposed. Because the tetrads apply exclusively to human utterances and artifacts, it follows that formal cause is uniquely and partic-ularly human. That is, and I believe this to be crucial, absent human agency or intel-lect there is no formal cause at all.[58] Certainly all of the elements of the tetrad, the four processes, are both formal and causal. And *con*formal. And I have elsewhere discussed the tetrad's identity with *logos* and definition.[59] The deep structure or "def-inition" of a thing is to be found in the nature and interaction of the four simulta-neous processes, amplification, obsolescence, retrieval, and reversal. Together they enact the verbal role of metaphor—*logos*. Some of that is in *Laws of Media*. Together, the four processes of the tetrad spell out the entelechy—and aetiology—of their sub-ject. They give its Grammar and nature. The active part of the *logos*, the transform-ing part, is the province of Rhetoric. Entelechies, just as clearly, side with etymology and manifold simultaneous levels of existence—and analogy as regards being, whether considered modally or absolutely. The word, Aristotle's coinage, serves as the central conception of the *De Anima*.[60] (Always bearing in mind the crucial dis-tinctions between Divine and human agency, and between uttering and re-utter-ing, and between cognition and recognition: "mirabilius condidisti et mirabiliter reformasti." Adam's first job in the Garden was the naming of creatures.) Single-level existence, stripped of all discontinuities, in these precincts, means death; and exactly that rarefied and sanitized locus of operation is the heaven of Dialectic: visual space. All modes and kinds of being, including our own, as we know, derive by analogy from the supreme Being; analogy requires discontinuity, not connectedness or logic. In that sense, we are all made "in the image and likeness . . ." meaning, by analogy. However, here let me address the imputation that McLuhan was involved in some form of determinism. His aim was always to explore and document and interpret the operation of formal causes, the making process at work in literature and in culture. He had no particular interest in efficient cause or final cause—either of which is in its own manner the domain of "determinism," and both of which are concerns of normal science.

What, then, is the main reason Dialectic has such difficulty with formal cause? It could be because formal cause is irrational, and Dialectic is above all else rational. Formal cause has other properties that Dialectic would find unwelcome: it is not sequential (it operates outside of chronological time, which in and of itself offends rationality), and it is too low definition, because it can never be hotted up to play *figure* to some other *ground*. Having no points of contact with Dialectic, therefore, it does not "belong to" Dialectic, neither does it belong in or with or around Dialectic. Formal cause is an *auslander*; it emanates from Grammar and Rhetoric at their most elemental and most profound. Moreover, etymology lies at the root of the grammatical instinct. Grammar has its roots in *the logos spermatikos*, the seeds of things and words and their formal structures. (Hence Grammar's two main areas of activity: etymology and interpretation of texts.) Dialectic, on the other hand, grows out of the *logos hendiathetos*, the unspoken "word" in the mind, the thought process abstracted from utterance and from hearer. The silent word.[61] Rhetoric itself derives from the *logos prophorikos*, the uttered word that goes forth to transform the hearer. A Dialectician seeks to change your mind, to convince you; A Rhetorician, rather, aims to change *you*, to modify *how* you think rather than what. These three modes of *logos* together constitute the old *logos* of the pre-Socratics and considerably pre-Aristotle and –Plato. Reborn as the trivium they have shaped our Western intellectual tradition from Roman times to the present.

Formal cause is in the end of no interest to Dialecticians because they have no use for it. It does not apply to things of the mind, it solves no problems for them; it poses no answers—or questions—that they are disposed to entertain. Formal cause concerns the *ground* as seedbed, as active process. Or if not exactly the *ground* then (much the same thing) the interval between *figure* and *ground*, so that the formal cause is also the conformal cause, as it were, and is the cause of the *figure* and its *ground* simultaneously.[62] That interval full of active interface is an active process of formation and counterformation, yet it is not diachronic. The restless pressures and counterpressures perform their isometric dance—with no need of uniform tempo, no need of uniform time. Ironically, although three-quarters of Aristotle's tetrad of causes operate outside time, formal cause alone is reckoned irrational. The modality of formal cause is that of abrasive interface, an exchange of pressures and textures between situations: consequently, it belongs to touch, kinesis, and proprioception. This is a world of constant isometric compression and tension. Material cause too is extratemporal; that is, time may be present but its chronological aspect is incidental at best, or simply irrelevant. Matter always needs being, but clearly does not always need becoming.[63] Final cause, too, is extratemporal. One has to make a constant effort to bear in mind that the final cause (that for the sake of which, as 'Arry continually reminds us; also, the end—*telos*—or purpose) is NOT the end-point of a chain or series of efficient causes. Final cause is present *in toto* from the outset, even before the sequence of making gets underway. The world of final cause, then, functions outside of chronological time. Yet it too is not considered irrational—which indicates that it too is presently misunderstood.

There is this important difference between efficient cause and final cause as regards time and temporality. Final cause does not lie at the end of a series of efficient causes because it is present in its entirety from the outset. It is, after all, not a result but a cause. It lies outside chronological time: it does not admit of degrees of completion. If chronology belongs to efficient cause, infinity belongs to final cause because infinity too is not gradual but sudden. There are no degrees of infinitude. Infinity too functions to one side of chronological time, an absolute. Final cause is absolute and simultaneous; it anticipates the chronological making process. Like infinity, it anticipates time. Formal cause, on the other hand, is not infinite but definite. Bound up in definition, it has no need for chronological time. And like final cause, formal cause concerns being. Formal cause, because it is absolute, does not admit of degrees.

Although he refrains from mentioning it by name, T. S. Eliot was much concerned with formal cause in his musings on poetry and poetics. It was integral to his theory of communication. In a meditation on "The Frontiers of Criticism," he offers this contrast between the material (subject matter used as material cause), efficient cause (producer and production), and formal cause, as regards poetry:

> . . . One can explain a poem by investigating what it is made of and the causes that brought it about; and explanation may be a necessary preparation for understanding. But to understand a poem it is also necessary, and I should say in most instances still more necessary, that we should endeavour to grasp what the poetry is aiming to be; one might say—though it is long since I have employed such terms with any assurance—endeavouring to grasp its entelechy.[64]

Aristotle uses "entelechies" to denote primal causes.[65] Human understanding is inseparable from the formal cause of the poem—as an active force. Some reader or critic must provide the understanding. Poems are not isolated objects, like consumer goods, but active processes that complete—achieve—their forms by interacting with audiences. The reader is the formal cause of the poem. And the audience is the formal cause of the advertisement, sculpture, song, or sofa—and the consumer of the consumer product. Joyce: "My consumers are they not my producers?"[66] A parallel term for entelechy might be vortex, as used above. Marshall McLuhan's idea of a medium as an invisible, ever-present vortex of services and disservices is exactly that of formal cause. As he wrote,

> [Fritz Wilhelmsen] is interested in working on St. Thomas' theory of communication, and I have pointed out to him that Aquinas designates his audience, the people he wants to influence and alter, in the Objections of each article. Then I realized that the audience is, in all matters of art and expression, the formal cause, e.g., fallen man is the formal cause of the Incarnation, and Plato's public is the formal cause of his philosophy. Formal cause is concerned with effects and with structural form, and not with value judgments.
>
> My own approach to the media has been entirely from formal cause. Since formal causes are hidden and environmental, they exert their structural pressure by interval and interface with whatever is in their environmental territory. Formal cause[s are] always hidden, whereas the things upon which they act are visible. The TV generation has been shaped not by TV programs, but by the pervasive and penetrating character of the TV image, or service, itself.[67]

A bad poem results from confusing—fusing together or merging—its formal and final causes. What Eliot said of the bad poet is true also of the reader of a bad poem: Eliot maintained that the inferior poet is conscious where he ought to be unconscious, and unconscious where he ought to be conscious: the same mixup happens to the reader of a bad poem. The inferior poem draws your attention to itself and its language, its tricks and devices, then does nothing, leaving you numb in that quarter. Or it tries to convince you of some doctrine. Ether way, it attempts to force-fit the formal cause inside the poem.

The poem by itself, in the abstract, is comparatively meaningless. Saying that the poem cannot be fully understood until you have taken into account the poet and the circumstances of the poem's creation is like saying that you can't understand the car—or a given car—until you have taken into account Detroit and the influences on, and actions of, and intentions of, all of the people who toiled to produce the car. The makers. Here we see that little tyrant, efficient cause, asserting itself.

> For myself, I can only say that a knowledge of the springs which released a poem is not necessarily a help towards understanding the poem: too much information about the origins of a poem may even break my contact with it. I feel no need for any light upon the Lucy poems beyond the radiance shed by the poems themselves.

... It is relevant if we want to understand Wordsworth; but it is not directly relevant to our understanding of his poetry. Or rather it is not relevant to our understanding of *the poetry as poetry*. I am even prepared to suggest that there is, in all great poetry, something which must remain unaccountable however complete might be our knowledge of the poet, and that that is what matters most. When the poem has been made, something new has happened, something that cannot be wholly explained by anything that went before. That, I believe, is what we mean by 'creation.'[68]

Wallace Stevens went Eliot one better when he performed his field experiment of formal cause. Here is the lab report he wrote, in the form of the poem, "The Anecdote of the Jar":

I placed a jar in Tennessee
And round it was, upon a hill.
It made the slovenly wilderness
Surround that hill.
The wilderness rose up to it
And sprawled around, no longer wild.
The jar was round upon the ground
And tall and of a port in air.
It took dominion everywhere.
The jar was gray and bare.
It did not give of bird or bush,
Like nothing else in Tennessee.

The jar provided the formal cause of all of the metamorphoses mentioned in the poem. (Considered in terms merely of the matter or actions of the agent, the poem simply concerns an act of littering.) This poem is the only example I know of where a poet, or artist of any ilk, consciously performed a perceptual experiment and reported the results in verse.

Early in his career, Eliot published a personal manifesto of sorts under the title of "Tradition and the Individual Talent." It is his own case-study of formal cause in the area of poetics. First, he establishes the acoustic nature of the Tradition as a set of simultaneous relations, *not* a sequence or parade of big reputations:

Tradition is a matter of much wider significance. It cannot be inherited, and if you want it you must obtain it by great labour. It involves, in the first place, the historical sense, which we may call nearly indispensable to anyone who would continue to be a poet beyond his twenty-fifth year; and the historical sense involves a perception, not only of the pastness of the past, but of its presence; the historical sense compels a man to write not merely with his own generation in his bones, but with a feeling that the whole of the literature of Europe from Homer and within it the whole of the literature of his own country has a simultaneous existence and composes a simultaneous order. The historical sense, which is a sense of the timeless as well as of the temporal and of the timeless and of the temporal together, is what makes a writer traditional. And it is at the same time what makes a writer most acutely conscious of his place in time, of his contemporaneity.[69]

The historical sense provides the appropriate perceptual stance, the requisite sensitivity. In the next sentences, Eliot puts formal cause on display as he details the process of con-forming or mutual forming of the individual talent and the tradition:

No poet, no artist of any art, has his complete meaning alone. His significance, his appreciation is the appreciation of his relation to the dead poets and artists. You cannot value him alone; you must set him, for contrast and comparison, among the dead. I mean this as a principle of aesthetic, not merely historical, criticism. The necessity that he shall conform, that he shall cohere, is not one-sided; what happens when a new work of art is created is something that happens simultaneously to all the works of art which preceded it. The existing monuments form an ideal order among themselves, which is modified by the introduction of the new (the really new) work of art among them. The existing order is complete before the new work arrives; for order to persist after the supervention of novelty, the *whole* existing order must be, if ever so slightly, altered; and so the relations, proportions, values of each work of art toward the whole are readjusted; and this conformity between the old and the new. Whoever has approved this idea of order, of the form of European, or English literature, will not find it preposterous that the past should be altered by the present as much as the present is dictated by the past. And the poet who is aware of this will be aware of great difficulties and responsibilities.[70]

In a word: the individual talent is the formal cause of the tradition. This finding is of the same order as that "*logos* is the formal cause of the *cosmos*" (see Appendix One, *infra*).

Ezra Pound found formal cause everywhere at work when he wrote about "The Serious Artist." The métier of the arts is the culture's sense and sensibility; the artist's particular job, which only he is trained for, is to report on it as exactly as possible.

This brings us to the immorality of bad art. Bad art is inaccurate art. It is art that makes false reports. If a scientist falsifies a report either deliberately or through negligence we consider him as either a criminal or a bad scientist according to the enormity of his offence, and he is punished or despised accordingly.

If he falsifies the reports of a maternity hospital in order to retain his position and get profit and advancement from the city board, he may escape detection. If he declines to make such falsification he may lose financial rewards, and in either case his baseness or his pluck may pass unknown and unnoticed save by a very few people. Nevertheless one does not have to argue his case. The layman knows soon enough on hearing it whether the physician is to be blamed or praised.

If the artist falsifies his report as to the nature of man, as to his own nature, as to the nature of his ideal of the perfect, as to the nature of his ideal of this, that or the other, of god, if god exist, of the force with which he believes or disbelieves this, that or the other, of the degree in which he suffers or is made glad; if the artist falsifies his reports on these matters or on any other matter in order that he may conform to the taste of his time, to the proprieties of a sovereign, to the conveniences of a preconceived code of ethics, then that artist lies. If he lies out of deliberate will to lie, if he lies out of care-lessness, out of laziness, out of cowardice, out of any sort of negligence whatsoever, he nevertheless lies and he should be punished or despised in proportion to the serious-ness of his offence. His offence is of the same nature as the physician's and according to his position and the nature of his lie he is responsible for future oppressions and future misconceptions. Albeit his lies are known to only a few, or his truth-telling to only a few. Albeit he may pass without censure for the one and without praise for the other.

. . .

We distinguish very clearly between the physician who is doing his best for a patient, who is using drugs in which he believes, or who is in a wilderness, let us say, where the patient can get no other medical aid. We distinguish, I say, very clearly between the fail-ure of such a physician, and the act of that physician, who ignorant of the patient" dis-ease, being in reach of more skilful physicians, deliberately denies an ignorance of which he is quite conscious, refuses to consult other physicians, tries to prevent the patient's having access to more skilful physicians, or deliberately tortures the patient for his own ends.

One does not need to read black print to learn this ethical fact about physicians. Yet it takes a deal of talking to convince a layman that bad art is "immoral". And that good art however "immoral" it is, is wholly a thing of virtue. Purely and simply that good art can NOT be immoral. By good art I mean art that bears true witness, I mean the art that is most precise.[71]

So the arts draw their form from the perceptions and sensibilities of the cul-ture, and this process also plays in the artist's "putting on" his audience. The *ground* always provides the formal cause of its *figures*.

In his poem "Esthétique du Mal" Wallace Stevens sings of the embrace of forms:

This is the thesis scrivened in delight,

The reverberating psalm, the right chorale.

One might have thought of sight, but who could think

Of what it sees, for all the ill it sees?

Speech found the ear, for all the evil sound,

But the dark italics it could not propound.

And out of what one sees and hears and out

Of what one feels, who could have thought to make

So many selves, so many sensuous worlds,

As if the air, the mid-day air, was swarming

With the metaphysical changes that occur,

Merely in living as and where we live.

He indicates that the slightest shift in the level of visual intensity produces a subtle modulation in our sense of our selves, both private and corporate. Since technologies extend our own physiology, they result in new programs of an environmental kind. Such pervasive experiences as those deriving from the encounter with environments almost inevitably escape perception. The formal causes of perception—and imperception[72]—they are made visible only by the action of a counterenvironment.

When two or more environments encounter one another by direct interface, they tend to manifest their distinctive qualities. Comparison and contrast have always been a means of sharpening perception in the arts as well as in general experience. Indeed, it is upon this pattern that all the structures of art have been reared. Any artistic endeavor includes the preparing of an environment for human attention. A poem or a painting is in every sense a teaching machine for the training of perception and judgment. The artist is a person who is especially aware of the challenge and dangers of new environments presented to human sensibility. Whereas the ordinary person seeks security by numbing his perception against the impact of new experience, the artist delights in this novelty and instinctively creates situations that both reveal it and compensate for it. The artist studies the distortion of sensory life produced by new environmental programming and tends to create artistic situations that correct the sensory bias and derangement brought about by the new form. In social terms the artist can be regarded as a navigator who gives adequate compass bearings in spite of magnetic deflection of the needle by the changing play of forces. So understood, the artist is not a peddler of new ideals or lofty experiences. He is rather the indispensable aid to action and reflection alike.[73]

If the vortex of effects arrives first then we can escape it, as Poe suggests, only by formal, structural study of its action. We can manipulate any environmental vortex by judicial design of counterenvironments and by controlling and designing the mix of technologies we release in our environments. But such an ecology of media, of culture, necessitates extensive training in the arts, and widespread training of formal awareness has ever been at odds with the demands of "practical" necessity. Perhaps it is time for the roles of artist and bureaucrat/entrepreneur to reverse positions. This New World of chaos and complexity is too volatile, too precarious, too important to be left in the hands of the merely practical administrator.

Appendix One

Formal Cause

Ground/figure
Interaction   stasis
The Name   numb

        E   **F**

        R   **O**

Simultaneous,   sequential, diachronic
configurational

Supplementary note

Communication Arts in the Ancient World

All human wisdom is manifest in words, and words come in three forms: silent, written, spoken. The *logos* is therefore *the* medium—of communication as well as of the cultural bond. But under the influence of alphabetic writing, the transforming *logos* of the pre-Socratics morphed into new elements that correspond to the three verbal modes of wisdom.

The silent word is that of Dialectic, the *logos hendiathetos*. It is the word in the mind, before speech. It is the skill of thinking in words. So dialectic places its emphasis on mental processes, on logic and philosophy, and thinking aright (2 polarities; 3 parts of syllogisms).

The written word is that of Grammar, the *logos spermatikos*—the *logos* as the seeds embedded in things, the seeds from which things grow and derive their essential nature. Consequently, Grammar places its emphasis on etymology and interpretation of both the written book and the Book of Nature. Grammar bridged the arts (4 levels) and sciences (4 causes). The grammarian regarded all of Nature and every written text as his province.

The spoken word is that of Rhetoric, the *logos prophorikos*. So Rhetoric emphasizes transformation, of audience, and decorum (and all 5 divisions).

The Theories
of Communication
# of Judaism and Catholicism

ERIC MCLUHAN

Five of the chapters above, numbers four, five, six, seven, and eight, and Appendix Two ("Cicero's Theory of Communication"), discuss the use of the five divisions of rhetoric as a means of structuring material for a particular mode of efficacy. The five divisions, taken together, constitute the *logos* of rhetoric, the *logos prophorikos*, which always aims at transformation of the audience. These rhetorical structures appear first in Roman rhetorical practice; they pervade every oration and every word in an oration. Perhaps the very first example of their use in structuring a group of books into a rhetorical unit can be found in Cicero's use to draw together his five key books on oratory.[1] Cicero did not announce that he was doing this; he simply did it, perhaps for his own aesthetic satisfaction. He never commented on his use of the five divisions in this manner, but it is obvious when his five books are considered together, as, indeed, they were intended to be and as scholars have traditionally done. And it is no surprise to find the same pattern picked up and used by writers over the centuries between his time and ours, although such use has always been tacit—no one has heretofore made public these matters. Poets such as Shakespeare,[2] Wordsworth and Coleridge,[3] and Yeats, Pound, Eliot and Joyce have used the five divisions consciously, deliberately, behind the scenes, to give their works force and integrity. We have always assumed that awareness of the rhetorical *logos* and its powers entered human understanding with Greek and Roman oratorical practice, so it comes as a surprise to find it used centuries before it was invented—and used in a completely different culture.[4]

Judaism

The Jewish *Torah* consists of five distinct books that contain an account of the creation of the world, the history of the Jews, their laws and rites. The order of the five books and their contents is not chronological, but it has been fixed as follows:

First, *Genesis*, which begins with the account of the creation, "The work of the six days."

Second, *Exodus*, much of which concerns the departure of the Jews from Egypt and their 40 years' wandering in the desert before arriving at the Promised Land.

Third, *Leviticus*, wherein is found instructions for forms and rites of worship, of sacrifice, and of offerings.

Fourth, *Numbers*, which is largely a history of the Jewish people.

Fifth, *Deuteronomy*, which is a recasting of the previous books and reformulation of the Law.

The five books are considered as constituting a single entity, rather like five atoms that constitute a single molecule. One atom (or Book) cannot be omitted without destroying the integrity of the whole; neither can a sixth atom be added for the same reason. For thousands of years, it has been understood that the integrity of the *Torah* depended not only on the presence of these five books but also on their proper sequence, which was somehow sacrosanct.

The relation of the five Books of the *Torah* to the five divisions of rhetoric is simple and clear:

The role of *Inventio* (invention) is played by the book of *Genesis*.[5] As used in rhetoric, "inventio" means "first things," and discovery of heaps of pertinent matter. The book of *Genesis* contains some of the best-known biblical stories, including the account of the creation, Adam and Eve, Cain and Abel, Noah's Ark, the Tower of Babel, and others. Structurally, it consists of the "primeval history" (Chapters 1–11) and cycles of Patriarchal stories (Chapters 12–50). Modern critical scholarship believes that the book of *Genesis* reached its final form in the 5th century BC, with a previous history of composition reaching back into the 6th and 7th centuries. For Jews, the theological importance of *Genesis* centers on the Covenants linking Yahweh to His Chosen People and the people to the Promised Land.

The role of the second division of rhetoric, *Dispositio* (arrangement), is performed by the book of *Exodus*, which sets forth the disposition and redisposition of the Jewish people living in Egypt. Moses leads the Hebrews out of Egypt and through the wilderness to the Mountain of God: Mount Sinai. There, Yahweh, through Moses, gives the Hebrews their laws and enters into a covenant with them, by which He will give them the land of Canaan in return for their faithfulness. The book ends with the construction of the Tabernacle.

The role of *Elocutio* (style) is taken by the book of *Leviticus*, which corresponds in its way to eloquence and to decorum in rhetorical practice. Here is set out the form of rites and offerings, governed, in this case as in rhetoric, by decorum (propriety). Arthur Wormhoudt[6] remarked that "Throughout the book of Leviticus we hear the voice of the Lord, Yahweh, giving his instructions to Moses. In no other book is there such an overwhelming display of the power of speech." The first 16 chapters and the last chapter make up the Priestly code, with rules for ritual cleanliness, sin-offerings, and the Day of Atonement. Chapters 17–26 contain the Holiness code, including the injunction in chapter 19 to "love one's neighbor as oneself." For the most part, the Book concerns "abominations," and dietary and sexual restrictions. The rules are addressed to the Israelites, except for several prohibitions applied equally to "the strangers that sojourn in Israel."[7]

The fourth division of rhetoric, *Memoria* (memory) is found in the fourth book of the *Torah*, *Numbers*, which provides the history. The period comprehended in the history extends from the second month of the second year, as measured from the Exodus, to the beginning of the eleventh month of the fortieth year, in all about 37 years and nine months; a dreary period of wanderings. They were fewer in number at the end of their wanderings than when they left the land of Egypt.

Delivery, the fifth and last division of classical rhetoric, is enacted by the book of *Deuteronomy*,[8] fifth and last in the *Torah*. It serves to "deliver" the first four books and welds them into a whole. A large part of the book consists of five sermons delivered by Moses reviewing the previous forty years of wandering in the wilderness, and the future entering into the Promised Land. Its central element is a detailed law-code by which the Israelites are to live within the Promised Land. Theologically the book constitutes the renewing of the covenant between Yahweh, and the "Children of Israel." One of its most significant verses is considered to be Deuteronomy 6:4, which constitutes the Shema, a definitive statement of Jewish identity: "Hear, O Israel: the LORD [YHWH] (is) our God, the LORD is one."

Whenever the five divisions of classical rhetoric are seen at work together in proper order, the effect aimed at is always the transformation of the target audience. That is the peculiar power of the *logos prophorikos*, the root of rhetoric.

The audience for the Five Books is the Jews, not any other group or race or nationality. And the intended effect is that of transforming a group of disparate tribes into a singular people: the People of The Book—the *Torah*. The People of the Book exist both in and outside of time, in an eternal present of their own making.

How can Greek and Roman rhetorical structures come to be found in use centuries before they were invented and in a culture thousands of miles distant from their area of origin?

There is no evidence whatever of transmission in either direction, geographically or temporally. I propose that whoever it was that organized the *Torah* and wrote Deuteronomy somehow intuited the structure of the word and used it to guide His pen.[9] There is a considerable literature on the Word in the Old Testament, and an entire tradition concerning the *logos*, having its origin in the statement that "God said . . ." at the creation of all things. The Creation is regarded as a speech, as proclaimed in Genesis; and that word is a transforming *logos* that literally makes and is all things. The uttered word of Creation is neither denotative nor connotative of things, as are human words; it *is* the things themselves.[10] The Greek and Roman rhetorical invention is a reinvention, evidently innocent of the original. The Christian doctrine of the *logos* flows from the Old Testament to and through the New Testament and unites them. Inasmuch as the created universe is a speech by God, Christian interpreters formulated the doctrine of the Two Books—the Book of Nature and the written Book, the Bible, as twin sources of God's revelation. The fourth Gospel, the Book of Revelation, begins, "In the beginning was the Word . . ." God spoke to humanity in two modes: each is intended to be read and interpreted, using the techniques of rhetorical and grammatical exegesis and etymology. Rhetorical analysis leads from the speech back to the speaker; etymology is the DNA code of words.

Catholicism

The central unifying event in Catholicism and Catholic liturgy is the Mass. At the heart of the Mass is the sacrifice on the altar that replays and reenacts the death and resurrection of Christ. It is no exaggeration to say that this sacrament is the unifying *logos* of the Catholic Church as much as the *Torah* is the unifying *logos* of Judaism.

Structurally, the Mass has two fundamental constituents: the Mass of the Catechumens and the Mass of the Faithful. Catechumens were those who had not yet been baptized and so not been fully accepted into the Church, so they could not participate completely in this holiest of sacraments. They could, however, attend the opening ritual prayers and hear the readings from the Old and New Testaments and the sermon, and they could recite the creed with the rest of the congregation. Traditionally, they would then leave the church while the Faithful stayed for the rest of the Mass.

First Part of the Mass: The Mass of the Catechumens—Prayers, chants, and readings.

I. Chants with Prayers

II. Readings with Chants

Second Part of the Mass: The Mass of the Faithful—The Sacrifice.

I. Offertory—Preparation of the Sacrifice

II. Canon—Oblation of the Sacrifice

III. Communion—Participation in the Sacrifice

Note that while the Mass of the Catechumens consists of two elements, the entire Mass—including the Mass of the Faithful—consists of a total of five elements, which follow the five divisions of rhetoric.

The first two divisions of rhetoric, Inventio and Dispositio, are traditionally associated with a completely separate component of the trivium,[11] Dialectic, where they are variously called matter and form or matter and arrangement, etc. In the context of the Mass, they signify that for the Catechumens the sacrifice of the Mass is still theoretical or ideological, more philosophy than real experience. Once the Catechumens have been admitted to the full mysteries, that is, once the remaining three elements are added, the Mass will turn from theory to actual transformation.[12]

The Offertory, as Elocutio, includes the offering of the bread and the wine, incensing, ritual cleansing (washing of hands), and prayers that the offering be found acceptable and proper.

The Canon, includes the reenactment of the Last Supper and the institution of the Eucharist. The priest repeats the actual words of consecration, by which the bread and wine are transformed into the actual Body and Blood of Christ (the transubstantiation), and ending with "in mei memoriam facietis"—"do this in memory of Me." Preserving the integrity and continuity of the Mass, and especially of the Canon, through the ages has been a particular concern of the Church.

The Communion section opens with the Lord's Prayer and includes the distribution (delivery) of the consecrated matter to the faithful and the dismissal (delivery), "Ite, Missa est"—"Go, you are dismissed."

With the Canon and the Communion, the sacrament steps outside time and into eternity. With the consecration, the sacrifice performed in the present on the altar joins instantly with every other performance of the same sacrifice past and future, as also with the original sacrifice at the Last Supper and on Calvary.[13] The communicants, furthermore, are joined with all other communicants, past, present, and future, and also with "the communion of saints."[14] So are conjoined the living and the dead into a single simultaneous congregation.

The Canon effects the transubstantiation of the *matter* of the sacrifice, the bread and wine; the Communion effects the transformation of the *communicants* from the present into eternal time. This latter is aided by the Lord's Prayer, which also exhibits rhetorical structure, as follows.

Inventio: the opening invocation, Our Father, who art in Heaven, hallowed be thy name

Dispositio/Arrangement: Thy kingdom come; Thy will be done on earth, as it is in Heaven

Elocutio: Give us this day our daily bread

Memoria: And forgive us our trespasses as we forgive those who trespass against us

Pronuntiatio/Delivery: And lead us not into temptation but deliver us from evil. Amen.

As well as the Eucharist, the other six sacraments of the Catholic faith are media of transformation. An entire separate study of the seven sacraments as transforming media is clearly indicated.

The *Torah*, the *logos* of Judaism, served and serves to transform the various tribes and sects of Jews, past, present, and future, into the Chosen People.

The Catholic Mass serves to transform the matter (bread and wine) into the Body and Blood of the risen Christ, and to transform the communicants into one Mystical Body with the Communion of Saints and with all other communicants, past, present, and future.

These spiritual transformations are brought about by human intention interacting with the Divine. Decorum demands that the energies of the human participants be aligned with the Divine ones to reach a spiritual end, that is, that we use the rhetorical *logos* to shape human physical and intellectual sensibilities in sympathy with the spiritual actions in progress.

Notes

Introduction

1. Letter of October 22, 1971. *Letters of Marshall McLuhan*, page 446.
2. Note: we used the rhetorical five divisions to structure the article, as we did also to structure the book, *Laws of Media*.
3. At about the same time, he wrote a separate study of "The Relation of Environment to Anti-Environment" to explore in greater depth many of the themes touched on here. Windsor, Ontario: *University of Windsor Review*, Vol. 11, No. 1, Fall, 1966, pp. 1–10. Rpt., Floyd Matson and Ashley Montagu, eds., *The Human Dialogue* (New York: Macmillan / Glencoe, Illinois: Free Press, 1967), pp. 1–10. Rpt., *Innovations*, Ed. Bernard Bergzoni (London: Macmillan, 1968).
4. In 1964, McLuhan wrote to Wilfred Watson: "Talk about blind spots in regions of maximal impact! Looking at [Wyndham Lewis's] *The Diabolical Principle* just now I read loud and clear that art must be totally environmental. It must be the content of nothing whatever. Ergo, the VORTEX = the totally environmental. . . . Lewis wants nothing less for Art than the power to create total environments for Life and Death. There must be no art as content of some other set of skills or interest . . . I find it a bit staggering to confront Lewis as a man who really wanted to be Pontifex Maximus of a magical priesthood. I suppose Yeats, Joyce and Pound had similar aspirations. Their priesthood was to create new worlds of perception. They were to be world engineers who shaped the totality of human awareness. Their pigments and materials were not to be paint or words but all the resources of the age. Such were the Pharaohs. They made of the world a perception Lab. . . . The mode of great Art. The environment as ultimate artefact."

5. See Appendix Two for an outline of Cicero's Theory of Communication.
6. Gingko Press, 2006.

Chapter one: World Communication Series

1. The note is dated May 10, 1977.

Chapter two: Wyndham Lewis's Theory of Art and Communication

1. Ed. Note: Refers to Mr. Lewis' artwork "Creation Myth No. 17," first of a collection of reproductions of Lewis' paintings which appeared in this issue of *Shenandoah* (pp. 90–94).

Chapter three: Formal Causality in Chesterton

1. G. K. Chesterton, *Dickens* (London: Methuen, 1906), page 1.
2. *Dickens*, page 2.
3. Joseph Conrad, "Preface" to *The Nigger of the 'Narcissus'* (London: Gresham Publishing Company, 1925), page x.
4. Arthur Miller, "1949: The Year It Came Apart," *New York Magazine*, December 30, 1974.
5. *Ibid.*
6. G. K. Chesterton, *Tremendous Trifles* (New York: Dodd, Mead, 1909), page 91.
7. G. K. Chesterton, "The Queer Feet," *The Father Brown Stories* (London: Cassell, 1966), page 51.
8. *Ibid.*, page 52.
9. John Henry Cardinal Newman, *An Essay on the Development of Christian Doctrine* (New York: Doubleday, 1960), page 62.

Chapter four: Francis Bacon's Theory of Communication

1. See *Of the Advancement of Learning*, Everyman ed., pages 37, 138; and *Novum Organum*, I, lxviii; xciii; II, lii.
2. Etienne Gilson, *The Philosophy of St. Bonaventure* (New York: Sheed & Ward, 1938), page 479.
3. lxiii–lxxxviii.
4. Jowett, *The Dialogues of Plato*, 4 Vols. (New York: Charles Scribner,s, 1895), Vol. I, page 678.
5. *Of the Advancement of Learning*, Everyman, page 66.

6. *Novum Organum*, II, xxvii.

7. *Novum Organum*, II, lii.

8. *Novum Organum*, II, xlviii.

9. *Advancement*, Everyman, page 132: *Cf.* "Idols of the Tribe," *Novum Organum*, I, xxiv–xxxi.

10. *Advancement*, Everyman, page 134: "Idols of the Cave," *N. O.*, I, xxxi–xxxv.

11. *Advancement*, Everyman, page 134.

12. For the entire section from Roger Bacon, see *Selections from Medieval Philosophers*, edited and translated, with introductory notes and glossary by R. P. McKeon (New York: Charles Scribner's Sons, 1930), Vol. II, pages 8, ff.

13. McKeon, *Selections from Medieval Philosophers*, II, pages 5–6.

14. *Advancement*, Everyman, page 32.

15. *Advancement*, Everyman, page 142.

16. *Advancement*, Everyman, page 7.

17. Tract entitled "Francis Bacon's Aphorisms and Advices Concerning the Helps of the Mind and the Kindling of Natural Light."

18. *Advancement*, Everyman, pages 34–35.

Chapter five: Pound, Eliot and the Rhetoric of *The Waste Land*

1. Ezra Pound,. *Personae* (New York: New Directions Books, 1926), p. 61 (hereafter cited in the text as *Personae*).

2. Wyndham Lewis, ed., *Blast: Review of the Great English Vortex*. (London: John Lane, The Bodley Head) No. I (20th June, 1914), p. 154. The words are Pound's.

3. Ezra Pound, *Gaudier-Brzeska: A Memoir* (London: The Marvell Press, 1960), p. 92.

4. M. C. Bradbrook, *T.S. Eliot* (London, New York, Toronto: published for The British Council and The National Book League by Longmans, Green & Co., 1950), p. 28.

5. T. S. Eliot, *For Lancelot Andrewes. Essays on Style and Order* (London: Faber and Gwyer, 1928), pp. ix–x.

6. Eliot, *After Strange Gods: A Primer of Modern Heresy*, the Page-Barbour Lectures at the University of Virginia, 1933 (London: Faber and Faber Limited, 1934), pp. 41–42.

7. Eliot, "The Method of Mr. Pound," in *The Athenaeum* (London: October 24, 1919), p. 1065.

8. Eliot, *Selected Essays* (London: Faber and Faber Limited, 1932, rpt. 1972), p. 289.

9. Ernst R. Curtius, *European Literature and the Latin Middle Ages*, tr. W. R. Trask. (New York and Evanston: Harper and Row, Publishers; first edition, 1963), p. 327.

10. Robert Hollander, *Allegory in Dante's* Commedia. (Princeton, New Jersey: Princeton University Press, 1969), p. 14.

11. Bishop Lancelot Andrewes, *Ninety-six Sermons* (in the *Library of Anglo-Catholic Theology*). (Oxford: John Henry Parker, 1841), I, 92.

12. Andrewes, III, 222.

13. St. Bonaventure, *The Breviloquium*, in *The Works of St. Bonaventure*, tr. Jose de Vinck (Paterson, N.J.: St. Anthony Guild Press, 1963), pp. 13–14.

14. Varro, *De Lingua Latina*, tr. R. G. Kent (Loeb Classical Library, Cambridge, Mass.: Harvard University Press; London: W. Heinemann Ltd., 1938. Rev. ed., 1958). Book V 7–8 (Vol I, p. 9).
15. Andrewes, V, 526.
16. Hollander, p. 45.
17. *Ibid.*, pp. 46–47.
18. *Ibid.*
19. Eliot, *To Criticize the Critic* (New York: Farrar, Straus & Giroux, 1965), p. 125.
20. *Ibid.*, p. 134.
21. Valerie Eliot, ed., *The Waste Land: A Facsimile and Transcript of the Original Drafts Including the Annotations of Ezra Pound*. (New York: Harcourt Brace Jovanovich, Inc., 1971).
22. *Writers at Work: The* Paris Review *Interviews*, Second Series. (New York, 1965), pp. 104–5.
23. St. Thomas Aquinas, *De Potentia Dei. On the Power of God* (*Quaestiones Disputatae De Potentia Dei*) tr., English Dominican Fathers (Westminster, Maryland: The Newman Press, 1952), II, 9.
24. Preface to G. Wilson Knight's *The Wheel of Fire* (1930) and to *Thoughts after Lambeth* (1932) [Miss Bradbrook's note].
25. Bradbrook, *T. S. Eliot: The Making of* The Waste Land (Harlow, Essex, 1972), p. 23.
26. "Virgil and the Christian World," in *On Poetry and Poets* (1951), pp. 122–123 (Miss Bradbrook's note).
27. R.P. Blackmur, "Irregular Metaphysics," in *T.S. Eliot. A Collection of Critical Essays*, ed. Hugh Kenner (Englewood Cliffs, N.J., Prentice-Hall, Inc., 1962), p. 63.
28. *Ibid.*, p. 59.
29. D. D. Paige, ed., *The Letters of Ezra Pound 1907–1941* (New York: New American Library, 1964), p. 170 (hereafter cited in the text as *Letters*).
30. Charles Dickens, *Our Mutual Friend* (New York: New American Library / Signet Classics, 1964), p. 226.
31. Curtius, pp. 307–8.
32. Etienne Gilson, *The Philosophy of St. Bonaventure*, tr., Dom Illtyd Trethowan and Frank J. Sheed (Paterson, N. J.: St. Anthony Guild Press, 1965), p. 208.
33. Henry James, *What Maisie Knew; In the Cage; The Pupil*, Novels and Tales, Series No. 11 (New York: C. Scribner's Sons, 1908).
34. *Ibid.*, p. 376.
35. *Ibid.*, pp. 377–378.
36. Included in *Literary Essays of Ezra Pound*, ed. and introd. T. S. Eliot (New York, 1968).
37. Bradbrook, *T. S. Eliot* (London, 1950), p. 35.
38. T. S. Eliot, *The Use of Poetry and the Use of Criticism: Studies in the Relation of Criticism to Poetry in England* (London: Faber and Faber Limited, 1933), pp. 118–19.
39. Quintilian, *Institutio Oratoria*, Book I.iv.1–4, tr., H. E. Butler, Loeb Classical Library (Cambridge, Mass., and London, 1963), I, 63.
40. *Ibid.* Book III.iii, 1–3, I, 385.
41. Petronius Arbiter, *The Satyricon*. tr., William Arrowsmith (New York, 1959), p. 57.
42. *Ibid.*, p. 61.
43. *The Waste Land*, ll. 43–46.

44. Blackmur, p. 63.
45. Donald Gallup, *T. S. Eliot & Ezra Pound: Collaborators in Letters* (New Haven: Henry W. Wenning / C. A. Stonehill, 1970), p. 24. The remark is in a letter from Pound to Harriet Monroe. He wrote: "You might also concede the constructive value of my kicking about mutilations. *Propertius* and *Mauberly* were cut, but on the strength of my howling to high heaven that this was an outrage, Eliot's *Waste Land* was printed whole. In which action I also participated. Dragging my own corpse by the heels to arouse the blasted spectators" (*Letters*, page 230).
46. Marjorie Crump, *The Epyllion from Theocritus to Ovid* (Oxford: Basil Blackwell, 1931).
47. Seon Givens, ed., *James Joyce: Two Decades of Criticism* (Rpt. 1948; New York, 1963).
48. W. B. Yeats, *Essays and Introductions* (New York: Macmillan, 1961), pp. 215–16.
49. Quoted in Hugh Kenner, *The Invisible Poet: T. S. Eliot*. New York: McDowell, Obolensky, 1959. Pages 151–152.
50. *Ibid*. Page 152.
51. *Ibid*.
52. Ed. Note: See Chapter Seven, hereunder, "Rhetorical Spirals in Four Quartets," pp. 65–73

Chapter six: Thomas Aquinas's Theory of Communication

1. So, Chesterton pointed out: "Everyone knows that the Nominalist declared that things differ too much to be really classified; so that they are only labeled. Aquinas was a firm but moderate Realist, and therefore held that there really are general qualities; as that human beings are human, and other paradoxes. To be an extreme realist would have taken him too near to being a Platonist. He recognized that individuality is real, but said that it coexists with a common character making some generalisation possible . . ." G. K. Chesterton, *St. Thomas Aquinas—The Dumb Ox* (Sheed & Ward, 1933; Doubleday/Image Books, 1956).
2. *De Anima* 415 b 12.
3. Question 3, Article 16, ad 22.
4. Etienne Gilson observes, "The second consequence of the Thomistic reform of metaphysics has been to introduce a clear-cut distinction between the two orders of formal causality and efficient causality. Formal causality is that which makes things to be *what* they are, and, in a way, it also makes them to be, since in order to be, each and every being has to be a *what*. But formal causality dominates the whole realm of substance, and its proper effect is substantiality, . . . It is then literally true to say that existence is a consequence which follows from the form of essence, but not as an effect follows from the efficient cause . . . In short, forms are "formal" causes of existence, to the whole extent to which they contribute to the establishment of substances which are capable of existing." *Being and Some Philosophers* (Toronto: Pontifical Institute of Medieval Studies, 1949), pages 182–183. His concern with the difference between formal causes and efficient causes is another main theme of his thinking, especially in the *Summa Theologica*. See for example, his comments on the action of grace in the soul in *S.T.*, Q. 113, Art. 7, ad 5. Formal cause is always sudden and transformative; efficient cause, gradual and sequential.

5. *Summa contra Gentiles*, Book I, chapter 53.

6. *Summa contra Gentiles*, Book I, chapter 54. See the comment, for example, by F. C. Copleston, *Aquinas* (Great Britain: Penguin Books, New York: Viking / Penguin, 1955), page 185.

7. *Summa contra Gentiles* Book III, part 2, chapter 152.

8. *Patrologia Latina*, CCX, 579 A. Cited in E. R. Curtius, *European Literature and the Latin Middle Ages*, Trans. W. R. Trask (New York and Evanston: Harper & Row, Harper Torchbooks / The Bollingen Library, 1953), page 319; and *vide* page 326 for a brief overview of the medieval trope of the world as a book.

9. "Henry IV, a Mirror for Magistrates" by H. M. McLuhan (Toronto: *University of Toronto Quarterly*, Vol. XVII, No. 2, January, 1948, page 159).

10. M. D. Chenu showed that St. Thomas used rhetorical decorum as a guide in deciding the order of presentation of texts in the *Summa Theologiae*: St. Thomas himself tells us expressly the intention of his new work: he wants to remove the obstacles which official instruction then presented, in that: "*ea quae sunt necessaria ad sciendum non traduntur secundum ordinem disciplinae, sed secundum quod requirebat librorum expositio lectio), vel secundum quod se praebebat occasio disputandi (quaestiones).*"—"Those things which are necessary for knowledge are not taught according to the order of the discipline, but according to the requirements of the *explication de textes*, or according to the demands of the occasion of the disputation."—"The Plan of St. Thomas' *Summa Theologiae*" in *Cross Currents*, Vol. II, No. 2, Winter, 1952 (New York: Cross Currents Corporation), page 67. A propos Thomas's education in the trivium he gives the merest sketch: "Such was the general method of instruction in the schools from the twelfth to the thirteenth centuries: the texts were "read," and the books which thus served as the bases of courses were officially inscribed in the programs of the various faculties. In grammar, Priscian and Donatus were read; in rhetoric, Cicero and Quintilian; in logic and in philosophy [i.e., dialectic], Porphyry, Boethius, then Aristotle; in medicine, Isaac Israeli, etc." (Page 68)

11. The same matter formed an argument in the *Summa contra Gentiles* (Book III, Part 2, Chapter 97, para. 13):

> Hence, the fact that creatures are brought into existence, though it takes its origin from the rational character of divine goodness, nevertheless depends solely on God's will. But, if it be granted that God wills to communicate His goodness to His creatures by way of likeness as far as it is possible, then one finds in this the reason why creatures are of divers kinds, but it does not necessarily follow that they are differentiated on the basis of this or that measure of perfection, or according to this or that number of things. On the other hand, if we grant that, as a result of an act of divine will, He wills to establish this particular number of things, and to bestow on each thing a particular measure of perfection, then as a result one finds the reason why each thing has such and such a form and such and such matter . . . .

This paragraph alone could provide the core of still another aspect of Thomas's theory of communication.

12. In the first Book of the O. T., *Genesis*, the creation takes place as each being is "spoken," that is, uttered: so beings, their degree, intensity, hierarchy, configurations, and organization, are as it were, "figures" or tropes of that mode of Divine speech.

13. *Vide* F. C. Copleston, *Op. Cit.*, page 112.

14. A clear reference to the discussion of *hamartia* in Aristotle's *Poetics*. *Hamartia* meant "off the mark," "off-centredness"; literally, eccentricity.
15. Copleston, *Op. Cit.*, page 127. Copleston remarks further, "Does any particular argument possess a special or pre-eminent importance? Modern Thomists often assert that the third proof, bearing explicitly on the existence of things, is fundamental. But if we look at the two *Summas*, we do not find Aquinas saying this. So far as he gives explicit preference to any particular proof it is to the first, which he declares, somewhat surprisingly, to be the clearest." (Page 127)
16. From "Joyce, Aquinas and the Poetic Process," by H. M. McLuhan, *Renascence*, Vol. IV, No. 1, Autumn, 1951, pages 3–11.
17. More copies of this work survive than of any other: it was a kind of fourth-century *Finnegans Wake*.
18. Bernard J. Muller-Thym, "St. Thomas and the Recapturing of Natural Wisdom," in *The Modern Schoolman*, May, 1941, pages 65–66.

Chapter seven: Rhetorical Spirals in *Four Quartets*

1. *James Joyce Quarterly*, 11 (Summer, 1974), 394–403.
2. *Language and Mind*, enlarged edition (New York, 1972), p. 19.
3. Ibid., p. 74.
4. Trans., Willard R. Trask, Bollingen Series XXXVI (New York, 1953), pp. 315, 317.
5. *The Philosophy of St. Bonaventure*, trans., Dom Illtyd Trethowen and F. J. Sheed (London, 1938), pp. 229–230.
6. Paris, 1922, p. 37.
7. See the four volumes of Henri de Lubac, *Exégèse médiévale, les quatre sens de l'Ecriture* (Paris, 1959–64).

Chapter eight: Poetic vs. Rhetorical Exegesis

1. The judgment of poetic evaluation indirectly involves a judgment of moral quality because poems, although not exhortations to action, are basically actions; and the quality of the poem involves the quality of the action. "What goes on in the poem" must be judged at least on the analogy of human ethics, but that is not to say that the poem advocates an ethic. The advocacy of any line of action is rhetorical; and thus "didactic poetry" is not organized poetically but rhetorically. As such it can enjoy a validity of its own. However, just as rhetoric and politics enter into a poem as matter or vehicle, ethics inheres as dramatic agency. Thus poetry cannot be organized without ethical vision but poetry can never, as such, perform the rhetorical task of inculcating morality. Insofar, therefore, as modern criticism has transferred its techniques of literary observation from psychology and anthropology, it has recovered a lost insight into many of the functions of language. Studies of language symbols as strate-

gy in neurosis and dreams, or language as gesture and phatic communion in the complex organic patterns of tribal communities have greatly deepened our perceptions in reading poetry. But neither psychologist nor anthropologist has approached his material with the means or intention of evaluation. The psychologist has studied neurosis as individual strategy and the anthropologist has viewed tribal cultures as communal strategies for coping with a hostile environment. This strategical viewpoint is essentially one of rhetorical exegesis.

Chapter nine: Joyce and McLuhan'

1. *The Role of Thunder in* Finnegans Wake. Toronto: University of Toronto Press, 1997.
2. R. A. Lanham, *The Electronic Word.* page 29.
3. From "James Joyce: Trivial and Quadrivial,'" pp. 83–85.

Chapter thirteen: The Emperor's Old Clothes

1. Erwin Straus, *The Primary World of the Senses,* New York, Free Press of Glencoe (1962).
2. Jacques Ellul, *Propaganda,* New York, Knopf (1965).
3. Alan P. Herbert, *Uncommon Law,* London, Methuen (1935), p. 14.
4. See E. J. Dijksterhuis, *The Mechanization of the World Picture,* Oxford, Oxford University Press (1961), pp. 418 ff.
5. Milič Čapek, *The Philosophical Impact of Contemporary Physics,* Princeton, N.J., Van Nostrand (1961).
6. Frank Kermode, *Romantic Image,* New York, Chilmark Press (1963).
7. Quoted by M. C. Bradbrook in his book *English Dramatic Form,* London, Chatto and Windus (1965), p. 125.
8. E. A. Gutkind, *Our World from the Air,* London, Chatto and Windus (1952).
9. R. Buckminster Fuller, in *World Resources Inventory,* Carbondale, Southern Illinois University Press, Phase I Document 3, p. 90.

Chapter fifteen: Culture and Communication

1. R. H. Trotter, "The Other Hemisphere," 218. The chart on the next page is taken from the article.
2. The chart reflects the scientific understanding of the cortical hemispheres, gained mainly in the last twenty years. The cortex of the ordinary human brain has two hemispheres, joined by a massive bundle of fibres called the *corpus callosum*, which seems to be the agency of dialogue between the hemispheres. It was only in the 1950s that these forebrain commisures in man were first deliberately severed, allowing the hemispheres to be studied independently. "The first important finding was that the interhemispheric exchange of information was totally disrupted following commisurotomy. The effect was such that visual, tactual, propri-

oceptive, auditory and olfactory information presented to one hemisphere could be processed and dealt with in that half-brain, but each of these activities went on outside the awareness of the other half-cerebrum. This observation confirmed the animal work done earlier by Myers and Sperry, except that in a sense the results were more dramatic. Since it is the left hemisphere that normally processes the natural language and speech mechanisms, all processes ongoing in the left hemisphere could easily be verbally described by the patients; information presented to the right hemisphere went undescribed" (Michael S. Gazzaniga, "Review of the Split Brain," 91). In subsequent tests of patients that had undergone commisurotomy, the complementarity of the two hemispheres became increasingly evident. Most surprising was the range of activities proper to the right hemisphere, which in the nineteenth century carried the label of "minor" or "quiet." So complete was our culture's visual bias at that time, it was seriously proposed that the right hemisphere made no contribution to human intellection or activity.

3. Page 244: "It is well known that the right brain is poor at comprehending consonants and does not do well at syntax, which is the left brain's special province. How far this is a sheer absence of function, and how far it is an effect of the left brain inhibiting the right across the corpus callosum is still not clear." If the right brain cannot even handle consonants they must have had their genesis in the left brain: this adds point to the mystery of what it was that urged the Greeks to invent them in the first place.

4. Joseph E. Bogen, "Some Educational Aspects of Hemispheric Specialization," 138. Bogen observes further: "What distinguished hemispheric specialization is not so much certain kinds of material (e.g., words for the left, faces for the right) but the *way* in which the material is processed. In other words, hemispheric differences are more usefully considered in terms of *process specificity* rather than material specificity."

5. Herbert Krugman, from a paper delivered to the annual conference of the Advertising Research Foundation, October, 1978. Cf. also Barry Siegel, "Stay Tuned for How TV Scrambles Your Brain," in *The Miami Herald*, C10. Krugman's original report was presented as a paper to the annual conference (1970) of the American Association for Public Opinion Research.

6. Jacques Ellul, *Propaganda: The Formation of Men's Attitudes*, 108–9. Harold Innis comments on the moment of transition: "For a brief period the Greeks escaped from the oral tradition and the written tradition. The oral tradition was sufficiently strong to check complete submergence in the written. The oral tradition supported Greek skepticism and evaded monopolies of religious literature." (*The Bias of Communication*, 111)

7. Benedict, *The Chrysanthemum and the Sword*, 249. "On" is an obligation passively incurred (*cf.* page 116).

8. *Novum Organum*, Book I, aphorism xl.

9. *Novum Organum*, Book I, aphorism xli: "The Idols of the Tribe have their foundation in human nature itself, and in the tribe or race of men. For it is a false assertion that the sense of man is the measure of all things. On the contrary, all perceptions, as well of the senses as of the mind, are according to the measure of the individual and not according to the measure of the universe. And the human understanding is like a false mirror, which, receiving rays irregularly, distorts and discolors the nature of things by mingling its own nature with it" (page 3). Vico's first axiom is this: "120. Because of the indefinite nature of the human mind, whenever it is lost in ignorance, man makes himself the measure of all things. 121.

This axiom explains those two common human traits, on the one hand that rumor grows in its course (*fama crescit eundo*), on the other that rumor is deflated by the presence [of the thing itself] (*minuit praesentia famam*). In the long course that that rumor has run from the beginning of the world it has been the perennial source of all the exaggerated opinions which have hitherto been held concerning remote antiquities unknown to us by virtue of that property of the human mind noted by Tacitus in his *Life of Agricola*, where he says that everything unknown is taken for something great (*omne ignotum pro magnifico est*) (*The New Science of Giambattista Vico*, 54).

10. *Novum Organum*, Book I, aphorism xlii: "The Idols of the Cave are the idols of the individual man. For everyone (besides the errors common to human nature in general) has a cave or den of his own, which refracts and discolors the light of nature; owing either to his own proper and peculiar nature or to his education and conversation with others; or to the reading of books, and the authority of those whom he esteems and admires . . . or the like. So that the spirit of man (according as it is meted out to different individuals) is in fact a thing variable and full of perturbation, and governed as it were by chance. Whence it was well observed by Heraclitus that men look for science in their own lesser worlds, and not in the greater or common world" (page 35). This Idol takes its name from the cave in the *Republic* of Plato (Book VII). Vico notes (axiom two): "122. It is another property of the human mind that whenever men can form no idea of distant and unknown things, they judge them by what is familiar and at hand. 123. This axiom points to the inexhaustible source of all the errors about the beginnings of humanity that have been adopted by entire nations and by all the scholars. For when the former began to take notice of them and the latter to investigate them, it was on the basis of their own enlightened, cultivated and magnificent times that they judged the origins of humanity, which must nevertheless, by the nature of things, have been small, crude and quite obscure" (page 54).

11. *Novum Organum*, Book I, aphorism xliii: "There are also Idols formed by the intercourse and association of men with each other, which I call Idols of the Market-place, on account of the commerce and consort of men there. For it is by discourse that men associate; and words are imposed according to the apprehension of the vulgar. And therefore the ill and unfair choice of words wonderfully obstructs the understanding. Nor do the definitions or explanations wherewith in some things learned men are wont to guard and defend themselves, by any means set the matter right. But words plainly force and overrule the understanding, and throw all into confusion, and lead men away into numberless empty controversies and idle fancies" (page 35). Vico translates this into his third axiom, as follows: "125. As for the conceit of the nations, we have heard that golden saying of Diodorus Siculus. Every nation, according to him, whether Greek or barbarian, has had the same conceit that it before all other nations invented the comforts of human life and that its remembered history goes back to the very beginning of the world" (page 55).

12. *Novum Organum*, Book I, aphorism xliv: "Lastly, there are the Idols which have immigrated into men's minds from the various dogmas of philosophies, and also from wrong laws of demonstration. These I call Idols of the Theater; because in my judgment all the received systems are but so many stage-plays, representing worlds of their own creation after an unreal and scenic fashion. Nor is it only of the systems now in vogue, or only of the ancient sects and philosophies, that I speak; for many more plays of the same kind may yet be composed and in like artificial manner set forth; seeing that errors the most widely different have nev-

ertheless causes for the most part alike. Neither again do I mean this only of entire systems, but also of many principles and axioms in science, which by tradition, credulity, and negligence have come to be received" (page 35). Vico renders this in his fourth axiom: "127. To this conceit of the nations there may be added that of the scholars, who will have it that whatever they know is as old as the world. 128. This axiom disposes of all the opinions of the scholars concerning the matchless wisdom of the ancients . . ." (page 55). Summing his great chapter on Poetic Wisdom, Vico reiterates: "779. We have shown that poetic wisdom justly deserves two great and sovereign tributes. The one, clearly and constantly accorded to it, is that of having founded gentile mankind, though the conceit of the nations on the one hand, and that of the scholars on the other, the former with ideas of an empty magnificence and the latter with ideas of an impertinent philosophical wisdom, have in effect denied it this honour by their very efforts to affirm it. The other, concerning which a vulgar tradition has come down to us, is that the wisdom of the ancients made its wise men, by a single inspiration, equally great as philosophers, lawmakers, captains, historians, orators and poets, on which account it has been so greatly sought after" (page 265).

13. Mario Bunge, *Causality: The Place of the Causal Principle in Modern Science*, 32. *Vide*: *Metaphysics*, Bk. I, ch. iii, 983a, b; Bk. V, ch. ii; and *Physics* Bk. II, ch. iii and vii.

14. George Steiner, *After Babel: Aspects of Language and Translation*, 149. He illustrates: "We *know* what will happen to Agamemnon when he enters the house, each instant of the agon has been announced and prepared for. We *know* precisely what Oedipus will discover—in a crucial sense he too has known all along. Yet with each narration or performance of the fable our sense of shock is renewed. The tragic vision of Greek literature turns on this deep paradox: the event most expected, most consequent on the internal logic of action, is also the most surprising" (page 149).

15. *Novum Organum*, Book I, aphorism xlviii. See, too, his remarks in *The Advancement of Learning*, Book II, 5 and 7.

16. Aristotle, *Generation of Animals*, xliv, 3. Aristotle opens Book I by presenting formal cause as "the *logos* of the thing's essence."

17. W. K. Wimsatt, Jr., and C. Brooks, *Literary Criticism—A Short History*, 7–9. In their footnote they cite Frye's "My [Critical] Credo," 91–110, and add: "'Archetype,' borrowed from Jung, means a primordial image, a part of the collective unconscious, the psychic residue of numberless experiences of the same kind, and thus part of the inherited response-pattern of the race."

18. For over a thousand years, based on the Book of Genesis, the West has propounded a theory of nature as one of the forms of Divine revelation. There were two books, the Book of Nature and the Book of Scripture, parallel texts in different idioms as it were, both subject to exegesis. Shakespeare frequently alludes to this tradition of multilevel exegesis: in *As You Like It*, the exiled Duke remarks to his companions, the woods "are counsellors / That fleetingly persuade me what I am . . . And this our life, exempt from public haunt / Finds tongues in trees, books in the running brooks, / Sermons in stones, and good in everything" (ll.1.10–17). "The Book of Nature was an encyclopedia of being: only God spoke in events. In the minds of the Middle Ages every event, every case, fictitious or historic, tends to crystallize, to become a parable, an example, a proof, in order to be applied as a standing instance of a general moral truth. In the same way every utterance becomes a dictum, a maxim, a text. For every question of conduct, Scripture, legends, history, literature, furnish

a crowd of examples or of types, together making up a sort of moral clan, to which the matter in question belongs." (J. Huizinga, *The Waning of the Middle Ages*, 227).

Chapter sixteen: Marshall McLuhan's Theory of Communication

1. An itinerant professional safe-cracker. Most dictionaries will give that much. But see Eric Partridge's *A Dictionary of the Underworld British and American: Being the Vocabularies of Crooks, Criminals, Racketeers, Beggars and Tramps, Convicts, The Commercial Underworld, The Drug Traffic, The White Slave Traffic, Spivs* (London: Routledge & Kegan Paul Ltd., 1949/1950), pp. 783–784: He gives more than a column to the history and uses of *yegg*, which was still current at mid-century.
2. From "Education in the Electronic Age." Printed as Chapter 12.3 in *The Best of Times / The Worst of Times: Contemporary Issues in Canadian Education*. Eds., H. A. Stevenson, R. M. Stamp, and J. D. Wilson. Toronto and Montreal: Holt, Rinehart and Winston of Canada Limited, pages 515–531. Rpt. from *Interchange* (Toronto: Ontario Institute for Studies in Education), Vol. 1, No. 4, 1970, pp. 1–12. Text of an address to the Provincial Committee on the Aims and Objectives of Education of the Schools of Ontario, on January 19, 1967. This passage forms the last two pages, pp. 11–12.
3. Stephen Hawking, *Black Holes and Baby Universes* (New York, London, Toronto, Sydney, Auckland: Bantam Books, 1993), p. 44.
4. Anti-environments, or countersituations made by artists, provide means of direct attention to environments and enable us to see and understand more clearly.
5. McLuhan, Marshall and Harley Parker, *Through the Vanishing Point: Space in Poetry and Painting* (New York: Harper & Row, 1968), page xxiii.
6. *Op. cit.*, pages 237–238.
7. *Op. cit.*, page 240.
8. *Laws of Media* devotes a chapter to this theme, reprinted here as Chapter 15.
9. T. S. Eliot, *To Criticize the Critic and Other Writings* (New York: Farrar, Straus & Giroux, 1965), page 134, The next two passages are from the same page.
10. In *The Sacred Wood*. New York: Barnes & Noble, 1960, pages 47–59. Also in *Selected Essays*.
11. In *Literary Essays of Ezra Pound*. New York: New Directions, 1968, pages 41–57.
12. Harold Bloom, *The Western Canon: the Books and School of the Ages* (New York: Harcourt Brace and Company, 1994), page 479.
13. "An Introduction for My Plays," in *Essays and Introductions* (London: Macmillan & co. Ltd., 1961), page 529.
14. Note: it is still in fashion in the twenty-first century. Pernicious habits die hard.
15. *Novum Organum*, aphorism lx.
16. From *The Advancement of Learning and New Atlantis* (London: Oxford University Press, 1906, Rpt., 1951), page 39.
17. *The Advancement of Learning*, *Op. cit.*, page 163.

18. From "The *Hot and Cool* Interview with Gerald Emanuel Stearn" (1967). Rpt., *Marshall McLuhan Essays, Media Research: Technology, Art, Communication Edited with Commentary by Michael A. Moos* (Amsterdam B.V.: Overseas Publishers Association, 1997), page 49.

19. University of Toronto Press, Rpt., 1964, 1968, included in this volume as Chapter 11. All of the Innis quotes are from this text.

20. From "The *Hot and Cool* Interview with Gerald Emanuel Stearn" (1967). Rpt., *Marshall McLuhan Essays, Media Research: Technology, Art, Communication Edited with Commentary by Michael A. Moos* (Amsterdam B.V.: Overseas Publishers Association, 1997), page 58.

21. *Op. cit.*, pages 62–63.

22. First issued in 1938; Rpt., (Third edition) New York: Holt, Rinehart and Winston, Inc., 1960. On the flyleaf of my copy, he wrote, "Cleanth Brooks, a long-standing friend of mine, did revolutionize the teaching of literature in USA with this book."

23. By I. A. Richards. Rpt., New York: Harcourt, Brace & World, Inc. (Harvest Books), 1956.

24. Richards summarizes the experiment:

> For some years I have made the experiment of issuing printed sheets of poems—ranging in character from a poem by Shakespeare to a poem by Ella Wheeler Wilcox—to audiences who were requested to comment freely in writing upon them. The authorship of the poems was not revealed, and with rare exceptions it was not recognized. (*Practical Criticism*, page 3.)
>
> Writers were given a week to make their comments. Richards is sensitive on one point: "The standing of the writers must be made clear. The majority were undergraduates reading English with a view to an Honours Degree" (page 4). Such however was not the scuttlebutt around the university when McLuhan arrived. It was generally accepted that the subjects had been graduate students and members of faculty. The "scandal" was that they could not even agree as to the meaning of a poem let alone any other aspects.
>
> In *Practical Criticism*, Richards quotes extensively from the written comments ("protocols") and seeks order amid the chaos, eventually proposing the "four kinds of meaning": Sense, Feeling, Tone and Intent.

25. Vol. 6, No. 3 (Summer 1944), pages 322–332. Rpt., 1945, in *Gerard Manley Hopkins. Kenyon Critics Edition* (Norfolk, Connecticut: New Directions Books), pp. 15–27. Rpt., 1966, in *Hopkins*, Ed., G. H. Hartman. Rpt., 1969, in *The Interior Landscape: The Literary Criticism of Marshall McLuhan 1943–1962*, edited by Eugene McNamara. Toronto: McGraw-Hill, pp. 63–74.

26. The four levels are the Literal, and the figurative levels, the Allegorical, the Moral (Tropological), and the Spiritual Levels. (Despite the coincidence of the first exegetical level with the Literal Sense of Practical Criticism—they are practically the same—the two sets of four are not otherwise in parallel.)

27. *And There Was Light*, Tr., Elizabeth R. Cameron (Boston and Toronto: Little, Brown and Company, 1963), pages 143–144.

Appendix 1: Aristotle's Theory of Communication

1. Copyright, Eric McLuhan, 2009.
2. *"Aristotle: On the Soul, Parva Naturalia, On Breath*. Trans., W. S. Hett (Heinemann / Harvard, 1957), III. vii; 481a.14–17, p. 177. The Greek original: *Te de dianoetike psyche ta phantasmata oion aisthemata hyparchei. Otan de agathon he kakon phese he apothese, pheuge he diokei. Dio oudepote noei aneu phantasmatos he psyche* . . . (Loeb, p. 176.)
3. Barry Sanders, *A Is for Ox: The Collapse of Literacy and the Rise of Violence in an Electronic Age* (New York: Random House / Vintage Books, 1994), page 32.

Appendix 2: Cicero's Theory of Communication

1. Translated and Revised with the Author's Co-operation by Max Meyer and Robert Morris Ogden. Second edition. New York: G. E. Stechert & Co., 1932.
2. *Op. cit.*, page 45.
3. Paul Fussell, Jr., *Poetic Meter and Poetic Form* (New York: Random House, 1965), page 110.
4. *Op. cit.*, page 36.
5. See the longer treatment of these matters in Chapter seven, above.
6. See the second Note added to the end of Appendix four, "On Formal Cause" for a brief explanation of the Logos and its relation to the elements of the trivium, Rhetoric, Dialectic, and Grammar.
7. Grammar, of course, means literature and therefore encyclopedism—ability with both Books—hence the coinage, "encyclopaedic wisdom" (another buzz-phrase for Grammar).

Appendix 4: On Formal Cause

1. The concluding paragraphs of Marshall McLuhan's essay, "Education in the Electronic Age"—The text of an address to the Provincial Committee on the Aims and Objectives of Education of the Schools of Ontario, on January 19, 1967. Printed as Chapter 12.3 in *The Best of Times / The Worst of Times: Contemporary Issues in Canadian Education*. Eds., H. A. Stevenson, R. M. Stamp, and J. D. Wilson. Toronto and Montreal: Holt, Rinehart and Winston of Canada Limited, 1972, pages 515–531.
2. Perhaps this is what Aristotle had in mind when he remarked, about thinking and perceiving, that "the exercise of their functions comes before the faculties themselves" (*Aristotle: On the Soul, Parva Naturalia, On Breath*. Trans., W. S. Hett (Heinemann / Harvard, 1957), II.4.19–20, page 84, 85: proteron gar eisi ton dynameon ai energeiai kai ai praxeis kata ton logon).
3. *After Babel* (London, New York, Toronto: Oxford University Press, 1975), page 149.
4. *The Economy of Cities* (New York: Random House, 1969), pp. 1–2.
5. *Op. cit.*, p. 38. The operation of formal cause is clearly evident in detective stories, where the detective is presented first with the effects and has to use formal cause to work backwards to the (efficient) cause of the crime. My father, who loved detective stories, noted in pencil

on the front flyleaf of one such paperback novel that Watson was the formal cause of Holmes as Jeeves was of Bertie Wooster. (*The Seven-Per-Cent Solution: Being a Reprint from the Reminiscences of John H. Watson, M.D., as edited by Nicholas Meyer.* New York: Ballantine Books, 1974, 1975.) I earnestly hope the reader will also look up three essays by Marshall McLuhan in which he discusses formal cause in relation to matters he studied. The first is the essay on "The Relation of Environment to Antienvironment," in *University of Windsor Review*, Vol. 11, No. 1, Fall, 1966, (Windsor, Ontario), pp. 1–10. Rpt., Floyd Matson and Ashley Montagu, eds., *The Human Dialogue* (New York: Macmillan, 1967), pp. 1–10. The second, "*The Argument: Causality in the Electric World*," by Marshall McLuhan and Barrington Nevitt, appeared in *Technology and Culture*, Vol. 14, #1 (University of Chicago Press, January, 1973), pp. 1–18. The responses by Fr. Joseph Owens (pp. 19–21) and Dr. Fritz Wilhelmsen, pp. (22–27) also merit attention. The third, "Formal Causality in Chesterton," appeared in *The Chesterton Review*, Spring / Summer, 1976, Vol. 11, No. 2, pp. 253–259.

6. *Great Books of the Western World*, Ed. R. M. Hutchins. Volume Two (the first half of the *Syntopicon*), *The Great Ideas: I*, Ed. Mortimer Adler. University of Chicago; ©Encyclopædia Britannica, Inc., 1952. Page 156.

7. Marshall and Eric McLuhan, *Laws of Media: The New Science*. Toronto: University of Toronto Press, 1988.

8. *Aristotle: Posterior Analytics*, trans., Hugh Tredennick; bound with *Topica*, trans., E. S. Forster. (London: William Heinemann / Cambridge, Mass., Harvard University Press: Loeb Classical Library, 1960), Book I, Ch. xxxiii.89a (end), pp. 170, 171.

9. A propos the moral outlook, McLuhan remarked, "Don't ask me if this is a good thing. I don't feel that any person is able yet to make value judgments of that sort. Our job is diagnosis and observation prior to judgment. But I have noticed over and over again that when people ask in the middle of some effort to chart an actual development, "Is this a good thing?" they always mean, "Is this a good thing for me?" "How does it affect me?—I'm a doctor." Or "How will it affect me? - I'm an architect." They don't mean, "Is it good?" They mean, "What will it do to me?" It took me years to find out what they really meant by this strange constant request for value judgment. It's a Protestant sort of fixation, this "Is it a good or a bad thing?" It comes from an obsession with efficient causes at an applied moment. The actual obsession with efficient causality—what you call activism—is basic to the Protestant outlook." (From a transcript of an informal address, given at the 12th annual seminarians' Conference, St. Michael's College, University of Toronto, 29–31 August 1959, and published in the volume, *Communications and the Word of God*, by St. Michael's College, pp. 9–22. Rpt., *The Medium and the Light* (Toronto: Stoddart, 1999), p. 37.) In a letter to the editor of *Commonweal* about their review (issue of May 25, 1979) of Elizabeth Eisenstein's study, he wrote: "[My book] *The Gutenberg Galaxy* makes no personal value judgments because it is concerned with *formal* causality and the study of effects, with reception aesthetics. Professor Eisenstein is concerned with *efficient* causality: her title is *The Printing Press as an Agent of Change*! This level of descriptive narrative leaves ample room for the noting of *content* and the making of value judgments, both of which are alien to the level of formal causality.
"In a utilitarian society, untrained in the formal structures and patterns of effect, efficient causality and moralizing is the only acceptable norm. Having written *The Gutenberg Galaxy* by way of turning in a fire alarm, it is curious to find some readers have charged me with arson . . .""

10. Stephen Hawking, *Black Holes and Baby Universes and Other Essays* (New York, London, Toronto, Sydney, Auckland: Bantam Books, 1993), p. 43. He adds, "The person who called me a positivist went on to add that everyone knew that positivism was out of date—another case of refutation by denigration." (Page 44.) McLuhan has enjoyed precisely the same sort of attention from his critics and from academic experts alike.

11. Translated and Revised with the Author's Co-operation by Max Meyer and Robert Morris Ogden. Second edition. New York: G. E. Stechert & Co., 1932.

12. *Op. cit.*, page 45.

13. Paul Fussell, Jr., *Poetic Meter and Poetic Form* (New York: Random House, 1965), page 110.

14. *Op. cit.*, page 36.

15. *Metaphysics*, I.6.30 (987b). The translation is by W. D. Ross; it agrees exactly with McKeon's.

16. Let us not casually assume that he means what we do by "definition." He is thinking in Greek; we, in Latin and English. *De*-finite, means being sensitive to the boundaries of the thing, the edge that circumscribes things finite. Observing the *figure/ground interface* between it and non-finitude. Where does it depart from or o'erleap finitude?

17. Aristotle, *Parts of Animals*, Book I, Ch. 1, 18–22 (642a.18–22). Loeb, pp. 76–77.

18. Each time the womb "speaks" through its mouth, the speech is a child. At the birth, the native midwife stands nearby the mother and calls out various names until the child, hearing its name, decides to be born.

19. So, Gilson remarks, echoing Aquinas, "God *knows* essences, but He *says* existences, and He does not say all that He knows." Etienne Gilson, *Being and Some Philosophers* (Toronto: Pontifical institute of Mediæval Studies, 1949, Rev., 1952), p. 169.

20. In modern science, the theory has the same effect as the name. Stephen Hawking observes that "it makes no sense to ask if [a theory] corresponds to reality, because we do not know what reality is independent of a theory. . . . It is no good appealing to reality because we don't have a model independent concept of reality. . . . The unspoken belief in a model independent reality is the underlying reason for the difficulties philosophers of science have with quantum mechanics and the uncertainty principle." *Black Holes and Baby Universes*, *Op. cit.*, pp. 44–45.

21. McKeon's translation: opening of *De Anima*, Book III, Chapter 8; 431'b20–432a.

22. Loeb, pp. 178–180. Keep this in mind in the discussion below: For Aristotle, *nous* and *aisthesis* are both *eide*.

23. Jowett (New York, 1895), I, page 678.

24. Marshall McLuhan, unpublished Ph.D. thesis, *The Place of Thomas Nashe in the Learning of His Time*. "Chapter One (The Trivium until St. Augustine) A. Grammar."

25. *Metaphysics*, V. 2.25, 30 (1013a).

26. In an aside suffused with delicacy, our translator of *Physics* exclaimed, "it does violence to the English idiom to call the material out of which a thing is made, or the distinctive attributes which define it, its 'causes,' whereas the Greek *aitia* and the corresponding adjective *aitios* can be applied to anything that is 'guilty of' or 'responsible for' a thing, or 'to the account of which,' for praise or blame, the thing may in any sense be put down. Paraphrase or barbarism offer the only escape from using English words in a sense that they cannot really bear." *The Physics*, Trans., Philip A. Wicksteed and Francis M. Cornford. In two volumes. Vol. I, pg. 127. Loeb (Harvard / Heinemann), 1980.

27. *Metaphysics*, I.3.25–30 (983a).

28. *Metaphysics*, VIII.4.10 (1044b).
29. *Metaphysics*, VIII.4.35 (1044a).
30. *Physics*, IV.1.22–23 (209a). Loeb, pp. 282–285.
31. *Metaphysics*, XII.5.29 (1071a).
32. *Commentary on the Metaphysics of Aristotle*, Trans., J. P. Rowan (Chicago: Henry Regnery Company, 1961), Book V, Lesson 2, paragraph 764.
33. *Op. cit.*, pp. 35, *ff.*
34. *The Role of Thunder in* Finnegans Wake. Toronto: University of Toronto Press, 1997.
35. Eric A. Havelock, *Preface to Plato.* Cambridge, Mass.: Harvard University Press, TheBelknap Press, 1963.
36. Pedro Lain-Entralgo, *Therapy of the Word in Classical Antiquity.* Ed. and Trans., L. J. Rather and J. M. Sharp. New Haven and London: Yale University Press, 1970.
37. In *Physics*, II, 3 (195a20–21), Aristotle speaks of *ti en einai*—which he uses there to denote formal cause—as "in the sense of the *essence*—the whole or the synthesis of the form." (*to de holon kai he synthesis kai to eidos.*) Loeb, pp. 132, 133. Also, in *Posterior Analytics*, II, 11 (94a35): " . . . this is the same as the essence, inasmuch as it is what the definition implies." (. . . *to ti en einai, to touto semainein ton logon* . . .) See also *De Anima*: *eti tou dynamei ontos logos he entelecheia* (415a.14–15), "the actuality of that which exists potentially is its essential formula." (*Aristotle: On the Soul, Parva Naturalia, On Breath.* Trans., W. S. Hett (Heinemann / Harvard, 1957), II.4, page 86, 87)
38. Eric A. Havelock, *The Muse Learns to Write: Reflections on Orality and Literacy from Antiquity to the Present* (New Haven and London: Yale University Press, 1986), page 113.
39. "Now for the thinking soul images take the place of direct perceptions; and when it asserts or denies that they are good or bad, it avoids or pursues them. Hence the soul never thinks without a mental image." (Loeb, p. 177 *Aristotle: On the Soul, Parva Naturalia, On Breath.* Trans., W. S. Hett (Heinemann / Harvard, 1957), III.vii; 481a.14–17) The Greek original: *Te de dianoetike psyche ta phantasmata oion aisthemata hyparchei. Otan de agathon he kakon phese he apothese, pheuge he diokei. Dio oudepote noei aneu phantasmatos he psyche* . . . (Loeb, p. 176.)
40. *Aristotle, De Anima*, Ed., Sir David Ross (Oxford: Clarendon Press, 1961), p. 39. There is not room here to enter the discussion of modern observations about the "disability" of thinking in images and its relation to split-brain research, although it is absolutely pertinent. At least one extremely suggestive study has discussed thinking in images in relation to autism, which in the present context ought to cast a most illuminating light on Aristotle's difficulties: Lance Strate, "Narcissism and Echolalia: Sense and the Struggle for the Self." *Speech Communication Annual* 14, 2000, pp. 14–62.
41. *Physics, Op. Cit.*, p. 129; the Greek version is on p. 128.
42. Translators continually struggle to render *logos*, for which English has no adequate equivalent. Also lacking one, Latin resorted to the hendiadys, *ratio atque oratio*, which they understood as "wisdom and eloquence" and used as a foundation for the alliance of Grammar and Rhetoric. The translator of *Generation of Animals* remarks in a note, that "we have here a term of wide and varied application, with which a number of correlated conceptions are associated, one or other of which may be uppermost in a particular case. The fundamental idea of [*logos*], as its connexion with [*legein*] shows, is that of *something spoken or uttered*, more especially a *rational utterance* or *rational explanation*, expressing a thing's *nature* and the *plan* of

it; hence [*logos*] can denote the *defining formula*, the *definition* of a thing's *essence*, of its *essential being* (as often in the phrase [*logos tes ousias*]), expressing the structure or character of the object to be defined." Aristotle: *Generation of Animals*, trans., A. L. Peck (Cambridge, Mass., Harvard University Press / London: William Heinemann Ltd., 1963), page xliv. This is the new (conventional) translation, not the manifold, transformative *logos* of the pre-Socratics.

43. Long, Marcus, *The Spirit of Philosophy*. Toronto: University of Toronto Press, 1953. Pages 142–3.

44. Book III, Chapter 2, 996b.5.

45. Thomas Aquinas, *Qu. Disp. De Anima*, art. 14, ad 4ᵐ. Cf. Ad 5ᵐ; and *In Boethium de Trinitate*, q. V, art. 4, ad 4ᵐ, ed. P. Wyser, p. 50, l. 19-p. 51, l. 11. (Gilson's note.) In his Commentary on *Metaphysics* Aquinas remarks, "In another sense cause means the form and pattern of a thing, i.e., its exemplar. This is the formal cause, which is related to a thing in two ways. In one way it stands as the intrinsic form of a thing, and in this respect it is called the formal principle of a thing. In another way it stands as something which is extrinsic to a thing but is that in likeness to which it is made, and in this respect an exemplar is also called a thing's form. It is in this sense that Plato held the Ideas to be forms. Moreover, because it is from its form that each thing derives its nature, whether of its genus or of its species, and the nature of its genus or of its species is what is signified by the definition, which expresses its quiddity, the form of a thing is therefore the intelligible expression of its quiddity, i.e., the formula by which its quiddity is known. For even though certain material parts are given in the definition, still it is from a thing's form that the principal part of the definition comes. The reason why the form is a cause, then, is that it completes the intelligible expression of a thing's quiddity."—Commentary on the *Metaphysics* of Aristotle, Trans., J. P. Rowan (Chicago: Henry Regnery Company, 1961), Book V, Lesson 2, Paragraph 764.

46. Gilson, *Being and Some Philosophers*, *Op. cit.*, pp. 168–169.

47. *Op. cit.*, p. 170.

48. See Gilson's discussion, *Op. cit.*, pp. 172, ff.

49. *The Question Concerning Technology and Other Essays, Translated and with an Introduction by William Levitt*. New York: Harper Colophon Books (Harper & Row, Publishers), 1977. Heidegger provides an extended criticism of the four causes as received, which he regards nevertheless as indispensable to understanding technological transformations of culture.

50. *The Question Concerning Technology*, pp. 26–27.

51. *Anatomy of Criticism—Four Essays*. Princeton, New Jersey: Princeton University Press, 1957, Rpt., 1971, page 132. Cf. Gilson, *Op. cit.*, p. 174: "In short, form is the cause of actual existence, inasmuch as it is the formal cause of the substance which receives its own act of existing. This is why, as Thomas Aquinas so often says, *esse consequitur formam*: to be follows upon form." And p. 175: "In order to receive its to be, a form must needs be in potency to it. 'To be,' then, is the act of the form, not *qua* form, but *qua* being."

52. *Fables of Identity: Studies in Poetic Mythology* (New York: Harcourt, Brace & World, Inc.), page 11.

53. For a delightful history of final causation (teleological cause), see Etienne Gilson's *From Aristotle to Darwin and Back Again: A Journey in Final Causality, Species, and Evolution* (Notre Dame, Indiana: University of Notre Dame Press, 1984).

54. See Ivan Illich, *In the Vineyard of the Text: A Commentary to Hugh of St. Victor's* Didascalion (Chicago and London: University of Chicago Press, 1993), pp. 51 ff. Reading was far from passive, and recommended throughout antiquity as strenuous exercise: "Hellenistic physicians prescribed reading as an alternative to ball playing or a walk. Reading presupposed that you be in good physical form; the frail or infirm were not supposed to read with their own tongue. At one solstice, Nicholas of Clairvaux had submitted with all the other monks to the customary quarterly purging and bleeding, but this time the fast in combination with the cupping had left him too weak for a while to continue his reading. When Peter the Venerable had a cold which made him cough when he opened his mouth, he could not read, neither in the choir nor in his cell 'to himself.'" (Illich, pp. 57–58.) He notes: "The most readable and dense description of monastic reading is still Jean Leclerq, *Love of Learning*, especially '*Lectio and Meditatio*,' pp. 15–17, where these two anecdotes and their sources are given." (p. 58.) See Jean Leclerq, *The Love of Learning and the Desire for God* (New York: Fordham University Press, 1982).

55. This passage from my essay, "Francis Bacon's Theory of Communication."

56. Tract entitled "Francis Bacon's Aphorisms and Advices Concerning the Helps of the Mind and the Kindling of Natural Light." *The Works of Francis Bacon, Lord Chancellor of England. A New edition: with a Life of the Author, by Basil Montagu, Esq.,* In Three Volumes (Philadelphia: Parry & McMillan, 1854), Vol. I, page 454.

57. You can apply the four laws (we state them as questions) to any human artifact, hardware or software alike. What does the thing set aside / obsolesce? What much older thing does it retrieve / update in a new form? What, already present, does it amplify / enhance? What complementary form does it reverse into / put on when pushed too far? These four laws have among themselves the ratios of proper proportionality—a is to b as c is to d—that characterize the logos, and every word, and the nature of metaphor. There is no sequence: they apply simultaneously. They bridge the hitherto separate worlds of technology and the arts.

58. This explains the difficulties facing anyone who tries to discern formal causes in Nature or to separate them there from final causes. Cf. the remarks in the Great Books' explanation (used above):

But the formal cause is not as apparent in nature as in art. Whereas in art it can be identified by reference to the plan in the maker's mind, it must be discovered in nature in the change itself, as that which completes the process. For example the redness which the apple takes on in ripening is the formal cause of its alteration in color. The trouble with the final cause is that it so often tends to be inseparable from the formal cause; for unless some extrinsic purpose can be found for a natural change—some end beyond itself which the change serves—the final cause, or that for the sake of which the change took place, is no other than the quality or form which the matter assumes as a result of its transformation.

59. See *Laws of Media: the New Science.*

60. See *Aristotle, De Anima,* Ed., Sir David Ross (Oxford: Clarendon Press, 1961), p. 10. On p. 11 he supplies a complete list of the occurrences of the word *entelecheia* in Aristotle's works.

61. Plato's Ideas, his ideal forms are mental images. They would appear natural consorting with the word in the mind before speech; some images may not be spoken as verbal embodiments are still inadequate. By contrast, Aristotle's *logos* as formal cause clearly associates with an embodied word. Gilson warns (*Being and Some Philosophers, Op. cit.*, p. 183): "To posit essence or supreme essentiality as the supreme degree of reality is therefore the most disastrous of all metaphysical mistakes, because it is to substitute *essentia* for *esse* as the ultimate root of all being. The whole of metaphysics is here at stake. . . ."

62. See below, T. S. Eliot on "Tradition and the Individual Talent."

63. Or unbecoming, but not decay. Decay belongs to transformation; unbecoming—one-half the process of decay—does not.

64. *On Poetry and Poets.* New York: Noonday Press (Farrar, Straus & Cudahy), 1943, *Rpt.* 1961, page 122.

65. *Cf.*, "eti to prôton entelecheiai" (*Metaphysics*, XII.5.35—1071a).

66. *Finnegans Wake*, 497.01. Joyce is a prime source of insight into the workings of formal cause, in literature as in life. *Finnegans Wake* is a formal teaching machine.

67. Letter, written 19 June, 1975, to Fr. John Culkin.

68. *Ibid.*, page 124.

69. "Tradition and the Individual Talent," from *The Sacred Wood*, pages 47–59. These remarks, p. 49.

70. *Ibid.*, pp. 49–50.

71. "The Serious Artist," in *Literary Essays of Ezra Pound, edited by T. S. Eliot* (New York: New Directions, 1968), pages 43–44.

72. Francis Bacon has articulated the formal causes of imperception in his doctrine of the four Idols, taken from his medieval kinsman, Roger Bacon. Whereas the four causes do cause something, the Idols are forms of inertia, death, uncausing, noncausing.

73. Marshall McLuhan, opening of the last chapter of *Through the Vanishing Point: Space in Poetry and Painting*, "The Emperor's New Clothes."

Appendix 5: The Theories of Communication of Judaism and Catholicism

1. See Appendix Two, above.

2. Shakespeare uses the five divisions, for example, in his sonnets, and in his formulation of the five-act play.

3. Coleridge and Wordsworth use the five divisions in their declaration in the celebrated Preface to the *Lyrical Ballads*. Wordsworth himself was a devotee of rhetoric and used the seven parts of a classical oration to pattern the stanzas in his "Ode to Duty."

4. It makes little difference whether the *Torah* is ascribed to the fifteenth century BC, or the seventh, or the fifth. Whatever the case, it greatly antedates the establishment of Roman rhetorical structures such as the five divisions, which concern us here.

5. Greek: Γένεσις, "birth," "origin," from Hebrew: בְּרֵאשִׁית, Bereishit, "in the beginning."

6. *The Five Books as Literature: Two Essays in Biblical Interpretation.* Eton, Windsor, Great Britain: The Shakespeare Head Press, 1961, page 44.

7. *The Catholic Encyclopedia*. Vol. 11. New York: Robert Appleton Company, 1911: "The voice of tradition, both Jewish and Christian, is so unanimous and constant in proclaiming the Mosaic authorship of the *Torah* that down to the seventeenth century it did not allow the rise of any serious doubt." Modern biblical scholars believe Leviticus to be almost entirely from the priestly source, marked by emphasis on priestly concerns, composed *c* 550–400 BC, and incorporated into the *Torah c* 400 BC. The Book of Numbers, too, with its dry style and emphasis on censuses is thought to derive from the same source and at the same time.

8. Deuteronomy (Greek: Δευτερονόμιον, "second law") or Devarim (Hebrew: דְּבָרִים, literally "things" or "words").

9. Orthodox Jews believe in the undisputed authorship of the *Torah* by Moses. They hold, moreover, the Divine origin of the entire *Torah*, and the eighth of the thirteen articles of faith formulated by Maimonides and incorporated into the prayer-book reads: "I believe with full faith that the entire *Torah* as it is in our hands is the one which was given to our teacher Moses, to whom be peace." (*The Catholic Encyclopedia*, 1912, Vol. XIV, p. 780) Moses lived in the 13th century B.C. and the early part of the 12th.

10. Analogously, each time the womb utters a word, it brings forth—it speaks—a baby.

11. The trivium, the "three roads," are Grammar, Dialectic, and Rhetoric. See the Note at the end of Appendix Four, "On Formal Cause," above. The main departments of Dialectic are logic and philosophy.

12. In his book, *This Is the Mass*, H. Daniel-Rops explains that it was "declared in the Catechism of the Council of Trent that no part of the Missal ought to be considered *vain* or *superfluous*; that not even the least of its phrases is to be thought wanting or insignificant. The shortest of its formularies, phrases which take no more than a few seconds to pronounce, form integral parts of a whole wherein are drawn together and set forth God's gift, Christ's sacrifice, and the grace which is showered upon us. This whole conception has in view a sort of spiritual symphony in which themes are taken as being expressed, developed, and unified under the guidance of one purpose." (London, 1959), page 34.

13. Michael Davies writes, "A Catholic knows that the most vital moment in human history took place outside Jerusalem nearly 2000 years ago when a mother stood weeping by a cross upon which her torn and broken Son offered His life to unite mankind with God once more. This is the event which the Catholic Mass makes present, whatever the rite, throughout the world and throughout the centuries. (*Cranmer's Godly Order*, Devon, Great Britain: Augustine Publishing Co., 1976, page 81)

14. It is above all in the distribution of the Eucharistic Bread that one realizes the unity of the Mystical Body; all the members in every age are nourished at the same table by the very same Body and Blood of Christ. St. John Chrysostom expresses this thought in a striking manner: "We are that very Body. For what is the Bread? The Body of Christ. What therefore do those communicating become? The Body of Christ—not many bodies but one Body. For just as bread is formed from many kernels of wheat, . . . so we are joined together with one another and with Christ." (Introductory note to a *Daily Missal* edited by the Maryknoll Fathers, New York: P.J. Kennedy & Sons, 1960)